WITHDRAWN

DENISE LEVERTOV

UNDER DISCUSSION

Donald Hall, General Editor

Denise Levertov

Selected Criticism

Edited with an Introduction by Albert Gelpi

Ann Arbor

THE UNIVERSITY OF MICHIGAN PRESS

60106309

Copyright © by the University of Michigan 1993
All rights reserved
Published in the United States of America by
The University of Michigan Press
Manufactured in the United States of America

1996   1995   1994   1993   4   3   2   1

Library of Congress Cataloging-in-Publication Data

Denise Levertov : selected criticism / edited with an introduction by
   Albert Gelpi.
        p.   cm. — (Under discussion)
      Includes bibliographical references and index.
        ISBN 0-472-09416-5 (alk. paper). — ISBN 0-472-06416-9 (pbk. :
   alk. paper)
        1. Levertov, Denise, 1923–   —Criticism and interpretation.
   I. Gelpi, Albert.   II. Series.
   PS3562.E8876Z63   1993
   811'.54—dc20   93-18170
                                                              CIP

A CIP catalogue record for this book is available from the British Library.

*Every effort has been made to trace the ownership of copy-
righted material used in this book and to secure permission
for its use.*

This book is dedicated to my brother
Donald Gelpi, S.J.

Contents

Part Two   Poetics

Part Three   Politics

Part Four   Gender

Part Five   Religion

ALBERT GELPI

Introduction

Centering the Double Image

The titles of Denise Levertov's first collections of poetry suggest that experience originates for her, as for most of us, with seeing—and seeing double: *The Double Image, Here and Now, With Eyes at the Back of Our Heads*. There was much in the circumstances of her life to make her feel divided in her affiliations and commitments. She has been acclaimed as an American poet—not just by citizenship but in the quality of poetic eye and ear; but she was born in England in 1923 and spent her formative years there: educated at home as her older sister Olga had been, studying painting and ballet, beginning nurse's training, publishing her first book of poems. *The Double Image* (1946) demonstrates in its metrical forms and neo-Romantic diction how much of the English poetic tradition she had absorbed by her late teens, when most of the poems in that book were written. Her inclusion in Kenneth Rexroth's anthology of *The New British Poets* (1949) places Levertov among the somewhat older "New Romantics"—George Barker, Dylan Thomas, Kathleen Raine—in the English poetry world of the 1940s.

The enduring importance of her roots is reflected in the locale of a number of poems over the years and in the persistence of certain distinctively English images, locutions, cadences that have become, if anything, more rather than less frequent in recent work. What's more, the cultural heritage of this English child was dual: a Welsh mother who sang, painted, and wrote; and her father a Hasidic Jew from Russia who converted to Christianity before his marriage in 1910 and settled ten years later in England, where he became an Anglican priest and a scholar and preacher dedicated to Jewish-Christian dialogue.

When marriage to the American writer Mitchell Goodman brought her to the United States and to residence in New York in December 1948, Levertov found herself immersed in a poetic and cultural scene for which London could not have prepared her. Postwar American poets were beginning to react against the academic legacy of the New Criticism in the teaching and writing of American poetry, and during the decade of the 1950s this revolt erupted variously in a number of groups: the Beat movement, which sent poets like Allen Ginsberg, Jack Kerouac, and Lawrence Ferlinghetti richocheting between New York and San Francisco; the already simmering San Francisco Renaissance, instigated by Kenneth Rexroth, which included William Everson, Robert Duncan, and Jack Spicer and drew recruits from the northwest like Philip Whalen and Gary Snyder; the New York School of Frank O'Hara, John Ashbery, and Kenneth Koch; and the Black Mountain poets, named after the experimental college of arts and letters in North Carolina where Charles Olson as rector presided over a community that came to include Duncan and Robert Creeley. These were the poets constellated a few years later in Don Allen's *The New American Poetry* (1960), and this anthology served as manifesto and manifestation of the new, self-consciously American poetry whose open form and oral, performative character rejected the academic formalism of poets like Allen Tate and Richard Wilbur as derivative of the settled conventions and assumptions of European and particularly English verse.

Under the stimulus of such a fierce challenge to what she had learned and practiced, Levertov remade herself as a poet, starting with the basic structural elements—line, rhythm, diction, image. Pound and Williams were the Modernist masters invoked by the postwar poets involved in the insurrection against what was perceived as the Eliotic domination of the New Criticism, and Levertov responded particularly to the power of Williams's poetry and poetics. Through him perhaps more than through anyone else she learned to see—and so to say—more precisely, more consciously, more incisively: modulating the varying propulsions of the voice-line to score the cadences of perception; determining the line breaks to graph the disjunctions and connections, turns and suspensions in that process of coming to awareness; shaping in speech her marveling concentration upon the particularity and diversity of the objects of experience. By the time Ferlinghetti's City Lights Books published *Here and Now* in 1956, her indebtedness to Williams was clear, as well as her association with the central figures in the loose confederation already dubbed the Black Mountain poets. Though she had never attended Black Mountain (or any other college) and was never personally close to Olson, she accepted the aesthetics of "composition by field" and found in her intense friendships with

Duncan and Creeley the peers she needed for inspiration and confirmation.

The very fact that she saw double images from eyes at the back as well as the front of her head made Denise Levertov intent upon precision and accuracy to focus polarity into clear-sightedness and, further, into clairvoyance. Astigmatism, myopia, spliced images—these have more and more painfully afflicted the modern capacity for seeing, and split vision has polarized every aspect of experience: inner/outer, mind/matter, subject/object, body/spirit, male/female, private/public, psychological/political, individual/community, particular/universal, physical/metaphysical. But Levertov's poetry, for all its awareness of doubleness, has been more remarkable for its centeredness: its tenacious grasp of the one grounding the two. For her, the double propounds not contradiction but paradox, aspects of relationship twinned in concentricity. If the two adhere as one, the one inheres in doubleness. This conviction has become increasingly explicit during the course of her career, but it was the implicit assumption and the underlying inclination of her poetry almost from the start, and pronouncedly so after coming to her own voice and form by the early 1960s under the impetus of Williams and company.

In his essay "Plato," Emerson declared:

Two cardinal facts lie forever at the base: the one and the two.—1. Unity, or Identity, and 2. Variety. We unite all things, by perceiving the law which pervades them; by perceiving the superficial differences, and the profound resemblances. But every mental act,—this very perception of identity or oneness, recognizes the difference of things. Oneness and otherness. It is impossible to speak, or to think, without embracing both.

Levertov agrees with Emerson that the resemblances between things are profound, but she also agrees with Thoreau that the differences between things, never trivial or superficial, are in fact telling signs. Unlike Emerson, she characteristically begins with particulars and only ends with abstractions. Her words, like Williams's, discriminate aspects of appearance, but for an end different from Williams's. She attends on particulars in the expectation, like Thoreau, that a fact will flower into a truth; for them both, immanence is the key to transcendence.

For—quite astonishingly—Denise Levertov breathed in the

American tradition in one great inhalation of the imagination: *both* the Transcendental mysticism at the heart of our Romantic poetry *and* the hard-edged Modernist formalism that informed the poetry of the first half of this century. In fact, her simultaneous absorption of Emerson and Thoreau as well as Williams and Pound—her reconciliation of those antiphonal strains in her imaginative comprehension and expression—gives her poetry its distinctive timbre and force yet makes it central to the entire tradition.

In the poetry of Denise Levertov's early maturity, most luminously and consistently perhaps in *The Jacob's Ladder* (1961) and *O Taste and See* (1964), the details, expertly deployed in the short, irregular, often enjambed lines, yield an intuition of the mystery of the living thing, of the thing's vital energy. Her Jewish and Christian heritage is not specified, nor does she wish it to be. At this point she cannot, or at one rate does not, name the mystery, and it is not experienced in terms of a specific theological reality or tradition. Nevertheless, the poems again and again break into a celebration of the sacredness, even the sacramentality of temporal experience: not just the organic beauty and sublimity of natural creation but intimations of essentializing spirit breaking through even the ugly, violent brutality of urban life. At the same time, she had begun writing essays like "Some Notes on Organic Form" and "Line-Breaks, Stanza-Spaces, and the Inner Voice" in order to give open-form poetics a more concise and practical formulation than either Williams or Olson or Duncan had managed. For Levertov, poetry sought to be organic so as to enact verbally the psychological, moral, and spiritual effort to realize—in landscape, cityscape, human relationships, marriage, motherhood—that essentializing sense of individual wholeness and of individual participation in the whole.

The crisis of Levertov's life and poetry came, after *O Taste and See,* with the desolating recognition that most human effort was bent not on participating in life's mystery but, on the contrary, on violating it. How could personal epiphany avail, even survive, within and against a public, political world dedicated not to creating a community consonant with the whole of creation but to exploiting nature and fellow humans, especially the more vulnerable and less advantaged? *The Sorrow Dance* (1967), particularly in the "Life at War" section, and the next several volumes contain an increasing number of poems about the atrocities afflicting society in this country and around the world: the Vietnam War, the oppression of the Third World by capitalist imperialism, ecological devastation, engrained racism and sexism. The problem of evil, particularly collective and institutionalized violence, split open Levertov's sense of harmony, and her resistance was immediate and vehement.

The stress of protest and opposition, however, threatened to consume her energies and to block access to those areas of experience and feeling that had been the wellspring of her poetry. Could she sound a poetry of moral outrage without sacrificing a poetry of celebration? It is a question that all prophets come to face. The titles of the volumes—*Relearning the Alphabet* (1970) and *To Stay Alive* (1971)—indicate the desperateness of the situation—not just for Levertov herself but for the survival and reconstruction of the world. The long title-sequences of those volumes live the dilemma out and through. Her voice would not be stilled; she would continue to denounce political, economic, and racial injustice, struggle for peace over war, for community over oppression—and at the same time strive to remain open to whatever lyric and mystical intimations might still sometimes break upon her.

The volumes of the 1980s, *Candles in Babylon, Oblique Prayers, Breathing the Water, A Door in the Hive,* represent a fresh but organic development—clarification and resolution, really—in Denise Levertov's poetry. Gradually and unsparingly, these recent poems begin to test out, define, and affirm the transcendent third term that bridges the rupture between individual epiphany and public calamity. Immersion in the immediate and divided world is still the way to an experience of immanence and so of transcendence, but now the centering mystery takes on a name, the Christian Incarnation, and with that name a history and a tradition. Its perfection is betrayed again and again by alienated, selfish individuals and groups, but its Spirit persists nonetheless in the dualisms of natural creation, the contradictions of human nature.

The recent poems make it increasingly clear that Levertov's Christian faith is the source of both her inspiration and her politics, her poetry of celebration as well as her poetry of opposition; it informs her sense of tragedy and of transcendence. For her, as for contemporary prophets like Daniel Berrigan, mysticism and liberation theology are the double face of the Word in the world. The sequence "Of God and of the Gods" (in *Oblique Prayers*) recognizes and posits an evolutionary continuity between the pantheism of the early poetry and the explicit Christianity of the new work. In the first poem of the sequence, the myriad rivers with their particular deities nonetheless "know, in unknowing flowing, / the God of the gods, whom the gods / themselves have not imagined," and the poem exists to acknowledge what the rivers can never become conscious of.

A poem of the 1960s called "A Vision" is quintessential Levertov. The double image came to her in a waking dream or vision, and the words came to her in a single sitting pretty much as they stand in the published text, which is prefaced with an epigraph from Spinoza, as quoted by Pound: "The intellectual love of a thing is the understanding of its perfections." It is revealing to note that this visionary poem is placed in *The Sorrow Dance* at the end of a section called "Perspectives" and just before the concluding section of political poems, "Life at War."

Two angels among the throng of angels
paused in the upward abyss,
facing angel to angel.

Blue and green glowed the wingfeathers
of one angel, from red to gold the sheen
of the other's. These two,

so far as angels may dispute, were poised
on the brink of dispute, brink of
fall from angelic stature,

for these tall ones, angels
whose wingspan encompasses entire
earthly villages, whose heads if their feet touched earth

would top pines or redwoods, live by their vision's harmony
which sees at one glance
the dark and light of the moon.

These two hovered dazed before one another,
for one saw the seafeathered, peacock breakered
crests of the other angel's magnificence,
different from his own,

and the other's eyes flickered with vision of
flame petallings, cream-gold grainfeather glitterings,
the wings of his fellow,

and both in immortal danger of dwindling, of dropping
into the remote forms of a lesser being.

But as these angels, the only halted ones
among the many who passed and repassed,
trod air as swimmers tread water, each gazing

on the angelic wings of the other,
the intelligence proper to great angels flew into their wings,
the intelligence called *intellectual love,* which,
understanding the perfections of scarlet,

leapt up among blues and greens strongshafted,
and among amber down illumined the sapphire bloom,

so that each angel was iridescent with the strange newly-seen
hues he watched; and their discovering pause
and the speech their silent interchange of perfection was

never became a shrinking to opposites,

they remained free in the heavenly chasm,
remained angels, but dreaming angels,
each imbued with the mysteries of the other.

Angels are of course God's messengers, negotiating the space
between the divine and the human, but in Levertov's vision two
angels, treading the "upward abyss" or "heavenly chasm" be-
tween spheres, all but fall into human egotism and envy. The
ravishingly gorgeous blue-green of one angel's wings contrasts
with the equally gorgeous red-gold of the other's wings. The first
recognition of the other's particular perfection threatened to alien-
ate them from themselves and divide them from one another.
Jealously eyeing the splendor opposite, "each gazing / on the
angelic wings of the other," the pair "hovers" on the verge of a
"drop." Emerson defined the fall as a coming to consciousness,
and so to self-consciousness, and so to an isolating awareness of
"oneness and otherness," and he saw life thereafter as a halting,
often balked process of realizing the oneness of the divisive two.
But here, between angels, the process is completed. During the
course of the poem the distinctive colors of the wings become, in
the eyes of the angels and of the beholding readers, interchange-
able and interdependent; the intellectual love that permits the rec-

ognition of the other's perfections subsumes differences and binds the opposites together. The pair of angels becomes twinned, "each imbued with the mysteries of the other." In the harmony of translunar comprehension the different colors permeate one another without losing the particularity that distinguishes, among the angelic orders, seraphim from cherubim.

Levertov knows that in our fallen, sublunary world oppositions are more obdurate, more fraught with retaliatory violence, but she is convinced as well that in our breakthrough moments, those epiphanies that are meant to light and guide the rest of our cloudy lives, we too, however fleetingly, however fragilely, can know and participate in the loving "intelligence" that links the angels. The sinuous turns and leaps, pauses and rushes of the poem's lineation and the metaphysical wit suffusing the gorgeousness of the presentation serve to carry the intensity of the poem to its resolution, as angels' paradoxical union glosses our halting human effort to grasp "at one glance / the dark and light of the moon."

I have chosen the essays and reviews in this collection to offer, within a single volume, a wide-ranging and balanced assessment of Denise Levertov's poetic achievement. They take up different aspects of her work and come to differing conclusions about it, and I have included the publication dates of the books being reviewed and the initial dates of the essays' publication in order to specify the point in Levertov's development from which the critic is speaking. I have presented the reviews chronologically but organized the essays, with publications dates, under the useful but overlapping rubrics "Poetics," "Politics," "Gender," and "Religion." The reader will soon find (as even the titles of several essays indicate) that these areas of vital concern become increasingly interlinked in Levertov's thinking and in her writing.

Barry Maxwell's bibliography, complied for this volume, lists all Levertov's published books and offers a selection of the best books, chapters, essays, and reviews dealing with her work. I want to thank Barry for his assistance in preparing this book; his perceptiveness about poems and about the texture of human experience that makes for poems is incisive and inspiriting.

The opinions and judgments about Levertov vary from critic to critic, but a strong, clear consensus acknowledges the range and coherence of her large and still growing body of work and confirms her as a major poet of the second half of the twentieth century.

PART ONE *Reviews*

KENNETH REXROTH

The Poetry of Denise Levertov

In my opinion Denise Levertov is incomparably the best poet of what is getting to be known as the new avant-garde. This may sound to some, committed to the gospel of the professor poets—the first commandment of whose decalogue of reaction is: "The age of experiment is over"—like saying that she is very much better than her associates, Charles Olson, Robert Creeley, Allen Ginsberg, Cid Corman, Chris Berjknes, Gil Orlovitz and others who published in *Origin* and the *Black Mountain Review*. I don't believe these are bad poets—in fact, I think they are the best of their generation and the only hope for American poetry. It is just that Denise Levertov has several things they haven't got, at least yet.

In the first place, she is more civilized. One thing she has which they lack conspicuously is what Ezra Pound calls culture (which he himself is utterly without). She is securely humane in a way very few people are any more. This is not because she is English, of Welsh and Jewish parentage, although the fact that her father was a learned rabbi, a leading authority on the Kabbalah, who became an Anglo-Catholic priest, may have helped. She seems to have grown up in a household full of mildly Bohemian scholarship, freewheeling learning of the type Theodore Gaster made well known in his reminiscences of his own father (Rabbi Gaster and Paul Levertov were friends). Certainly this is a humanism older than the Renaissance, so well founded that it penetrates every bit of life. This is far from the humanism of Sigismondo Malatesta or even Henry Luce—it is more like Lao-tse. If it is really absorbed and manifest in an individual it becomes that rare thing, wisdom. I don't need to labor the point that there exist practically no wise poets nowadays and few for the last two hundred years.

This means that Denise Levertov knows more than her colleagues, far more than most; she is far sounder than Olson,

Review of *Here and Now* (1956). Reprinted from Kenneth Rexroth, *Assays* (New York: New Directions, 1961), 231–35. Copyright © 1961 by Kenneth Rexroth. Reprinted by permission of New Directions Publishing Corporation. World rights.

whose learning suffers from the same sort of Frobenius-Lost Atlantis provincial oddity as Pound's. Many of them know practically nothing, not even French and algebra. Because it is humane, her knowledge is the result of doing what came naturally. She may have read Donne from her father's library at the age of ten—perhaps, like the Bible, for the dirty words. That is the way to read Donne. Cultured people do not discover him when they go to Harvard and use him to intimidate the yokels back home in St. Louis. This means too that she has an almost perfect ear. Reading her, especially hearing her read aloud, you feel she must have literally absorbed the rhythms of great poetry with her mother's milk. It is all so natural and so utterly removed from English 7649328 A—Forms and Techniques of English Verse (4 credits).

Nothing shows this better than the actual evolution of idiom and tone. During the years of the Second World War, Denise Levertov came up as one of the best and one of the most individual of the young English Neo-Romantics. Comfort, Woodcock, Gascoyne, Gardiner, Tambimuttu, Read, the whole "leadership" of the "movement" were quick to recognize her as something very special indeed. She was naturally "romantic." She didn't have to believe in it or belong to it as a movement. She was built that way. I said of her then that "in poets like Denise Levertov this tendency (a sort of autumnal-evening *Wienerwald* melancholy) reaches its height in slow, pulsating rhythms, romantic melancholy and indefinable nostalgia. Once these qualities would have been considered blemishes. Today they are outstanding virtues. For the first time, *Schwärmerei* enters English verse." The only thing wrong with this statement in those days was that there weren't any "poets like Denise Levertov." She was unique. None followed her. The next crop, represented, say, by Heath-Stubbs, seem like muggy little Böcklins cut out of cardboard in comparison. It was as though for a moment in the October moonlight a girl's voice sang faintly across the Danube, "Knowest thou a land where the pomegranate blooms. . . ." And then she gave it all up. "Hospital nurse, land girl, charwoman, children's nurse, companion to an alcoholic . . ." Hitchhiking over France the year after the Second World War ended, she married a GI and came to the States. "She'll probably end up a professor's wife," said a friend in London in 1949, "pushing a pram in a supermarket."

Denise turned out to be made of tougher stuff . . . and the GI, himself a writer, was on the side of the angels. At first she fell under the influence of the Southern Colonels and the Country

Gentlemen. It didn't last long. We were all horrified. "So and so is a lot like our Empson," said she to me. Said I to her, " 'Ceptin' that he never seen a book until he went to school and his folks still got cotton seeds in they hair. And besides, you are a leader of the very generation of revolt against the impostures of Empson, Richards, Eliot and their sycophants." She allowed as how that was true. But nobody "influenced" her to turn away, pretty quick, from the smoking dogs and bicycling seals of the American academicians. It was her own good sense, the good sense of bona fide tradition and an infallible ear. W. H. Auden has spent years in America and never learned to use a single phrase of American slang without sounding like a British music-hall Yank comic and his verse has remained as British, as specifically "school," as Matthew Arnold. In no time at all Denise came to talk like a mildly internationalized young woman living in New York but alive to all the life of speech in the country. Her verse changed abruptly. It would be easy to say that it came under the influence of William Carlos Williams. It would be more true to say that it moved into the mainstream of twentieth-century poetry. She writes like Williams, a little, but she also writes "like" Salmon, or Reverdy, or Char—or Machado, or Louis Zukofsky, or Parker Tyler, or Patchen, or the early Lowenfels, or me. After all, as Shakespeare said, we are all civilized men. I think Miss Levertov is a better poet than Salmon, as Williams is a better poet than Reverdy. If all her work of the past ten years were collected, I suspect she would show as the equal of Char and as superior to all but a handful of American poets born in this century. Certainly she is better than any post–Second World War French poet—than Frenaud, or Cadou, or Becker, or Rousselot. Her only rival among the younger women in England is a poet once described by an older colleague as writing like an exquisitely well-bred lady's maid, and who hasn't been up to her early snuff in many years. The only trouble with *Here and Now* is that it is much too small a collection and it is a collection of her easiest verse.

The fact that Denise Levertov has had to wait so long for publication and now is able to publish so little is a shame to American publishers, who year after year put out the most meretricious, pompous, academic nonsense, which gets meretricious, pompous, academic reviews in the literary quarterlies—and wins countless millions in Fellowships, Scholarships, Consultantships and Visiting Poetships. The official position is that people like Denise Levertov do not exist. Officialdom to the contrary, they very much do, and they will out-exist the jerry-built reputations of the *Vaticide Review* by many, many long years. Nothing could be harder, more irreducible, than these poems. Like the eggs and birds of Brancusi, they are bezoars shaped and polished in the vitals of a powerful creative sensibility. No seminar will break their creative wholeness, their presentational immediacy. No snobbery will dissolve their intense personal integrity. However irrefrangible as objects of art, it is *that,* their personalism, that makes them such perfect poetic utterances. Denise may never have pushed a pram in a Cambridge, Massachusetts, supermarket, but these are woman poems, wife poems, mother poems, differing only in quality of sensibility from thousands of other expressions of universal experience. Experience is not dodged, the sensibility is not defrauded—with any ambiguity, of seven types or seventy. One meets the other head on, without compromise. This, I was taught in school, many years ago in a better day, is what makes great poetry great. And the rhythms. The *Schwärmerei* and lassitude are gone. Their place has been taken by a kind of animal grace of the word, a pulse like the footfalls of a cat or the wingbeats of a gull. It is the intense aliveness of an alert domestic love—the wedding of form and content in poems which themselves celebrate a kind of perpetual wedding of two persons always realized as two responsible sensibilities. What more do you want of poetry? You can't ask much more. Certainly you seldom get a tenth as much.

JEAN GARRIGUE

With Eyes at the Back of Our Heads

Denise Levertov is concerned with making a certain kind of poem and achieving a certain kind of aesthetic effect by means of it. So far as I see it, it is a kind of askance impressionism, proceeding by indirections indirectly and by allusion, pitched in a low key, the approach quasi-conversational, informal, deliberately casual, rather intimate—a low key, yet by means and manner of juxtaposition striving to move into the high key of perception, "the quick of mystery" as she says, into that surprise that gets the poem off the ground into the shimmer and tremor of Possibles.

One especially sees this manner at work in certain poems, such as "A Straw Swan," "The Room," "The Vigil," "Girlhood of Jane Harrison," "Relative Figures Reappear," where the particulars are given a kind of abstract notation and where the large interest is simply in setting up relations between them or in giving proportions to those relations of a highly subtle and elusive kind. Attendant upon all this is her great interest in the look of things. She has a cultivated "painterly" eye and likes to isolate the looked-at thing in all of its detail, the looked-at thing as more or less the thing in itself, not involved in a conceptual order. So the lustre of surfaces and the glister of appearances is given much heed, and so is her concern to say the poem with as little stiffening of rhetoric as is possible. In "A Ring of Changes" she glides from point to point as in a dream. Many of her poems seem to begin from the middle of reverie and end there, in a suspension of meanings. She is all for the undertone and the overtone and for that mystique of the arrangement of things whereby mysterious doors open briefly onto a view of other dimensions.

The only trouble is the doors don't stay open long enough or you don't know how or why they open. There is too much withheld. We are asked to move in a landscape of secrets but we're not quite allowed to share the secret. There is too much fragmentation, almost too much intentional disorganization, the

Reprinted from *Chelsea* 7 (May 1960): 110–12.

opposing of jagged edges. I, for one, welcome the hard definiteness of "The Goddess,"

> She in whose lipservice
> I passed my time,
> whose name I knew, but not her face,
> came upon me where I lay in Lie Castle!

That "Lie Castle" is original, moral, imaginative, a vigorous conception that keeps the poem firmly in rein, closing:

> [she] without whom nothing
> flowers, fruits, sleeps in season,
> without whom nothing
> speaks in its own tongue, but returns
> lie for lie!

Levertov would appear to have learned much from W. C. Williams but the wonder of Williams is that all that life going on and after gets subsumed somehow in the barbed vitality and cultivated roughness of the instant he chooses to let fly forth his hot arrows on. The "aesthetic" is fully trained upon existence; it serves as a transparent frame for its sources. What Williams didn't want of a contrapuntal organization and a formal subduing proceeded also out of innovation. He was inventing and he was the only bronco out there in the original wild American field of weeds and cinders. His radical strength and rootedness, his capacity to get and keep the poem in a uniqueness of reality belongs to him and is perhaps a secret that can't be passed on. If he was of the tribe that wanted to purify language this does not mean that his tribe has founded a school where all the lovely technics can be learned. For what technic does not go hand in hand with substance? Levertov's eye and flexible rhythms need to sharpen themselves on denser bodies of substance.

JAMES WRIGHT

From "Gravity and Incantation"

Miss Levertov has published several books during the past few years. Born in England, she first wrote with startling skill in a traditional iambic style. After moving to the United States, of which she is now a citizen, she began to write poems in a measure which is sometimes called (mistakenly, I believe, as does Miss Levertov herself) "free verse." I have neither the space nor the full understanding required to discuss her prosody, but it should be discussed, for it is one of the most rewarding features of her moving poetry. Perhaps Miss Levertov herself will eventually write on the subject in relation to her own work. I hope she does. I have the impression that she is often misread and misinterpreted. I once read, in a foolish review, that Miss Levertov was simply writing imitations of W. C. Williams, whose style itself, compact of originality and even eccentricity, could not be imitated. Elsewhere, I have seen Miss Levertov associated, almost identified, with the Beats. (It is as though one had described Horace as one of the hangers-on of Byron during the later, riper part of his career.) Whether or not some person has approached her at a party to ask why she isn't Yeats, I do not know; but I would not be surprised; she apparently has had to put up with every other critical inanity imaginable, and she may as well finish the course. At any rate, she cannot be understood as a British poet who came to America and tried to assimilate the American language through the expedient of appropriating Dr. Williams's language bag and baggage. She has made her own discovery of America. The character of her poetry is remarkably American precisely *because* it is genuinely international. I have read that her father was a great Jewish scholar and that she was educated at home. Her father must have been delighted; he must have felt like one of her readers; for her imagination is always religiously open, and it always responds to what touches it awake. It is a quick, luminous mind, protected by

Review of *The Jacob's Ladder* (1961). Reprinted from *Minnesota Review* 2 (Spring 1962): 424–27.

wisdom against falsity till its spirit is strong enough to do its own protecting. Her poetry caresses the English landscape, as in "A Map of the Western Part of the County of Essex" in her new book. It naturally embraces the local details of America, as in so many of her new and earlier poems. I begin to believe that her poetry is so beautifully able to acclimate itself to different nations (to their true places, not to their latest political lies) because her imagination was given its first shape and direction by a spirit of culture that traditionally has belonged to different nations. As far as I know, Miss Levertov's work has rarely been judged from this perspective—Kenneth Rexroth seems to have pointed it out only to be ignored by subsequent reviewers. In any case, the advantages offered this poet by her international heritage are displayed inescapably in her new book *The Jacob's Ladder.*

She has poems that lovingly touch the places of America, country and city alike, each with its continuous spirit and body. There are some poems—like the really splendid "In Memory of Boris Pasternak" and the difficult, harrowing sequence about the Eichmann trial—which explicitly confront international themes. But the international spirit blossoms most fully in the new poem entitled "A Solitude." Here the poet helps a blind man find his way through and out of a subway in New York city; and she allows the international inspiration to find its own fulfillment. For it touches the great theme: the particularly human. Her considerable talent blooms in this poem, which is, in Johnson's phrase, "a just representation of general nature." "A Solitude" is a special joy to those who have always felt the deep gravity which underlies Miss Levertov's work. "A Solitude" can stand up in the presence of Rilke's poems on the blind. Yes, I know what I am saying. And if it is justified, then it is easier to see why Miss Levertov's poems have been so maddeningly categorized by fools among fools. If Rilke, completely unknown in the United States, were to publish *Neue Gedichte* right now, it would probably be brushed off in an omnibus review. Let's see, now . . . where did I leave that box of prefabricated phrases for omnibus reviews? . . . Ah, here it is: "Mr. Rilke should realize that, after all, Dr. Williams's notorious 'new territory' is really inseparable from his methods of arriving there, and it cannot be explored by the young. It is a pity that such a promising young writer should waste his energy by following roads already travelled by others. Besides, why isn't he Yeats?" Well, I am not called, much less chosen, to console Miss Levertov for the frustration of being misread by dead asses. Anyway, it just doesn't matter. "A Solitude" will outlive misreaders, and categorizers, and her, and me, and perhaps that isn't enough. The poet must judge for herself. I will merely record my gratitude for the appearance of a noble poem—indeed, for a noble book.

GILBERT SORRENTINO

Measure of Maturity

Denise Levertov has always been a meticulous writer, one whose poems exhibit a great degree of care and polish. In this new volume, however, she adds to her usual excellence a measure of maturity that has not been seen before. It is a long journey from the "pre-Williams" poems, when she was still working in England—

> A painted bird or boat above the fire,
> a fire in the hearth, a candle in the dark,
> a dark excited tree, fresh from the forest,
> are all that stand between us and the wind.

—with its almost regular iambics and staid progression, the "argument" resolved with the passive "are" as verb, through

> let it scissor and bounce its denials
> on concrete slabs and black
> roadways. Flood the streets.
> . . . .
> vague skies, the tedium
> up there.
> Under scared bucking trees
> the beach road washed out

in which the voice, the tone, the measures are all American and very heavily laced through with the Williams influence; to, finally, in this new volume:

> one knew
> that heart of fire, rose
> at the core of gold glow,
> could go down undiminished,

Review of *The Jacob's Ladder* (1961), from *Nation,* 10 March 1962, 220–21. This article is reprinted from *The Nation* magazine / The Nation Company, Inc., © 1962.

for love and
or if in fear knowing
the risk, knowing
what one is touching, one does it,

each part
of speech a spark
awaiting redemption, each
a virtue, a power

in abeyance unless we
give it care
our need designs in us. Then
all we have led away returns to us.

She has come into her own movement, the words are charged
with meaning, one must read the poem carefully or the beauty
escapes. There is a great tightening up of the "margins" of the
poem. That is, she has almost given up the concept, so explicit in
the second quote, of breaking the sequence of idea and image,
and jumping from one block of words to another. It seems to me
that this is all to the good, for her talents are not in that direction.
She is at her best when the poem moves quietly from the first
line through to the last, without the sudden breaks learned from
Williams.

The book has many fine poems, and some failures, but they
are never absurd failures. I disagree with the blurb-writer who
lauds her sequence *During the Eichmann Trial:* here she uses her
above-mentioned talents for a direct movement *through* the
poem, in a narrative fashion, without imbuing the words (in the
first two sections, at least) with poetic power. In other words,
there is a very thin feeling here—not emotionally, but poetically.
The poem does not carry its own weight, and we have

he scales the wall
enters the garden of death
takes the peach
and death pounces

mister death who rushes out
from his villa
mister death who loves yellow

who wanted that yellow peach
for himself
mister death who signs papers
then eats

—a kind of loose prosy manner that is like the papier-mâché
verse of Prévert or Ferlinghetti.

The book, however, is almost totally successful and the indica-
tions are that Denise Levertov is taking her place as a solidly
important American poet.

THOM GUNN

From "Things, Voices, Minds"

The healthfulness of his [Williams's] influence can be seen from the variety of the young poets who seem to have learnt from him: David Ignatow, Philip Levine, Denise Levertov, Robert Creeley, for example—each seems to owe something to Williams, but to owe it in the most open and grateful way, for he has helped them to realize their own very different poetic attitudes. It is unusual in Denise Levertov's latest book to feel that she is borrowing his tone of voice: she is fully individual, even though her outlook is often very similar to his. It is relevant to quote her opening poem, "To the Reader":

> As you read, a white bear leisurely
> pees, dyeing the snow
> saffron,
>
> and as you read, many gods
> lie among lianas: eyes of obsidian
> are watching the generations of leaves,
>
> and as you read
> the sea is turning its dark pages,
> turning
> its dark pages.

If Williams is behind this poem, he is distantly so, and only as Jonson was behind Pope. One is at once aware of its "rightness," and the rightness is at least partly a matter of the delicate yet firm movement with which it progresses. It is like the movement of Williams at his best, yet, as I have said, Miss Levertov is far from a mere follower. The poem confidently and completely establishes the range of subject matter in the book that it prefaces. The first image is of the present: the bear's impulse is part of the

Review of *The Jacob's Ladder* (1961). Reprinted from *The Yale Review* 52 (Autumn 1962): 129–38. Copyright © Yale University.

natural process of life, which is beautiful because it is authentic, neither graceful nor awkward; the second image is of the past, continuing into the present in a special way; and the third laps the whole within the mystery of general tendencies. These things are to be "read," like the poems in the book; and conversely the poems are to be treated like things of the world, each distinct and unclassifiable. In fact, in presenting us with particularities, Miss Levertov is constantly trying to break down categories and dismiss them from our minds: she implies that if we are to feel sympathy with the flux of life (such sympathy is the dominant emotion of the book) we must disregard the classifications into which we have come to divide the constituents of the world and regard each thing and process as special, unique. The purpose of her very metaphor is often to get rid of our preconceptions. New York City, for example, the background to many of the poems, becomes a kind of temple:

> The lights change: the avenue's
> endless nave echoes notes of
> liturgical red.

The Jacob's Ladder is a very distinguished book indeed, and the concluding thirteen poems from an earlier collection help to show up its virtues. She has abandoned the slightly tenuous fancifulness around which some of the early poems are organized, for a solid acceptance of the solid. It is not a glib acceptance, either, merely borrowed from the nineteenth-century romantics, but one which surely reflects (as any good poetry must) a manner of living, a personal discipline, in this case the discipline of tolerance. The book gives us confidence, of a sort that we can feel rather seldom, in the considerable and still expanding talent of a poet whose world is based on the world we share.

HAYDEN CARRUTH

An Informal Epic

In rereading all Denise Levertov's earlier poems, and then this
collection of new poems, O *Taste and See,* I have been im-
pressed, very forcibly indeed, by one aspect of her development
which has not been remarked publicly before, at least as far as I
know. Usually attention has been called to her technical accom-
plishments, which are great. Anyone interested in the composi-
tion of poetry can learn much, certainly, from her use of the
line, from the way she has discarded mannerisms as she pro-
gressed, from her molding of the whole poem to a swift, wide
gesture of sensibility (like a dancer's), and also from her dic-
tion, which is another part of her work that has been insuffi-
ciently discussed. But what I wish to speak of now is the mean-
ing of her poetry.

Miss Levertov began with an obsessive theme: art itself, the
life of the imagination, the artist as an exemplary figure, the
esthetic comprehension of reality. Without counting, I should
say that far more than half her poems consolidate around this
idea. It was endemic, of course, in the generations preceding
hers; from the void of post-Nietzschean nihilism sprang up the
tribe—cubists, futurists, expressionists, twelve-tonalists, surreal-
ists, revolutionaries of the word—which attempted to reconsti-
tute ontological validity solely in terms of art; or, more properly
speaking, in terms of style. For them the word became the thing.
As it happens, I have spent too much time and energy condemn-
ing this fantasy not to condemn it also in Miss Levertov's early
poems. There, in her immaturity, Miss Levertov wrote like her
forebears who, in the throes of their self-divisive faithlessness,
thrust up, by an act of desperation, an art which would, they
hoped, stand against the meaninglessness of both cosmic and
social existence. Hence these early poems are divided against
themselves, against experience, against the world; their feeling is
self-created, and often empty and dry. Among her early poems

Review of O *Taste and See* (1964). Reprinted from *Poetry* 105 (January 1965):
259–61.

those on other themes, such as the love poems or descriptive poems, are the more successful.

But two points must be emphasized. First, Miss Levertov was not genuinely a creature of the nihilist age. Perhaps because the peculiar circumstances of her early life denied her any formal education whatever, she apparently missed the epochal experience of intellectual despair. Instead she followed her own inclination, which led her, one surmises, in the direction of Jewish mysticism, but not so far that she got more than she could comfortably absorb. Second, because she nevertheless is, like all of us, a post-nihilist, she has been washed clean of all sentimentalism. She does not find meaning where none exists. In consequence she sped, so to speak, back through Hopkins, through Wordsworth, through Jacob Böhme—yes, and through Plato too, for that matter—to a stage of sensibility which I would call primitive if the word weren't associated with technical incompetence. Perhaps "pre-classical" or "pastoral" would be better, signifying the unitary culture in which esthetic cognition is identical with the whole structure of consciousness.

Actually we use these backward-looking terms at all only because the future has not yet been invented. Miss Levertov is not backward-looking; she is so modern that few readers have caught up with her. She is commonly called a lyricist, for example, because her verbal sense is undeniably musical; but for me her poems are far less lyrics than epics, using the term as Brecht used it in his "epic theater." They are moments in which the unenterable, unleavable drama of totality turns back upon itself, like a seasonal revolution; moments, in other words, when we who are totally involved are nevertheless permitted to see what has happened. The reason for Miss Levertov's success is clear: she stuck with her obsessive idea until, in a gradual fusion which is evident in the books, her esthetic mode of being combined inextricably with all her being and then with being itself. This is her modernity, her futurity; a remarkable feat in the era of self-consciousness. In technical terms she has projected the existentialist sensibility beyond anguish, and beyond any extemporaneous leap from anguish, to a simple—but how thoughtful and varied!—celebration of what is, to a spiritual but actual cognizance of reality, reasonable and joyous, arising chiefly from considerations of the body. This is what we have in a dozen or more of the best poems in *O Taste and See*.

Fine work sometimes makes us ask intemperately for more while we are content to take that which is less than fine for what it is. The flaws in Miss Levertov's poems are not worth talking about; but she has limits, and the analogy with Brecht makes them clear. Her "moments" are intensely personal, her vision radiates from the narrowest possible aperture, even to such a degree that readers who do not know her as a person cannot understand some of her poems. This may be—though here I am on uneasy ground—a necessary, natural function of her femineity, which we would be fools to wish to modify. One merely wonders what might happen if she were to embark on a work of larger scope, a work in which the epical sensibility was more formally organized as such. Would the eye become The Eye? Sartre, in *Les Mots,* has disclaimed his early work on the ground that the position, the office, of authorship is untenable, logically, morally, and psychologically. An extreme view; but possibly a premonition of what the coming age will bring.

Meanwhile we have the informal epic, Miss Levertov's five books. (I do not know her first small book, published in England.) It is poetry which brings us the kind of satisfaction we associate with the epical sensibility: a communion—but concrete, nothing hazy or suppressive of individual consciousness—in a known world.

SISTER BERNETTA QUINN, O.S.F.

Review of *Relearning the Alphabet*
(1970)

In her latest volume Miss Levertov inquires of the cold spring "what if my poem is deathsongs?" The singular *poem* suggests the elegy as unifying principle, like the city in Williams or the grass in Whitman, whereas the plural *deathsongs* defines her role as singer, a character developed in section four, where in a dramatic monologue a tree narrates the Orpheus myth. All human music has a dying fall, though few writers can so well analyze its poignancy as this Margaret who realizes full well she mourns first of all herself, experiencing death by imagination; then she grieves for the "burning babes" of Asia and the starved children of Africa; for young David, dead, and her friend Bill Rose, whose unanswered postcard haunts her; for the "wild dawns" of youth. An extract from her 1968–1969 notebook asks: "Is there anything / I write any more that it is not / elegy?" Perhaps the answer is no. At any rate, one is grateful that with her beautiful honesty she looks squarely at the fact so many dare not face.

Gifted in seizing upon the unregarded image, Miss Levertov uses also the great traditional ones—for example, the moon. She identifies it with the ocean ("the great nowhere"); with mown grass; with a tiger that enters a bedroom to threaten lovers; with a coldness capable of burning the speaker to cinders.

Equally opposed to daytime reality is her symbolic employment of the dream. In *Riders at Dusk* she canters through a castled landscape, bewildered by the presence of a beloved but unknown companion: the situation is reminiscent of Emmaus. *The Rain* shows her trying "to remember old dreams"; in the constant rain, life itself—voices, rooms, birds, hands—has become dream. *A Dark Summer Day* pleads for a jazz band to waken her with the news that life has been dreaming her. The entire book closes with her prayer to the *lares* of a house left to its profound dreams.

Related to the problem of reality vs. dream is that of identity.

Reprinted from *Poetry* 118 (May 1971): 97–98.

Keeping Track tells how she leaves her occupation of hulling strawberries or writing poems to check in a mirror as to whether or not she is still there. *Wind Song* reveals her search for a deeper self through a series of fiery metamorphoses. A related facet is the identity of others as treated in *Dialogue:* the difficulty of "reaching" another and the importance of believing that persons are not objects but figures of more numinous being than sight perceives.

The title lyric, *Relearning the Alphabet,* explores insights stemming from the twenty-six letters. If its lines resemble in their prosody the author of *Paterson,* they do so without diminishing the force of Miss Levertov's own genius, almost blazing in its impact. It completes a collection rising from a season analogous to Keats's "golden year"—Keats, whose phrases weave in and out of these songs and whose *Ode to a Nightingale,* as an autobiographical passage declares, is the only poem she ever memorized.

An enlargement of the spirit is effected by contact with Denise Levertov's dances, agonies, and playing on the ten-stringed lute. Like Orpheus, she uproots and then plants again in a new soil. No simplest sentence of daily life remains the same for this scholar, now that she has acquired a second alphabet, nor for those to whom she here teaches it. Prophet in the Flannery O'Connor sense, Miss Levertov has arrived at a vision counteracting the pain of mortality. She has discovered what Hopkins meant by "the dearest freshness deep down things."

MARIE BORROFF

From "Recent Poetry"

Denise Levertov's *To Stay Alive* presents itself explicitly in politi-
cal as well as personal terms; it is frankly offered as a "document
of some historical value, a record of one person's inner / outer
experience in America during the '60's and the beginning of the
'70's." Levertov has come, she tells us, to understand that "oppo-
sition to war . . . cannot be separated from opposition to the
whole system of insane greed, of racism and imperialism"; the
"guardians of life" are "not only those who 'disdain to kill' but
all who struggle, violently if need be, to pull down this obscene
system before it destroys life on earth."

As a document, the book is heavy with fact: names are
named, places and dates given, accusations made, praise be-
stowed. Its major fault—in the geological sense of a fracture-line
between opposed forces—results from the attempt to absorb
these materials into a specifically *poetic* dramatization. Levertov's
poetic sensibility is deeply informed by the classical English tradi-
tion (phrases from Keats, Hopkins, and Swinburne float in italics
on the page). The time-honored impulse to celebrate, to wonder,
to sing is basic in her, and this impulse is, literally, disturbed by
the knowledge that an unassimilable evil exists which must be
hated and which must be fought on the level of action. Poetic
forms are repeatedly laid aside, as if felt inadequate for the render-
ing of actual life. Pages of the book are devoted to "real" ex-
cerpts, in prose, from pamphlets, postcards, letters, simulated or
actual newspaper items, and a page from *The Instant News* pub-
lished in Berkeley at the time of the People's Park confrontations
(in which Levertov was a participant), telling "What People Can
Do." At times the effect is one of collage; the reader has an
irritating sense of being made to switch back and forth between
poetic and moral response. A holiday by the sea awakens the
lyric impulse, but this is soon thrust aside by the nagging remem-

Review of *To Stay Alive* (1972). Reprinted from *The Yale Review* 62, no. 1
(Autumn 1972): 81–83. Copyright © Yale University.

brances of sacrifices that are being made by others now, while we watch the waves roll in:

> To repossess our souls we fly
> to the sea. To be reminded
> of its immensity, and the immense sky
> in which clouds move at leisure,
> transforming their lives ceaselessly,
> sternly, playfully.

> *Today is the 65th day since de Courcy Squire, war-resister,*
> *began her fast in jail. She is 18.*

Elsewhere, the resources of traditional rhetoric are eloquently marshaled in the attempt to bring home the unspeakable:

> delicate Man, whose flesh
> responds to a caress, whose eyes
> are flowers that perceive the stars,

> whose music excels the music of birds,
> whose laughter matches the laughter of dogs, . . .
> still turns without surprise, with mere regret
> to the scheduled breaking open of breasts whose milk
> runs out over the entrails of still-alive babies,
> transformation of witnessing eyes to pulp-fragments,
> implosion of skinned penises into carcass-gulleys.

The celebration is Shakespearian, reassuring; the indignation is as lofty as it is vain.

> burned human flesh
> Is smelling in Vietnam as I write.

Yes; one can only bow one's head. It is as a human portrait, not as a work of imaginative transfiguration, that this book remains with us, in delicate and anguished echo. Perhaps this is as its author would wish.

LINDA WAGNER MARTIN

Matters of the Here and Now

Thirteen years ago Kenneth Rexroth chose Denise Levertov as
the most interesting poet of the new generation—"the most
subtly skillful," "the most profound," "the most modest and the
most moving"; i.e., "the best of the lot." High praise indeed
from Rexroth, but praise that was echoed widely. Levertov estab-
lished herself thereafter as one of the most important younger
poets. Readers admired her poems; they also admired the serious-
ness with which she took her role as poet. Even then, Levertov
gave splendid readings, stirring in both their intensity and their
dignity. And whenever she was asked to write about her craft,
she did so, again with dignity and clarity.

The Poet in the World, a collection of essays and reviews, is the
natural result of one poet's involvement with her life as a writer. It
tells a great deal about Levertov's own aesthetic principles, but it
also reads like a handbook of contemporary poetics. She does not
assume great sophistication on the part of her readers, and thereby
hedge the most obvious—and sometimes the most difficult—
questions. Accordingly, reading this book can serve to educate the
uninitiated in modern poetry. Sections I and V, "Work and Inspira-
tion," and "Other Writers," are particularly interesting here. Her
essays on Paul Goodman, Robert Creeley, H.D., Pound and Wil-
liams and others (many of these written while she was poetry
editor of *The Nation*) show too how influential her criticism—and
that of other poets—has been in recent years. Each of these writers
either appeared for the first time or enjoyed a kind of renaissance
between the early 1960s and the present.

That Levertov is one of the first poets of her generation to
have published this kind of prolegomenon is not surprising. She
has consistently told her students to read criticism by poets, to
trust Coleridge, Wordsworth, Hopkins, Pound, Rilke, Duncan.
Yet she seems to be partly at odds with the image of herself as

Review of *The Poet in the World* (1973), from *Nation,* 22 June 1974, 795–96. This
article is reprinted from *The Nation* magazine / The Nation Company, Inc., ©
1974.

poet-critic, with its ivory-tower connotations, for she includes as a secondary category excerpts from her political writings. The title of the book itself reflects that antipathy against the idea of existing only as an artist; even poets must live in the world—or, perhaps poets especially must live in the world—and Levertov speaks in that connection of "the essential interrelatedness and mutual reinforcement of the meditative and the active."

One of the many significant ideas Levertov pursues is that of "the artist as translator." She objects to the notion that the poet attempts only a limited re-creation of simple experience, or therapeutic self-expression. A poet must do more than label or confess. He must find a way to bring his understanding of the world to his reader in such a way that the reader too feels a part of the "translation."

> We must have poems that move away from the discursively confessional, descriptive, dilutedly documentary *and* from the fancies of inauthentic surrealism to the intense, wrought, bodied-forth and magical—poems that make us cry out with Carlyle, "Ah, but this sings!"

To reach this point of involvement, Levertov suggests what she terms "an ecstacy of attention, a passion for the thing known, that shall be more, not less sensuous, and which by its intensity shall lead the writer into a deeper, more vibrant language. . . ." One thinks of her own poems, so well described here—tulips, the iris and squirrel in "A Day Begins," the mutes on the subway, human bodies, the title poem from *O Taste and See:*

> The world is
> not with us enough.
> *O taste and see*
>
> the subway Bible poster said,
> meaning *The Lord,* meaning
> if anything all that lives
> to the imagination's tongue,
>
> grief, mercy, language,
> tangerine, weather, to
> breathe them, bite,
> savor, chew, swallow, transform

into our flesh our
deaths, crossing the street, plum, quince,
living in the orchard and being

hungry, and plucking
the fruit.

Given her high moral seriousness, her role as translator of experience into *claritas,* Levertov has provided contemporary writing with a direction, a tone, even an organ bass. It is true that her poems have shown great variety of form—although the pervasive Levertov voice is serene, moderate, marked by verbal music and metaphor. Yet, varied as their shape may be, the poems speak consistently for Levertov's solemn view of life. She sees life as renewing, joyful, majestic; a promise to be held tenderly; a duty to be performed earnestly; and her poetry, as an art originating in, and expressive of, that mysteriously compelling vision.

Just as Levertov's poems create this unmistakable sense of personal commitment, to both art and life, so do these essays. Each one is solid. It blocks off an area, defines its limits, and comes to terms with that definition. In the process, the reader learns a great deal about Levertov, about modern poetry, and about art through the ages. *The Poet in the World* is thus a book that does much translating of its own.

DAVID IGNATOW

Review of *The Freeing of the Dust* (1975)

It may be that the critical return in recent years of the genteel tradition has had the effect of obscuring the name and fame of Denise Levertov. *The Freeing of the Dust* is her eleventh book of poems. Levertov, through her forceful and compassionate presentations of urban lives, has been associated with the work and traditions of William Carlos Williams and Walt Whitman. She also has been praised for the beauty and sensuousness of her nature poems. By nearly unanimous agreement Levertov was well on her way to becoming one of our leading poets. The onset of the Vietnam War began the decline of her reputation, coinciding with the reemergence of the genteel tradition of polite and ultrasophisticated writing, a fantastic paradox in the face of the disaster of the war. Levertov, like so many other poets socially and personally involved, began to write her passionate Vietnam poems and to help lead large demonstrations against the war. In midst of our terrible spiritual dilemmas, nationwide, we can no longer afford to ignore her.

In *The Freeing of the Dust,* her power to move us has not diminished. If anything, it has gone into new, vital areas. Poems against the Vietnam War are still present, several of superb pathos, but beyond that are poems of a way of looking at life that we never before met in her work. She has changed. I am referring to her poems of love and divorce, for instance. At her center there now seems to be an acceptance of imponderable limits, yet without the bitterness one would expect from a disillusioned humane idealist. Rather there is a sweetness, a tenderness towards life; a change rises from her poems that is inspiring to read. For Levertov the circle of human frailty has been completed and forgiven and even blessed, because of life, as in "Living Alone (III)":

Reprinted from the *New York Times Book Review,* 30 November 1975, 54–55. Copyright © 1975 by The New York Times Company. Reprinted by permission.

35

I said, the summer garden I planted
bears only leaves—leaves in abundance—
but no flowers.
And then the flowers,
    many colors and forms,
    subtle, mysterious,
came forth.

I said, the tree has no buds.
And then the leaves,
    shyly sparse, as if reluctant,
in less than two days appeared,
and the tree, now,
    is flying on green wings.

What magic denial
shall my life utter
to bring itself forth?

The beauty of this acceptance of the self is found in many other poems, whose themes are familiar to us but are now transformed by this new spirit. Besides war, she touches on her love of friends and friendship, the Hasidic ecstasy, the love for and identification with the poor and nature, and her celebration of poetry, subjects that she has dwelt on before but not nearly in the same tone. Outstanding among her poems is "Conversation in Moscow," in which a Russian poet surrounded by his friends in an apartment talks with Levertov on the hidden springs of poetry. When we are finished reading, we have experienced a new depth to Levertov's understanding of these sources, an understanding that we share with her, through the power and simplicity of their evocation—the bitterness, for one, that like dust must be swept away.

HARRY MARTEN

Review of *Life in the Forest* (1978)

Artistic longevity is always risky. A poet who with the passing
of years settles into a style becomes not a maker of poems but of
artifacts. It is a pleasure to note, then, that with the publication
of *Life in the Forest,* her twelfth book of verse, Denise Levertov
continues to write exquisitely crafted lyrics. In their reverence
for language and life, they make the reader continually aware
that the poet's task is, as Levertov has said elsewhere, "to clar-
ify . . . not answers but the existence and nature of questions."

Early linked by friendship to Robert Creeley and his *Black
Mountain Review,* to Robert Duncan by shared imaginative re-
sources, to Cid Corman, Charles Olson and Paul Blackburn by
frequent publication in Corman's magazine *Origin,* to the Beats
by various anthologists, and especially to William Carlos Wil-
liams, clearly a great source of nourishment for her as well as for
most American writers of the last quarter century, Levertov
nonetheless refuses category. She is like Wallace Stevens's "man
of glass . . . the transparence of the place in which / He is," able
both to reflect and reveal the truth in its inconsistencies.

The poet's "Introductory Note" to *Life in the Forest* explains at
the outset a bit of the book's imaginative terrain. Having re-
cently discovered in the stark simplicity of Cesare Pavese's
poem-stories of the 1930s, *Lavorare Stanca (Hard Labor),* "a kind
of ratification for a direction" her work "was already obscurely
taking," Levertov notes an intention to "try to avoid overuse of
the autobiographical, the dominant first-person singular of so
much of the American poetry—good and bad—of recent years."
Yet differences between *Life in the Forest* and *Lavorare Stanca*
reveal as much as sympathies. Not even in "Homage to Pavese,"
the first section of Levertov's book, does she insist upon what
Pavese himself called the "*austerity* of style" or the "close, posses-
sive, passionate adherence to the object" and the "surrendering
to the plot" that impelled so many of his poems.

Levertov shares the honesty of Pavese's descriptions, the inci-

Reprinted from *New England Review* 2, no. 1 (Autumn 1979): 162–64.

siveness and clarity with which he was able to sketch landscapes and the people who inhabit them—

> There are places in the city
> where there are no streets, only alleys where the sun
>   doesn't reach
> and the wind never blows.
>
>   ("A Season," trans. W. Arrowsmith)

> In the winter fog
> the man lives jailed between streets, drinking
> his cold water, biting his crust of bread.
>
>   ("Simplicity," trans. W. Arrowsmith)

Nonetheless she gives her attention not so much to the qualities of the object perceived, or alternatively to the interior of the perceiver's mindscape, as to the relationships between the world "out there" and its apprehension by a receptive sensibility. In the far-ranging geographies of *Life in the Forest,* seer and things seen are mutually activating—whether we are in the rain and heat of Oaxaca where a seller of serapes makes his endless rounds, or amidst the assembled memories, possessions and sickroom detritus of an old woman dying too slowly, "at home, yet far away from home, / thousands of miles of earth and sea, and ninety years / from her roots."

The mysterious process of discovery in which interior and exterior meet and define one another is nowhere clearer than in the intense evocations of Levertov's mother-daughter poems:

> Now mother is child . . .
>   at the mercy
> of looming figures who have the power
> to move her, feed her, wash her, leave or stay
> at will. And the daughter feels, with horror,
> metamorphosed: *she's* such a looming figure—huge—a
>   tower
> of iron and ice—love
> shrunken in her to a cube of pain
> locked in her throat.
>
>   ("A Daughter (I)")

And wherever we turn in this splendid collection we find "the seed of change . . . seeing not only *what is* but *what might be*"—in the designs of "Blake's Baptismal Font," in the presence of "Chekhov on the West Heath," or when sharing the articulation of an extreme privacy in the entries of "Metamorphic Journal."

Levertov mixes long lines which propel poetic narratives ("Writing to Aaron," "The Cabdriver's Smile") and sharp images that crystallize moments of immediate experience ("A Visit," "The Blue Rim of Memory," "A Woman Pacing Her Room . . ."). She plays logical syntax against the brief hesitations in thought and feeling that, in large part, determine line breaks—

> Among sharp stones, below,
> of the hospital patio,
> an ugly litter of cigarette stubs
> thrown down by visitors leaning, anxious or bored,
> from other balconies.
>
> ("A Daughter (II)")

And the tensions of tone and meaning that result dislocate the reader, compelling him out of complacencies of observation and into active participation as he reads. Levertov's introductory remarks even invite one to take a hand in reassembling the shifting shapes that comprise the whole book—suggesting that in reading from section to section we perceive overlapping sections, kinship groups, internal associations from poem to poem.

Not all of the poems of *Life in the Forest* are fully created. The sequence of love poems, "Modulations for Solo Voice," is especially disappointing. The emotional declarations often seem strained, offering clichés which convince us simply that the experience is too self-serious and self-enclosed to make good poetry:

> I wanted to learn you by heart.
> There was only time
> for the opening measures. . . .
>
> ("From Afar")

Still, the "Epilogue" to the series which Levertov calls from a "cheerful distance" *Historia de un amor* has an exactness of irony and a satisfying emotional resonance which goes a long way toward rescuing the whole, sending us back to reconsider even the weak poems of the sequence in light of such final insights as "I thought I had found a fire / but it was the play of light on bright stones."

If one believes with Octavio Paz, as I do, that "poetry is metamorphosis, change, an alchemical operation" and that "the poem is a work that is always unfinished, always ready to be completed and lived by a new reader," one can only be pleased to have Levertov's latest effort, whatever its lapses. More than thirty years after her first volume, she reminds the reader that her best poems fulfill as well as any poetry can her own stated goals for fine writing. *Life in the Forest* "sets in motion . . . elements in the reader that otherwise would be stagnant. And that movement . . . cannot be without importance if one conceives of the human being as one in which all the parts are so related that none completely fulfills its function unless all are active."

FREDERICK GARBER

From "Geographies and Languages
and Selves and What They Do"

However different the work of Bill Knott from that of Denise
Levertov—and we are speaking here of abysses—she shares his
understanding of the likeness of being and doing and of the
poem as radical act. Indeed, the push toward exposing the radical
in word and phrase, thing and event, creates and defines Lever-
tov's work, taking it as far as poems can go from Knott's elabora-
tions. "Decipherings," the first poem of *Oblique Prayers,* offers a
set of instructions for reading what is to follow. We see and then
make images ("Half a wheel's / a rising sun: without spokes, / an
arch"); what we see opens out to stand for greater, the greatest,
acts ("half a loaf / reveals / the inner wheat: / leavened / transub-
stantiation"); the life outside, "Felt life / grows in one's mind" as
children do in the womb, becoming the energy of images which
tie themselves and us into moving wholeness: "each semblance
// forms and / reforms cloudy / links with / the next // and the
next." What follows in the book moves out from this poem,
though "Decipherings" does it better than some of the poems
which follow. The language is characteristic Levertov, brief,
tight and spare both in word and phrase, these leading into state-
ments of equal spareness. The ideal is to be lean and rich, dense
but never crammed. Levertov has always looked for a kind of
essentialism in which seeing and saying are alike, pure and direct
and to the bone, no gap in quality between vision and language
and therefore no gap between their activities. Such activities ask
of the poet a concomitant purity of consciousness, self not only
the agent of vision and language but their partner in quality as
well. Of course such language comes from Williams but she puts
it to the service of an ecstasy especially her own. The best of
Levertov shows how she has so mastered economy that she can
do minimalist work, shows how the essence of things is insepara-

Review of *Oblique Prayers* (1984). Reprinted from *American Poetry Review* 14
(September/October 1985): 18–19.

ble from movement, shows also the alertness of consciousness (itself lean and rich) for moments of surprise. "Blue Africa" puts her on a freeway in winter, yet seeing and hearing, in sudden interspace, the stride and quiet of the African elephants as "each in turn / enters . . . a blue river of shadows."

Yet Levertov's poems ride on a razor's edge. She practices a difficult lyricism which always aims for the delicate but often finds only the soft. It is breathtaking and unnerving to see her so frequently waver between Williams and Edna Millay. "Of Necessity" hovers between the two, never quite certain of where it is, while "Mappemonde" slips effortlessly into the sticky: "O Geography! / On your thick syrops / I float and float, / I glide through your brew / of bitter herbs." But to counter these there are others like the very fine "Presence," on the spirit of Jim Wright in the Ohio landscape, where the touch never falters, the razor's edge becoming the broadest of places on which to work. Essentialism leaves no room, has no mercy, for the slightest hesitation in touch or tonality.

Oblique Prayers builds toward its final section with hints in poems like "Presence" of dimensions beyond the tactile, of the making of spaces for the self beyond the textures of Ohio yet somehow contained within them, emergent from them. As the final section shows, this is more than a matter of spooks. That section seeks to put it all together, with some of her most delicate seeing and some subtly intoned moments of (essentially religious) ecstasy. "Of Rivers," "Of Gods," "The God of Flowers," "This Day": these and several others harbor the book's finest moments, where she is fully in touch with things, querying their capacities and showing the range of her own. Self can dwell in dimensions available only in certain conditions, dimensions that she seeks to open within the words that make the poems. The book ends in stillness and peace and (for the most part) a deftness of touch, the blood of El Salvador elsewhere than here, "great suffering, great fear— // withdrawing only / into peripheral vision." The politics which take up the second part of the book are put by for "this need to dance, / this need to kneel: / this mystery." All those moments of Millay have to be countered by moments like these where it all comes together, with seeing, making and being at their surest and most essential.

JANE MILLER

From "Working Time"

In *Breathing the Water,* Denise Levertov's fifteenth book published by New Directions, there is a consistency of free verse form throughout her steady writings, deeply affected by Robert Duncan's formal thinking on free verse. And there is, too, Levertov's long-time political sensibility in her poems, articulated early on in the seminal collection of essays, *The Poet in the World.* The political sensibility develops from the spirit, a spirit whose "presences" are Emerson, Hopkins, Rilke. She speaks of the "inscape of a sequence or constellation of experience," and that "back of the idea of organic form is the concept that there is a form in all things." She is most herself, most inspired in her essays in her articulation of a "reverence for life," valuing "the poet who more than others recognized language as a form of life and a common resource to be cherished and served."

More than ever Levertov is a poet of the world, here especially of an underworld. *Breathing the Water* is energized by spiritual presences, figures, shades, vivified darknesses, intuitions:

> a tremulous
> evanescence which is wood
> or which is the tardy sungleam from under cloudbank
> just before evening settles. . . .
>
> ("Athanor")

Her most intense poetry, the poetry of mystery, of illumination, is here in two groups of spinoffs. She explains,

> A spinoff, then, is a verbal construct which neither describes nor comments but moves off at a tangent to, or parallel with, its inspiration.

In the first instance, the poems spin off of photographs by Peter McAfee Brown, and the language is swift, prescient. This is the end of "A Doorkey for Cordova":

Review of *Breathing the Water* (1987). Reprinted from *American Poetry Review* 17 (May/June 1988): 17–19.

> patterns tight-closed
> eyes used to make in childhood when
> the greenish thickwoven cotton tablecover,
> frayed and become an ironing sheet, linked itself somehow
> to a September casbah imagined
> before any casbah became knowledge. . . .

The diction is swift, but the transformational language "linked itself somehow" is vague. "The Spirits Appeased" is unadulterated—

> This is the way
> you have spoken to me, the way—startled—
> I find I have heard you. When I need it,
> a book or a slip of paper
> appears in my hand, inscribed by yours. . . .

She proceeds to take up the issue of what happens "when our attention is somewhere else." And the poetry is strongest when it confronts the basic tremors of our lives—"We are not well but while we look away, / . . . a very strong luminous arm reaches in / . . . And though it may have nothing at all to do with us, / . . . nevertheless our condition thereby changes" ("Window-Blind").

In her essay "Work and Inspiration: Inviting the Muse," Levertov insightfully speaks of her process: "poems that seem to come as 'givens' often seem to have that aura of authority . . . that air of being mysteriously lit from within." She speaks frankly, as she goes through drafts, of sometimes "straining" to write; of sometimes "extraneous allusions." She also refers, in an interview, to composition:

> thinking and feeling are really working together . . . so let's call it perception. . . . But articulations—in the sense that our bones, our fingers are articulated, right? they have joints, they can bend—occur. These occur within the rationale of the syntax, and the line break is a particularly sensitive means of recording these things.

This is a well-known defense, and her line can bring what is most disquieting about free verse, its looseness, to account in a naturally expedient fashion. But didactic, trite articulations in the book slow this darting bird-like freshness to:

From the divine twilight, neither dark nor day,
blossoms the morning. Each, at work in his art,
perceived his neighbor. Thus the Infinite
plays, and in grace
gives us clues to His mystery.

This break-up of a fairly prosaic expression into lines has neither the power nor surprise of the Rilkean ambulatory line. This is a "Variation on a Theme by Rilke," without his voice that makes the whole century bear down. As he puts it in a letter to Ilsa Jahr: "The comprehensible slips away, is transformed; instead of possession one learns relationship." But Levertov can rise to that occasion in the same poem:

whose windows' ruby
and celestial sapphire can be seen
only from inside, but then
only when light enters from without?

In the image and out from the image comes the relation between spirit and matter:

Not one by one but in passionate clusters
we pressed the grapes to our lips.
Their bloom was bloom,
the dust plain dust,
a time of happiness.
We had suffered,
only a little, still,—our ignorance grown
only a little more shallow.

("Girls")

This mobility from the short to the long line has a sensuous existence, its rhetoric a light touch, much better than the sentimental

I trusted
utterly that at last,
however late, we'd get home.
No owl, no lights, the dun ridges
of ploughland fading. No matter.
I trusted you.

("To Olga")

This isn't enacted, and therefore lacks body. She can be vapid: "Traces / of blue shadow / melting like ice" ("August Daybreak") or close and sensuous again:

> There was blue, there was brown paler than ivory, a half-curtain,
> there were other blues and an aspiration to whiteness,
> there were preludes to green, pink, gold and aluminum. . . .
>
> ("The Spy")

If there are doubts about the flashes of imagery, the flashes of insight, they are corroborated by some of the sketchier poems. They are piquant, not poignant. "Captive Flower" ends, "I had not thought myself / a jailor." And where there is the simple statement there is the risk of the simplistic: "Missing Beatrice" ends. "But you— / you're gone and we never / really saw you." This middle section is weak—here, again, the end of "Every Day": "Every day, every day I hear / enough to fill / a year of nights with wondering"—but the book begins to pick up its language. Levertov seems to be at her tough essences when she is working off of themes, photos, other poetry. The second set of spinoffs do so from sentences taken out of context from her readings. She is here more powerful in the image than in the loose metaphor. Compare "Here's the cold inn, / the wanderer passed it by"—so palpable—to

> A world, the world, where *live shell*
> can explode on impact or, curled elaborate bone,
> be an architecture, domicile
> of wincing leisurely flesh.
>
> ("Wavering")

"Wincing leisurely flesh"? Or

> a presence,
> an energy field more intense than war,
> might pulse then,
> stanza by stanza into the world,
> each act of living
> one of its words, each word
> a vibration of light—
>
> ("Making Peace")

A beautiful sentiment. But poetry, as she puts it, is like goodness:

Goodness was
a fever in you. Anyone

might glow in the heat of it,
go home comforted—

for them a shawl, for you
fire at the bone.

("Missing Beatrice")

DONALD REVELL

From "The Memory and Future of Ourselves"

Over the past three decades, no poet has urged her readers more consistently toward the elsewhere of their uttermost humanity than Denise Levertov. Like Akhmatova, she has invented a language in which desire is indivisible, in which the oppressive precedents of bad faith, bad custom, and bad government disintegrate under the pressure of a will to ecstasy so strong and sincere that it fuses liberty and humanity into one luminous object of desire. And again like Akhmatova, Levertov's ecstasies communalize rather than isolate the experience of human freedom, abandoning the habitual inattention that nurtures repression in favor of a synthetic restlessness in which to see is to move outward and to imagine is to join. In *A Door in the Hive,* the revisionism of desire moves deeply into political and intimate venues: into the mendacious terrors of El Salvador ("Land of Death Squads"), into hagiography ("St. Thomas Didymus"), into the most private mind imagining its own mortality ("A Sound"). In each venue, the metaphor of the collection's title works beautifully, commending the pluralism that results from the poems' attentions, which are themselves means of escape *into* an ever more various material world. Every piece originates at a brink, as in "The Blind Man's House at the Edge of the Cliff":

> At the jutting rim of the land he lives,
> but not from ignorance,
> not from despair.
> He knows one extra step from his seaward
> wide-open door would be
> a step into salt air,
> and he has no longing to shatter himself
> far below, where the breakers
> grind granite to sand.

Review of *A Door in the Hive* (1989). Reprinted from *Ohio Review* 45 (1991): 92–96.

> No, he has chosen a life
> pitched at the brink, a nest on the swaying
> tip of a branch, for good reason. . . .

Here, attention obviates both ignorance and despair, two forms of blindness and repression. Here, brinkmanship is not a game with annihilation, but a constant readiness to witness and inhabit something where nothing was before. Precedents end at the cliff's edge, and elsewhere begins. There, in the poem's conclusion, Levertov's blind man "breathes face to face with desire," a free citizen of perpetual origin.

Yet the will to ecstasy does not wield an invariable authority. There is an ache as well as a freedom in desire, the ache of nostalgia for an answering, almighty otherness. When Levertov is elegiac, it is the elegiac worldview itself for which she grieves. In "Where Is the Angel?" she mourns the absence of creatures such as the one from whom Jacob wrestled his vision.

> A band of iron,
> like they put round a split tree,
> circles my heart. In here
>
> it is pleasant, but when I open
> my mouth to speak, I too
> am soundless. Where is the angel
>
> to wrestle with me and wound
> not my thigh but my throat,
> so curses and blessings flow storming out
>
> and the glass shatters, and the iron sunders?

Inspiration, like liberty, originates in the actions of individual consciousness, not in the beneficence of a divine other. It will neither come nor yield; it must be made. Indeterminate desire follows only its own voice. When it does not speak, it has nowhere to go. Thus, Levertov elegizes the classical Muse. Similarly, in a tremendously moving poem, she composes an anti-elegy for Robert Duncan ("To R. D., March 4th 1988") in which the loss precedes the death as "Love and long friendship / corroded, shrank, and vanished" long before the obituary date of the poem's title. The purpose of the piece, therefore, is not restoration but revision. Levertov does not wish her former mentor to be a mentor again; mentors, like muses, are demiurges of repression. Instead, she accomplishes a dream, inventing a relationship between herself and Duncan that never existed before it was dreamed.

> I had no need
> for a mentor, nor you to be one;
> but I was once more
> your chosen sister, and you
> my chosen brother.
> We heard strong harmonies rise and begin to fill
> the arching stone,
> sounds that had risen here through centuries.

In anti-elegy, desire designs an imagined future to be free of the past, not via restoration but via radical change.

If we sometimes ache for the past, the past, when imagined as possessing a humanity equal to our own, aches with loneliness for the future. In Levertov's strongest new poems, sincerity liberates posterity and present together, joining them in the community of projective desire. In this way, Levertov transcends the role of simple dialectician in order to take on the more generous, Dickinsonian task of remembering forward ("Life is over there") into a future where memory is no longer helpless and desire no longer uncompanioned.

THE PAST (II)

> My hand on chiselled stone, fitting
> into the invisible
>   print of the mason's own
>   where it lay
> a moment of that year the nave
> was still half-risen, roofless . . .
>
> There's a past that won't suffice:
> years in billions,
> walls of strata. My need roams
> history, centuries not aeons.
> And replica is useless.
>
> The new dust
> floated past, his mate
> from the scaffolding reached down
> for the water-jug.

            This stone
or another: no inch of all
untouched. Cold, yes,

    but that human trace
    will burn my palm.
    This is a hunger.

The imagination begins its work by annihilating repressive distinctions between then and now, absence and presence, process and completion. The first gesture of the poem locates the speaker in the finished church, joining hands with the remote, anonymous mason. So joined, both represent the insufficiency of their situations: in his moment, the mason's work is incomplete; in hers, the speaker discovers "There's a past that won't suffice." Each is a figure of need to be satisfied only by futurity. To each, "replica is useless" because image is no substitute for fact. Having a picture of the finished church in his mind does not relieve the mason of his labor. Having animated the past in *her* mind does not relieve the speaker of her desire to escape the stratifications of time. In one phrase, Levertov asserts the dysfunction of mimesis while creating a community of desire, a wedding if you will, in the vivid double church. And in keeping with her particular genre of sincerity, this wedding does not resolve desire so much as compound it. As visible hand joins invisible hand, cold stone burns living flesh. "This is a hunger." To contact is to want more than contact. To be wedded to the past at the brink of futurity only sharpens the will to departure.

A Door in the Hive offers us the alternatives of uncertain, prospective commitments. Even in those poems that most explicitly detail her Christianity. Levertov accentuates not the consolations of faith, but its speculative perils. The saint's vision is an "unravelling." The Annunciation of the Virgin draws its meaning not from God's design for salvation, but from young Mary's "consent, / courage unparalleled," which "opened her utterly." Such openness best characterizes both the motives and the forms of Levertov's espousal of desire. Each moment and each utterance verges on an unknowing more beautiful than any closure. And we, as readers, are urged yet never directed into that unknowing. As "The Book without Words" concludes, "You have come to the shore. / There are no instructions."

PART TWO *Poetics*

JAMES E. B. BRESLIN

Denise Levertov

We must have poems that move away from the discursively confessional, [the]
descriptive, dilutedly documentary and from the fancies of inauthentic surrealism to
the intense, wrought, bodied-forth and magical—poems that make us cry out with
Carlyle, "Ah, but this sings!"

—Denise Levertov

The formalist poetry of the fifties, passively reflecting broader social and cultural attitudes, constituted a literary *trend*. One ironic result of such trends is that they generate *movements* that are self-consciously dissident and programmatic. Poetry once again becomes critical, poetic theory polemical. One such movement in the fifties was that identified with the "beat," underground world peopled with thieves, junkies, and other decidedly unliterary and "angelheaded hipsters" that Ginsberg mythologized in "Howl." Another group, less mystical and less demonic, more literary than social in its disaffiliations, was that centered around Charles Olson and Black Mountain College.

Black Mountain, a small experimental college founded in 1933 in the foothills of western North Carolina, was floundering when Olson was brought in to direct it in 1951; and in the following and final five years of its life, Olson, putting its antitraditional, individualistic theories of education into practice, brought the college to a kind of final flowering. Under Olson's direction, Black Mountain became, according to Martin Duberman, a place distinctive

> not in endowment, numbers, comfort or public acclaim, but in quality of experience, a frontier society, sometimes raucous and raw, isolated, and self-conscious, bold in its refusal to assume any reality it hadn't tested—and therefore bold in inventing forms, both in life style and art, to contain the experiential facts that supplanted tradition's agreed-upon definitions.[1]

Such an innovative spirit seems a genuine extension of Olson's insistence on viewing only the man in the "field" of the present

Reprinted from James E. B. Breslin, *From Modern to Contemporary: American Poetry 1945–1965* (Chicago: University of Chicago Press, 1984), 142–75. Copyright © 1984 by the University of Chicago.

55

moment as real. But however much such a spirit may have penetrated the day-to-day activities of the school, it seems to have provoked accomplishment less among its students (with Ed Dorn and Robert Rauschenberg as the main exceptions) than its faculty, with the college less important for its experimental methods of education than as a meeting ground for artists (many of them exiles from New York City) who believed in "inventing forms" as a matter of human and artistic necessity. Thus, in the early fifties the faculty included important avant-garde figures from several of the arts—in music (John Cage), painting (Franz Klein), dance (Merce Cunningham), and poetry (Robert Creeley and Robert Duncan as well as Olson). Moreover, even under severe financial pressures, the college supported the *Black Mountain Review,* which had an importance far greater than its short life (seven issues between spring 1954 and fall 1957) might suggest. Not only did it provide an outlet for the work of poets not acceptable to the established quarterlies (Allen Ginsberg and Denise Levertov were two), but it allowed the inventive spirit of the college to become a visible and stimulating one in American poetry.

In a 1961 review of books by Gilbert Sorrentino, Le Roi Jones, and Paul Blackburn, Denise Levertov places these three poets "among the inheritors of a usable tradition, [who] have as ground under their feet all that Williams and Pound have given us." The three, moreover, "have been influenced in double strength, as it were: both from their reading of the older poets and through what Charles Olson and Robert Creeley have made of it (though none of the three actually studied under Olson or Creeley at Black Mountain College)."[2] Here, Levertov is also defining her own place in modern American poetry: as a poet who (as of the early sixties at least) had descended from Williams and Pound by way of Olson and Creeley, though she herself had never attended or even appeared at Black Mountain College. What the writers of the Black Mountain group shared, according to Robert Creeley, was that

> each one of us felt that the then existing critical attitudes toward verse, and that the then existing possibilities for publication for general activity in poetry particularly, were extraordinarily narrow. We were trying in effect to think of a base, a different base from which to move.[3]

Along with this common antipathy, these poets shared a view of the line as breath-spaced, emphasized use of the printed page as a means of scoring the poem for speech, and defined literary form as a dynamic unfolding or process. The new "base" these poets sought had been articulated, in short, in Olson's essay "Projective Verse."

As Levertov's identification of a line of succession clearly suggests, the Black Mountain response to the poetic crisis of the fifties was neither Ginsberg's plunge into the urban underground nor Lowell's descent into the "hell" of the private psyche; rather, poets like Olson, Creeley, and Levertov proposed to continue and advance the work of such then-marginal figures as Williams and Pound. Unlike Olson, however, Levertov remains at ease within such a line of succession and, as we shall see, she develops in O *Taste and See* an attitude toward literary predecessors (and male authority in general) that is more complex than Olson's rivalry. Not viewing the literary past as a Moloch threatening to swallow her up, Levertov never makes exaggerated claims of accomplishing an absolute break with the past; she avoids the grandiose histrionics of a Ginsberg or an Olson. At the same time, Levertov may be said to be less ambitious in proportion as she is less pretentious, and her modesty raises two key questions, to which we will return. Less inclined to take risks, does Levertov play it too safe and end up being too limited? If, as she says, she derives from Williams and Pound by way of Olson and Creeley, how different is that, say, from Wilbur's descent from Eliot by way of the New Criticism? The brief answer to the second of these two questions is that her stance was the more active one at the time and that Levertov finally alters what she inherits in a way that Wilbur does not; in fact, the notion of transforming that which is given and which has been repeated through human experience becomes a crucial one in both her theory and practice of poetry.

Among the Black Mountain poets, I select Levertov not because I think she is better (though she does merit much more attention than she has received) but because of the admirable richness and complexity of her development—moving from work in the late forties that was traditional in form and romantic in substance, to poetry in the late fifties that seemed innovative but actually derived from Williams, and finally in the midsixties, in O *Taste and See,* to a poetry of her own, a poetics of magical realism. Often Levertov's work is condescendingly dismissed as a poetry of intense perception, and it is true that she values "an ecstasy of attention" and that her poems break open traditional forms in order to admit the objects and energies of the immediate physical world.[4] Like many of her contemporaries, she steps outside the fifties' bounds of literariness by beginning with a poetic realism. Her stress on such externality leads to her negative critiques of both confessionalism and surrealism. Yet it is also the case that in the essay where she most fully attempts to place herself in contemporary poetry—"Great Possessions" (1970)—she spends most time attacking what she calls the style of "documentary realism" that has descended from the poetry of Williams.

> What began as a healthy reaction, a turning away with relief from sterile academic rhetorics, had proliferated in an unexampled production of *notations:* poems which tell of things seen or done, but which, lacking the focus of that energetic, compassionate, questioning spirit that infused even the most fragmentary of Williams's poems, do not impart a sense of the experience of seeing or doing, or of the *value* of such experience. (*PW,* 90)

To speak, as Levertov does here, of the value of such experience is, of course, to posit some external (and prior) framework from which it derives value. Increasingly, as Levertov's career has proceeded, she has come to identify that framework as "supernatural" (*PW,* 98). Unlike Ginsberg, she locates the visionary as immanent in the here and now, but she does seek the "form beyond forms" (*PW,* 7). Her colloquial, literalistic language strives to become numinous. "The substance, the means, of an art," she writes, "is an incarnation—not reference but phenomenon" (*PW,* 50). Such stress on the self-sufficient being of a work of art sounds modernist, as do her frequent characterizations of the poem as "disinterested" or "autonomous"; similarly, she emphasizes the work as a *verbal object* much more than beat or confessional poets usually do. Nevertheless, the poem for Levertov is not simply a self-reflexive object and the poet no mere cunning artificer. A poem, she says, is "the poet's means of summoning the divine"; as she contends, the poem is a "temple," the poet a "priest"—and the language of poetry, at once summoning and incarnating the gods, is magical (*PW,* 47). Such a line of thought, of course, invites substituting spiritual for literal reference, a danger Levertov seeks to avoid by insisting that the divine be discovered *in* the ordinary and that it be *embodied* in the language of the poem; she really means the incarnational metaphor, and a successful poem, for her, makes the word flesh in a language of magical realism. When her poems do fail, it is most often because a mythic dimension has been merely imposed upon the poem's material and the presence of the gods is merely asserted rather than convincingly summoned. At her best, however, Levertov gives us poems that are "intense, wrought, bodied-forth and magical—poems that make us cry with Carlyle, 'Ah, but this sings!' "

Levertov's first book, *The Double Image,* appeared in England in 1946 when she was twenty-three; the starting point for her poetry, as it was for such American contemporaries as Wilbur and Rich, was the dilemma of a centerless world, how to enter it, how to live and write in it. Participating in a symposium on myth in 1967, Levertov identified "the sense of *life as a pilgrimage*" as the myth informing "all of my work from the very beginning" (*PW,* 62–63). The poems of *The Double Image,* however, constitute a kind of failed pilgrimage. Divided into two sections, "Fears" and "Promises," the book is intended to record a journey that progresses from anxiety to acceptance—specifically, acceptance of life's double image, its fears *and* its promises. But while the poems do long to break out of the self-immolated solitude, they never succeed in doing so convincingly, and so the predominant feeling is one of loss and nostalgia, a lament for the absence of both vitality ("the lost élan," 12) and of intelligible order in experience. The first two poems, "Childhood's End" and "They, Looking Back," set the tone with their lamentations for the poet's exile from a "miraculous" Edenic world and her entry into the ambivalent temporal world of "love *and* death." Levertov's lost world is a magical one, where dreams are actualities and life a fairy tale.

> Trees in the park were wearing coats of mail:
> the nightly fairytale lived there by day—
> flying Mary Anna,
> little crying leaves,
> the eight wonderful stones.
> To bed by daylight meant a secret journey.
>
> (*DI,* 10)

But, Levertov continues, "time grew hostile," and she was cast out into what she later calls "the ravaged landscape of the lost" (20)—a realm of isolation, walls, "barricades" (14), divisions, "duality's abyss / unspanned by desire" (15). Poems in the "Fears" section stress the discrepancy between reality and the poet's idealized expectations of it. Her disappointments, however, prompt withdrawal and the conclusion that the external world is "alien and unreal" (30). Hence, throughout the book, physical objects are experienced as "shades," "phantoms," "ghosts," "images"— dim presences that mirror back her own subjective states. In reverie and withdrawal, the world, no longer "hostile," can be safely solipsized. Levertov no doubt has her own encapsulated condition in mind when she describes a man who "lay entranced, and heard / the soft forgetful murmur of his flowers / lovingly bent over their mirrored doubles"—an apt image of the drowsy solipsistic self, always at least one remove from reality, feeding on images rather than actualities (44).

In short, rather than accepting its loss, these poems seek to recover the lost magical world of childhood by transforming objects into manipulable images and poetry into reverie. Ideals, rather than being modified by contact with experience, are stubbornly clung to. And the poet that emerges is a self-protected and self-insulated figure, not unlike the authors of *The Beautiful Changes* and *A Change of World*. Moreover, like Rich, Levertov often criticizes the sterility of her defenses; even in the "Fears" section she sometimes tries to shake herself out of reverie and enter the present.

> Now when the night is blind with stars
> now when candles dazzle the day
> now
> turn from phantoms
>
> (*DI*, 21)

—the repeated "now" a reminder that her next book, *Here and Now,* will make the journey that she can here only exhort herself to. Similarly, in "Only Fear" she turns on her work, critiquing its subjects ("familiar images of mellow ruin") and its style ("pensive grace"), and hopes "to penetrate / the woolen forest and discover // an earthy path and unembroidered gate, / a credible living world of danger and joy"; and in the last of the "Fears" poems, "Meditation and Voices," she attacks her "vanity," questions why she must "hear your sorrows, count your sins, / and hope to rub a genie from your ring," that is, hope for magical absolution and deliverance.

But the poems of the second half of the book never make this transition from dream to reality; instead of "promises" kept, we get mere wishfulness. Affirming a living core hidden behind the "impassive mask" (33) or the "ravaged landscape," "Return" and "For B.M." open the possibility of spanning "duality's abyss";

"Ballad," "April (II)," "Days," "Midnight Quatrains," and "Listen!" affirm the "flame" of passionate experience. But in what will become a problem throughout all of Levertov's career, her resolutions here are simply asserted, either by uplifting discursive language or by ready-made symbolism, and in both cases a lack of specificity in her language makes it hard for us to feel she is in touch with a "*credible* living world." At the same time, the poems reveal some ambiguity about just what kind of world the poet is willing to enter: some accept a divided world of danger and joy, but others achieve acceptance only after discovering some hidden "core" or center, so that it is not clear whether Levertov is prepared to make a pilgrimage that is not made meaningful by some final end(s). "I need a green and undulating line / the hill's long contours in my words" (32), Levertov writes. Earlier she tells herself that "words must be flesh and blood, not ghosts" (17), anticipating her later conception of poetic language as incarnational. But the words of *The Double Image* remain ghostly rhetorical assertions, familiar symbols, and so at the book's close Levertov is still exhorting herself to leave "the comfortable myth and drowsy mansion" to wander through real life (44). As much as Levertov strains to put herself and her poems into motion, her first book remains static, fixated—with the poet's consciousness locked inside the "walls of dream" (14).

Throughout *The Double Image* Levertov appears at ease with set, traditional forms in a way American contemporaries such as Lowell, Wilbur, and Merwin were not; hers is not an artifice that continually calls attention to itself. Nevertheless, her poems remain even more narrowly circumscribed within a period style than theirs do. Her dreamy melancholy and her external forms, her "pensive grace," place her poems in the predominant movement in England after the Second World War, the neoromanticism in which poets such as Alex Comfort and Herbert Read were the leading figures. Levertov had by this time read Eliot and Auden, but her first book suggests that in postwar England the main strategy for dealing with the moderns, who probably appeared much less awesome against the background of the long British tradition, was to proceed as if they had never written and to return to the premises of romanticism.[5] But with *Here and Now* (1957) her view of the tradition and her sense of her own poetic genealogy radically altered.

"Only expected echoes / merit attention // not generosities," Levertov complains in "A Story, a Play," a poem responding to critical attacks on a story by Robert Creeley and a play by Wil-

liams (*OI*, 5). Now Levertov shuns "expected echoes," re-
nounces the advantages of a style that had already gained her
acceptance, and enters "new ground, new made" (*HN*, 22), a
ground she explores with just that generosity of attention that
had been missing in her first book. "Rules are broken," she says
in "A Story, a Play," to let us in, both to the here and now and
the poem itself, new made. Compare these lines from "Cassel-
den Road, N.W. 10" in *The Double Image:*

> Shadows of leaves like riders hurried by
> upon the wall within. The street would fill
> with phantasy, the night become
> a river or an ocean where the tree
> and silent lamp were sailing; the wind would fail
> and sway towards the light.

with these lines from "Laying the Dust" in *Here and Now:*

> The water
> flashes
> each time you
> make it leap—
> arching its glittering back.

In *The Double Image* the moment of poetry occurs when quotid-
ian reality is suddenly transformed by "phantasy," as if the physi-
cal world were an emptiness without a subjective presence to fill
it up. But in *Here and Now* the moment of poetry occurs when an
ordinary event, like wetting down dust with buckets of water,
generates a flash of sensual delight. The lines in "Laying the
Dust," rather than marking off predetermined units of measure,
mark off parts of a physical activity for careful attention at the
same time that they dramatize the processes of the mind attend-
ing to that experience: first we get an object ("water"), then its
thrust into brilliant motion with "flashes," then the generalized
activity of "flashes" is separated into "each time," then the in-
volvement and energy of the human agent ("make it leap"), and
then the poet's own metaphoric leap which makes the water
("arching its glittering back") seem animal-like, alive and inde-
pendent. "Laying the Dust" does not give us a world of phanta-
sies imposed by human subjectivity but an exchange between
self and world, "an / interpretation, both ways," as Williams
puts it.[6]

Ten years had passed between *The Double Image* (1946) and *Here and Now* (1956); "the early '50s were for me transitional, and not very productive of poems," recalls Levertov (*PW*, 67). For this English-born poet, too, midcentury was a time of personal change and poetic crisis. The year after publication of *The Double Image* she married Mitchell Goodman and, after a year's travel in Europe, they settled in New York City; in 1949 Levertov's son was born. In 1953 Allen Ginsberg would move from the East to the West Coast to free himself from both family and the established literary culture; Levertov moved from England to the East Coast for similar reasons, and with similarly liberating effects. "There are no miracles but facts," she declared in a 1951 poem (*OI*, 3), and with her removal to America she had not become the romantic wanderer she had exhorted herself to be in the closing poems of *The Double Image* but, with marriage and motherhood, she had rooted her life in domestic experience. As we shall see, acceptance of limits—physical, temporal, domestic—becomes integral to her definition of the creative process. At the same time there were specifically literary influences in helping her find an alternative to "expected echoes" and "the fabulous / poem" (*OI*, 2). Not long after coming to the United States, she met Robert Creeley, whom her husband had known at Harvard, "and through our friendship with him we later came to know a number of people connected with Black Mountain College."[7] She read Olson, including the essay "Projective Verse," and she came to know Williams, who "became the most powerful influence on my poetry" in the fifties (*PW*, 67).

Levertov had first read Williams, both poems and *In the American Grain*, while living in Paris in 1947, just after her marriage. She had "an *immediate* feeling that here was something, something that was going to speak to me," but at first she was bewildered by Williams's versification or his apparent lack of one. "I literally didn't know how [the poems] would sound. I couldn't read them aloud. I couldn't scan them, you know. I didn't understand the rhythmic structure."[8] Levertov has since attributed her difficulties with Williams to her lack of familiarity with American speech. With her actual experience of "American speech" and "the pace" of American life, "I picked up [Williams's poems] again, and I found to my joy that I could read them—and I think it was simply that my ear had gotten used to certain cadences."[9] By 1951 she was exchanging letters with Williams, and their correspondence reveals him relating to her as both loving paternal supporter:

Take care of yourself my dear and keep on with your writing. Because we love you. And don't bother to come out to the suburbs where you can do nothing to help us find ourselves in this mystifying dilemma in which we all find ourselves.

The poet is the only one who has not lost his way, and you are a poet. We must look to you. Keep on doing what you are already doing for us.[10]

And as tough artistic conscience:

Cut and cut again whatever you write—while you leave by your art no trace of your cutting—and the final utterance will remain packed with what you have to say.[11]

In fact, "Pare down, peel away" was exactly the advice that Levertov was urging upon herself in one of the earliest (1951) poems in her new manner—excellent advice for the author of the wordy poems in *The Double Image*.[12]

Williams thus encouraged Levertov to strip down her language and to expand the range of her work, leading her to conclude that "the artist doesn't impose form upon chaos," as so many poets and critics of the fifties supposed, "but discovers hidden intrinsic form."[13] According to Levertov, "The mountain is master of the landscape in which it is a presence," but "one does not emulate such a master, except by being more oneself" (*PW*, 243). In the early fifties, Levertov was drawn to the Williams of the shorter poems, with his "sharp eye for the material world" and his "keen ear for the vernacular" (*PW*, 67), but in *Here and Now* (1956) and *Overland to the Islands* (1958) she often emulated this figure (to adopt his own distinction) by *copying* his manner rather than by imitating his essential spirit.[14] To a significant degree, she was replacing "expected echoes" with unexpected ones.

"Silence / surrounds the facts. A language / still unspoken," Levertov writes in "A Silence." It is the language of fact ("precise / as rain's first / spitting words on the pavement," *HN*, 32) that she now proposes to speak, rejecting the ghostly diction and "mirrored doubles" of her first book. Yet even in her new poems it is quickly apparent how little the sharply defined visual image, the poem as "*notation*" engages her; her observations are exact, her poetry highly sensuous, but her perceptions are given value and force as manifestations of "the core / lost impulse" (*HN*, 31; compare "the lost élan") which she now locates in physical experience and in language itself. As we have seen with Olson, Levertov celebrates the "here and now," but she does so mainly because she finds hidden within it an absent core of energy. In her poems of the late fifties she avoids any open sacralizing or mythologizing of this force. She finds it in the vigorous "laughing" bird of "The Bird," the "intently haphazard" dog of "Overland to the Islands," the plunge of the "real rain, sensuous" in "The Way Through," the bird caught in her room who, after almost battering itself to death against the walls, finally soars "straight out" the window in "The Flight," in the "waterwoman" who "goes dancing in the misty lit-up town / in dragon-fly dresses and blue shoes," in the poet's dance "alone among the fireflies on the / dark lawn, humming and leaping" in "In Obedience."

As Levertov writes in "Beyond the End," "It's energy: a spider's thread: not to / 'go on living' but to quicken, to activate: extend"—and both the poem's argument and its title (which she at one time considered using as the title for *Here and Now*) suggest her renunciation of the weariness and detachment that characterized so much of American poetry in the fifties. Levertov now holds that it is "the will to respond," the manifestation of human energy, which allows us to do more than merely "go on living," to go "beyond the end / beyond whatever ends: to begin, to be, to defy," that allows the poet to break open those "walls of dream" which had enclosed her in *The Double Image*. Levertov's poems now mock the conventional wisdom that admonished us, "DISPOSE YOUR ENERGIES / PRACTISE ECONOMIES" (*HN,* 18); the "unlived life" (a phrase from Rilke, *HN,* 14) is, in a recurring figure, "caged," based on "civic prudence" (*HN,* 15) and issuing in sterile repetition, "passing / repassing, drooping, / senselessly reviving" (*HN,* 17), with "senselessly" a pun suggesting both "meaninglessly" and "without sensual content": for Levertov a life without sensual contacts *is* a life without meaning. Opposed to both caution and obsessive repetition is the pilgrimage, "the will to respond" extended into the world. "*It was thus and thus /* repeats the head, the fantasist"; instead of being caged in dreamy retrospectiveness Levertov now urges "*continuing variously*" (*OI,* 20). So, again, it is energetic motion (as in the dance) that holds her attention, not the static visual image. In "Turning," as she is describing a room full of objects—

> planes tilt, interact, objects
>   fuse, disperse,
>   this chair further from that table . . .

—Levertov suddenly tries to *fix* her attention: "hold it! / Focus on that: this table / closer to that shadow," but as the very necessity of locating the table in relation to the shadow reveals, holding the attention is as impossible as it is undesirable. "Turn, turn!" Levertov declares; "loyalty betrays"—a paradox based upon acceptance of change in an open and fluid universe.

The energy manifest in physical experience is also hidden within language itself; poems are therefore at least as much linguistic acts of discovery as they are discoveries of objects and forces in the "real" world. As a result, "copies of old words" will not do (*HN*, 9). Counter to such poetic repetition is what Levertov identifies in "Ink Drawings" as "energy, gay, terrible, rare, / a hope, man-made"; poetic energies are finally linguistic ones, man-made, and it often seems that the vital physical forces that engage Levertov are not fully accessible to human consciousness until they are embodied in language, in words that, because they are carefully chosen, are themselves alive, not mere copies. "The mirror caught in its solitude / cannot believe you as I believe," Levertov writes in "The Lovers." A mind that merely reflects the world may "go on living," but does so in solitude and silence, lacking the will to respond that makes us fully human. Similarly, poems that mirror the world—as (in Levertov's view) documentary notations and confessional poems do—are dead copies, while poems that are authentic acts of discovery give us that "rare" "man-made" energy. Such claims are, of course, vulnerable to the kinds of objections I raised in connection with Olson's "Projective Verse" in chapter 3. In particular, what Levertov "discovers" is hidden; presence, for her, turns out to be absent, and so the possibility is raised as to whether or not we are getting psychic projection or mythic imposition rather than actual discovery—a possibility that becomes all the stronger when we recognize that the energy she celebrates comes very close to a universal, mythic force, one perhaps all too man- (or woman-) made. At this point in her career Levertov is not yet ready to explore, as she will be in *O Taste and See,* some of these dilemmas of her poetic, but it is true that her stress on the poem as construction keeps her from adopting a naive conception of poetic presence. "Honesty // isn't so simple," she writes in "The Third Dimension," questioning the premises of the simpler forms of confessionalism before it had been invented: "a simple honesty is // nothing but a lie" because "the words / change it." Levertov, however, does not move from this perception into a never-ending meditation on the differences between language and its objects. Instead, she acknowledges poetic artifice, the status of the poem as a verbal illusion; poems are fictive, not actual incarnations. In "The Third Dimension" she refers to a love story she would like to write as a "fiction," reminding us that she had started reading Wallace Stevens when she found his work in the same Paris bookstore in which she had come upon Williams.[15] Levertov derives little from the style of Stevens, but she does share his sense that a phrase I used a few pages earlier, "the language of fact," contradicts itself, expressing an end the poet may pursue but which he will always miss because the words *do* change it. What attracted her to Stevens, Levertov told an interviewer, was "a sense of magic" in his early work, and she went on to say that a combination of the "realism" of Williams and the "illusionism" of Stevens would produce an ideal poet, one whose work, as we shall see, would embody a poetics of magical realism.[16]

For Levertov, then, a poem is a made object, a construction—but, as Olson had said, "a high-energy construct." In "Merrit Parkway" Levertov describes the perpetual movement of the cars speeding "relentlessly" along "the / sealed road" (*OI*, 8)—another version of the "unlived life" in which nothing changes, nothing is experienced, the highway a parody of Levertov's pilgrimage, which takes her from a "sealed" and "dreamlike" consciousness into an open world, from the closed autotelic poem to the poem as a field of action. The "new ground" she is claiming ("every step an arrival," *OI*, 1) is a world of fact *and* movement, not lost in "copies of old words" enclosed in copies of old forms but incarnated in "lines alive, *acts* of language" (*HN*, 16) that produce a poem that is "a dance of the words" (*HN*, 20).

But while Levertov repudiated the expected modes of the fifties, the ground she enters in *Here and Now* and *Overland* was not entirely new poetic territory. It is not just that her poetics, as I have been suggesting, derives from Williams by way of Olson, but that she also takes subjects and even tone of voice from Williams. "Sunday Afternoon," "Broken Glass," and "Jackson Square"—all poems where Levertov finds instinctive vitality in a "dusty" urban world—are close to Williams's proletarian poems. "The sink is full of dishes. Oh well," she begins "The Dogwood," a poem strongly reminiscent of "Le Médicine Malgré Lui," where Williams makes light of his medical obligations. Like the Ginsberg of *Empty Mirror,* she learned from Williams how to play prose sense against the brief pauses signaled by the end of a line—how, in short, to space and break lines, "the

67

proper space / holding existences in grave distinction" (*OI*, 36); but when she writes,

> I want to speak to you.
> To whom else should I speak?
>
> (*HN*, 27)

or

> We are faithful
> only to the imagination. *What the*
> *imagination*
>   *seizes*
> *as beauty must be truth.*
>
> (*HN*, 23)

she is trying to emulate her "illustrious ancestor" by becoming him. Williams did open possibilities that encouraged Levertov "to begin, to be, to defy"; but the here and now she enters in these poems is one that often seems to have been invented by Williams, experienced through his eyes and ears.

"The Shifting," published in *Origin* in 1952, announced a "change of pleasure," a pleasure *in* change; the shift from *The Double Image* to books like *Here and Now* and *Overland to the Islands* took Levertov from reverie to more immediate experience, from the "sealed" to the open poem. But in her next two books, *With Eyes at the Back of Our Heads* (1960) and *The Jacob's Ladder* (1961), Levertov continues to shift, now turning even more explicitly to discovery of what lies hidden within or beyond physical reality: "the quick of mystery" (*WE*, 49). In her work of the late fifties she had concentrated upon the surfaces of ordinary objects, but she now identifies "the real," as she writes in "Matins," as a "new-laid / egg whose speckled shell / the poet fondles and must break / if he will be nourished" (*JL*, 58); the poet still handles the surfaces of things lovingly, but she is now concerned to "break" the outside open and arrive at what she calls in "A Ring of Changes" the "true form" (*WE*, 39). At the end of "Matins" Levertov invokes a "Marvelous Truth" which can be found in the quotidian world, and her search for it leads her to view visible objects as "guises" (*JL*, 60), to be cracked open, like the speckled eggshell. In several poems she represents the muse as blind but "all-seeing" (*JL*, 40) because intuitive sight (of the sort accomplished with the eyes at the back of our heads) or the visionary ascent (of the sort accomplished by climbing the Jacob's Ladder) is what she finally stresses in these poems. In fact, what Levertov has done is to return to that magical world where form and content, being and becoming are one, from which she had been exiled at the start of *The Double Image*.

This change in Levertov's work—movement toward a kind of visionary poetry and toward a more elevated and more richly musical language—was not a totally abrupt one; signs of a mystical consciousness can be found in both *Here and Now* and *Overland to the Islands*. In "Homage," for example, Levertov praises a poet, "solitary in your empire of magic," who can "sing / dreaming wideawake" (*HN*, 20). Poems such as "The Sharks" and "Action" suggest that the way to activate, extend, is through the unconscious "depths" of the mind (associated with the sea); "The Instant," "Scenes from the Life of the Peppertrees," and "Pure Products" all seek to uncover "the old powers" manifest in the momentary. In "The Instant" (*OI*, 16–17), one of the strongest poems in these two books, Levertov recalls an early morning hunt for mushrooms with her mother, recreating the scene with precise detail: "Wet scrags / of wool caught in barbed wire, gorse / looming, without scent"; but suddenly the surrounding "mist rolls / quickly away" and her vision is swept up and outward:

> "Look!" she grips me, "It is
>   Eryri!
>   It's Snowdon, fifty
>   miles away!"—the voice
> a wave rising to Eryri,
> falling.
>   Snowdon, home
> of eagles, resting-place of
> Merlin, core of Wales.

Her mother's spontaneous use of "Eryri" (legendary Welsh name for Snowdon) helps make this instant a timeless one, as Levertov proceeds from the realistically observed to "the fabulous / poem" which discloses, by invoking the old powers, that remote world of magic and myth (both "home" and "resting-place," beginning and end) that she had sought in *The Double Image*. Ultimately *Here and Now* and *Overland* reflect a certain ambiguity in Levertov's assumptions about the nature of reality and of poetry. Yet it is easy to see how her focus on energy manifest in physical life could easily slide over to a sense of an underlying (and therefore eternal) principle, how the "here and now" can become the locus of "the old powers"—as happens, in fact, in the poetry of Williams himself.

The change in Levertov's work, however, did not result from a deeper reading of Williams, though in "Williams and the Duende" (1973) she claims a Williams who takes us to "the edge of the world, where all is unknown, undefined, the abyss of the gods" (*PW*, 265), a Williams who is consonant with her own new interests. Insofar as the origins of the change were specifically literary, they can be related to her reading of Robert Duncan and H.D. Levertov first met Duncan in the early fifties. Levertov's "The Shifting" "released my sense of a new generation in poetry," according to Duncan;[17] perhaps it did so partly because of the way the poem ("the shifting, the shaded / change of pleasure," it begins) enacts shifting in its transformations of full vowels and lush consonants—a quality that makes it very like Duncan's poetry. Duncan, in any case, acknowledged the impact of her work in "Letters for Denise Levertov: An A Muse Ment," published in the *Black Mountain Review* in 1955.[18] On the other side, Duncan's work, Levertov writes in "Great Possessions" (1970), "has for twenty years been appeasing my own hunger" for a poetry that is authentically magical (*PW*, 101). In 1959 she named Duncan and Creeley as "the chief poets among my contemporaries"; but, as she later told an interviewer, "Duncan has been for me much more of a stylistic influence," citing principally "the greater sort of fullness in his style."[19] Most important, perhaps, is the conviction behind that fullness that language "is not a set of counters to be manipulated, but a Power" (*PW*, 54); poetry then becomes the summoning of a god, the invoking of the old powers, that are hidden *in* language itself. It was Duncan, finally, who introduced Levertov to H.D. in London in the early sixties (*PW*, 247) and who, with the early chapters of the "H.D. Book," no doubt affected the way in which Levertov read H.D.[20] The Levertov who had descended from Williams by way of Olson, now turned to H.D. by way of Duncan.

While Levertov had been "for years familiar" (*PW*, 244) with the early short poems of H.D., it was not until she read "Sagesse" in the *Evergreen Review* (no. 5), that she experienced H.D. as a creative source, sensing "doors, ways in, tunnels through" in her work (*PW*, 244). From "Sagesse" Levertov proceeded chronologically backwards to the *Trilogy*—*The Walls Do Not Fall* (1944), *Tribute to the Angels* (1945), and *The Flowering of the Rod* (1946)—and then back to a rereading of the early "imagist" poems in light of the later mythopoeic work (*PW*, 245). Levertov then recognized that "the icily passionate precision" of the short poems "had not been an *end*, a closed achievement, but a preparation," developing a poetic strength that would enable H.D. to "carry darkness and mystery" in the later poems (*PW*, 245). As Levertov puts it in "H.D.: An Appreciation," "She showed a way to penetrate mystery; which means, not to flood darkness with light so that darkness is destroyed, but to *enter into* darkness, mystery, so that it is experienced" (*PW*, 246). "Let us substitute / enchantment for sentiment, // re-dedicate our gifts / to spiritual realism," H.D. wrote in *The Walls Do Not Fall;*[21] it was in this direction, toward a spiritual or magical realism, that Levertov now rededicated her own work. Williams had opened the sensuous world for Levertov; H.D., along with Robert Duncan, suggested ways to "tunnel through," "to penetrate mystery."

Toward such a passage—toward the poem, in Duncan's term, *as* "passage"—Levertov, at first hesitantly, begins to turn in *With Eyes at the Back of Our Heads*. Yet, even if the journey has taken on a spiritual dimension, the poem continues to be process, as it is in both Williams and H.D., Olson and Duncan. A poem like "A Straw Swan under the Christmas Tree," for example, begins with a concrete object, but it is the interplay between mind and object that generates—in fact, becomes—the poem.

> Its form speaks of gliding
>> though one had never seen a swan
>
>> and strands of silver, caught
>> in the branches near it, speak
>
> of rain suspended in a beam of light,
>
>> one speech conjuring the other.

Here Levertov is not concerned with evolving a language that will carry the presence of objects, as she had been in *Here and Now;* rather, external things (like the shape of the straw swan) *are* a kind of language, their suggestive appearances conjuring speech in her, as in the poem itself. Moreover, this power of objects is directed toward the imagination, since we need not literally to have seen a swan in order to "see" gliding in the shape of the straw figure. Objects, again, are less important than energies, motions; but the movement is now emphatically a linguistic and mental one. "All trivial parts" of the mundane world possess this power, Levertov goes on, to speak of "themselves" and of their metaphoric "counterparts," as the tinsel now speaks of "rain suspended in a beam of light"; she continues,

> Rain glides aslant,
>> swan pauses in mid-stroke,
>>> stamped on the mind's light, but aloof—

The real scene—straw swan, tinsel on a Christmas tree—fades as it conjures an imaginary (or perhaps remembered) one; it has been transformed by the "mind's light" or the imagination into a poetic image, an all-too-poetic image. For there is something unsatisfactory about the created scene; it may be "stamped" forever on the imagination but it remains "aloof" from the actual world that generated it in the first place. Moreover, the way Levertov switches the gliding from swan to rain, and the pause from rain to swan, reinforces the sense that she has moved too far from a world of objects, into a world of pure magic where words conjure words, instead of objects conjuring words. So the poem curves back from the "mind's light" to the physical "eye":

> and the eye that sees them refuses
> to see further, glances off the
> surfaces that
>> speak and conjure,
> rests
>
>> on the frail
>> strawness of straw, metal sheen of tinsel.

At first it may sound as if Levertov is simply moving back from imaginative flight to literal reality; but she does so only in a very special sense. The eye, which cannot get inside hard, opaque objects, glances (like a beam of light) off surfaces, to come to rest—the movement beautifully caught in the placement of the lines—on the "straw*ness* of straw." Levertov has now arrived at the "true form" of her object, the swan, and it is not form as external shape (as it was in the first line of the poem) but form as intrinsic being, a point supported by Levertov's allusion here to a remark by John Donne, "God is a straw in a straw," a sentence that she quotes in an essay, "Origins of a Poem" (1968), commenting that "the strawness of straw, the humanness of the human, is their divinity" (*PW,* 51). The poem, then, seems to come to a rest, and to an end, with the discovery of immanent form; but in fact the poem closes not with rest, but with motion, as Levertov asks herself:

> How far might one go
> treading the cleft the swan cut?

The closing line shows how Levertov can toughen what might be an idealized poetic image, that of the swan gliding across a lake or pond. Earlier, the sounds of "rain glides aslant" easily glide into each other, and the sounds of "swan pauses in mid-stroke" (a line that pauses at midpoint) are similarly soft; the smooth flow of both lines is part of what makes them beautiful but "aloof," while the hard *t*'s and *k*'s in "treading the cleft the swan cut" create a crispness of sound that assures us that the poet is carefully attending to her words: "lines alive, acts of language."

The question that Levertov raises, of course, is how far one might go in following out the suggestions of objects, the evocative powers of words themselves ("one speech conjuring the other"). In other words, how far can she go in pursuing the notion of art as magic that she found in H.D. and Robert Duncan? The danger in following such a lead all the way out is that the poet will end up in a world (and a poem) that is beautiful but remote, disembodied—one that only glances off the surfaces of things rather than perceiving form *in* matter. But it is also true that "A Straw Swan under the Christmas Tree" closes with a question, an open ending that is intended to provoke and to continue movement on the part of the reader, rather than to seal the poem off neatly. The journey continues, the interplay between mind and world persists, beyond the final lines, "beyond the end" of a poem that seeks to activate, extend.

In the midsixties the received critical estimate of Levertov's writing was that, while it showed superior craftsmanship, it lacked, as Robert Bly put it, "a vision."[22] A careful reading of even her earliest poems will, I think, show the superficiality of such a judgment; Bly is really complaining about the absence not of "a" but of his own kind of vision. In fact, *With Eyes at the Back of Our Heads* and *The Jacob's Ladder* both reveal an increasing commitment to a conception of art as magic, as the unveiling of the secret powers hidden inside things, and Levertov's style accordingly becomes fuller, more suggestive, a vernacular expanding to an oracular voice. At the same time, Levertov makes this change slowly, hesitantly, almost reluctantly, so intense is her attachment to concrete experience, and one of the reasons "A Straw Swan under the Christmas Tree" is so rich a poem is that it grows out of her hesitations and conflicts. Moreover, while the two books of the early sixties include many fine individual poems—"With Eyes at the Back of Our Heads," "Another Journey," "The Room," "The Communion," "The Goddess," "To the Snake," "To the Reader," "A Common Ground," "The Jacob's Ladder," "The Necessity," and "A Solitude" are among them—the overall impression created is that Levertov is moving toward a vision she has not yet fully articulated and which she cannot yet consistently embody in her style.

"I like to find / what's not found / at once, but lies // within something of another nature / in repose, distinct," Levertov writes in "Pleasures," one of the poems in *With Eyes at the Back of Our Heads*. She does not want to remain "composed," fully and finally formed, but to break open, to explore and discover, to leap into the world, now characteristically experienced as invigoratingly harsh, "intemperate" (*WE*, 23). "I'm tired / of all that is not mine"—all that is imposed upon or expected of her (*WE*, 22). So in "The Goddess" a demonic muse flings her out of Lie Castle, the poet landing face down in the mud where she finds, and eats, seeds, as if she were a hungry animal. The goddess brings Levertov back to her body because living in her body the poet becomes a goddess. The physical energy stressed in the two previous books is now explicitly transformed into a sacred power, the "animal god" the poet tries to summon in "The Vigil." Throughout *With Eyes*, Levertov conceives of the imagination as a dark, mysterious force, a sacred power, that lies within our physical nature, in repose, distinct.

In *The Jacob's Ladder*, Levertov has pushed even further toward the visionary, now thinking of the imagination as light, a form of spiritual illumination. "A Solitude" describes a blind man whose mind is still active, "filled / with presences," while in "The Illustration" the muse is given "closed all-seeing eyes." Together, the poems suggest the degree to which the physical world—a shell, to be fondled then cracked in "Matins"—recedes in importance for Levertov. The title poem thus defines life's pilgrimage (and the movement of "the poem" itself) as a slow, arduous ascent toward the light, a passage relieved by those moments when "wings brush past" and angelic presences are sensed. The stairway is made real in the poem; it is not a "radiant evanescence" but "of stone," "of sharp / angles, solidly built" and the climber "must scrape his knees" in ascending it; even the angels, who "spring" from one step to the next, "giving a little / lift of the wings," are made physical. Still, the process described is not that of finding the "true form" of a physical object, like a straw swan, but of making substantial a symbolic and spiritual conception, the same process that Levertov describes in "The Necessity." As she says in "The Jacob's Ladder," "the poem ascends," toward the light, and when she does confront immediate objects in this book, they typically become radiant. She speaks of "everlasting light" (15), "the dense light of wakened flesh" (25), "the walls of the garden, the first light" (20), "the heart of fire" (56).

In "The Message," one of the finest poems in her next book, *O Taste and See* (1964), the "Spirit of Poetry" appears "out of sea fog" in a dream, writing to Levertov to ask her to gather "seeds of the forget-me-not." The spirit, which seems to arise from the depths of her own being, bids her to "remember my nature, speaking of it / as of a power," and the poem stresses that the creative power, its seed, is to be found *within* the poet, as even the name of the seed (forget-*me*-not) confirms. At the poem's close, Levertov awakens at daybreak and starts to question the "message" delivered in the dream.

> Shall I find them, then—
> here on my own land, recalled
> to my nature?
>> O, great Spirit!

But what starts out as a question ends as an exclamatory affirmation, and a syntactic ambiguity allows us to read "O, great Spirit" *both* as direct address to an external presence *and* as in apposition with "my nature," and thus referring to an indwelling spirit. The spirit of poetry lies hidden inside the poet, a seedlike power that comes to fulfillment in a poem, the "*flower of work and transition.*" "Returning," she had written in "The Charge," "is a mourning or ghostwalking only" (*WE*, 11)—one of several poems in which she had urged a break with nostalgia or obsession, with repeating the past. But Levertov now imagines the poem as at once a return and an arrival—an old form, an ancient archetype, discovered in new experience, when the poet speaks out of her own nature, a power. Many of the poems in *O Taste and See* deal explicitly with such a return to origins, and they do so because Levertov, not so much shedding as internalizing her illustrious literary ancestors, returns to the whole of her own nature, now strengthened and deepened by the almost twenty years of living and writing since her first book. In *O Taste and See*, her poetry, integrating the dream consciousness of *The Double Image* with the realistic precision of *Here and Now*, achieves its most successful embodiment of magical realism, as her career, enacting the myth that is the seed of *O Taste and See*, becomes a "sequence / returning upon itself, branching / a new way" (12).

Indeed, the notion of a return that is also an advance ("a new way") generates a coherent mythology that informs all of the poems and the single short story that are collected in this distinguished book. Again and again the poems refer to origins, beginnings, sources that are not lost, distant, inaccessible (like Mount Snowdon in "The Instant") but are present, immanent, within the poet's own nature. In "Kingdoms of Heaven" paradise is at first identified as an "endless movie" that "draws you into itself"—a field in which "the attention / never wavers," the field of the poems of *Here and Now*.

> The attention
> lives in it as a poem lives or a song
> going under the skin of memory.

The comparison between the attention and the poem or song, however, shows how Levertov's attention lives among the words of the poem; the comparison speaks back to her, reminding her that works—poems, songs, movies—only live *on* because they live *in* us; they "get under our skin." So Levertov can make a leap of faith, suggesting a different location for the kingdom of heaven:

> Or, to believe it's there
> within you
> though the key's missing
> makes it enough? As if
> golden pollen were falling
>
> onto your hair from dark trees.

In this poem, too, the poet is recalled to her own nature; it is not in being drawn into otherness but, as the short line emphasizes, "within you" that paradise is to be found. Paradise, then, is not a place but, like the spirit of poetry, an energy, a power of the mind; the "key" to unlock it may be missing, but its living presence can be felt in sudden moments of discovery, as when "*golden* pollen" falls from "*dark* trees." "The Film" dramatizes the relation between the work of art and its audience, and Levertov similarly suggests that we deal with the external reality of the work by taking it inside of us; the work, a seed, flowers in our new perceptions of the world. Here she watches a symbolic movie in which "young Heroes," after an encounter with a threatening "Turtle Goddess," are then initiated into a vision of life as a "corridor / of booths," containing "scenes / of bliss or / dark action." But while others in the audience reject or forget the vision of the film, it gets under the skin of the poet's memory and lives on, not just in the poem we are reading, but in the very way Levertov apprehends experience. She equates the passage in the film from the Turtle Goddess to a "confused" life, blissful and dark, with the loss of her mother; she returns home after the movie to see "Mother is gone, / only Things remain. // So be it"—an acceptance that enables her to *begin* to live.

In *O Taste and See* the process of poetic transformation is now at once more magical and sacred and yet more intimately physicalized; creative activity becomes an incorporation, a taking into the body—as the title poem makes plain.

> The world is
> not with us enough.
> *O taste and see*
>
> the subway Bible poster said,
> meaning *The Lord,* meaning
> if anything all that lives
> to the imagination's tongue,
>
> grief, mercy, language,
> tangerine, weather, to
> breathe them, bite,
> savor, chew, swallow, transform
>
> into our flesh our
> deaths, crossing the street, plum, quince,
> living in the orchard and being
>
> hungry, and plucking
> the fruit.

Just as Levertov herself twists the well-known line from Words-worth ("The world is too much with us") and transforms the phrase on the subway Bible poster into her own "meaning," she urges actively taking the world into ourselves, transforming it "into our flesh our / deaths," into our very physical being; experience, in this way, is poetically *em*bodied, incarnated. Moreover, it is "all that lives" and even "our deaths" that we are exhorted to assimilate, any principle of selection, moral or otherwise, necessarily distancing us from experience. In the poem's closing lines Levertov, again enacting its theme, transforms both the myth of Eden and the world of the present by identifying the two, depicting us as "living in an orchard and being // hungry" and rather than deferring to biblical prohibitions, "plucking / the fruit," as Adam had done. In Levertov's mythology, of course, plucking and eating the fruit is precisely the "new way" to energize the self and expand its field of activity. All of this poem from the third line onward consists of a single sentence, the phrase "*O taste and see*" becoming a kind of seed from which, via Levertov's active reading of its "meaning," all the subsequent poem grows. A series of static nouns ("grief, mercy, language, / tangerine, weather") at first define experience; but then human activity is introduced in a series of infinitive phrases ("to breathe," "bite, / savor, chew, swallow, transform"), the infinitives characterizing an activity that, being untensed, seems eternal—as well as an activity that we are exhorted to carry on. But after "transform // into our flesh" all actions are rendered in present participles ("crossing," "living," "plucking"), the testing urged by the poster finally transformed into an activity, both concrete and mythical, that occurs in a continuous present. The self, hungrily taking in new experience, becomes a continually moving and constantly *re*formed center.

The recognition achieved at the end of "The Film," according to Levertov, is that "the house is occupied only by things, not by a psychic presence" (*PW,* 79). It sounds as if Levertov has purged herself of the parental images carried into adult life from childhood, along with the projections that stem from them, and managed to step, barefoot, into reality. But even her capitalization of "Things" in the poem implies an archetypal dimension to them; her poems are, in fact, pervaded with spiritual presences, clearly extensions of psychic ones. Such presences are often female and when they are, they are not simply versions of "the archetypal dominating Mother" (*PW,* 79) like the Turtle Goddess: they are more ambiguous figures, half demonic, half benign, as in Levertov's representation of the muse, evident in the recurrent figure of the moon, in the "Song for Ishtar" (a moon goddess), and most fully and explicitly in "To the Muse." What is striking about this poem is the way Levertov locates her muse within the domestic world, but without domesticating her. The muse in fact manifests the presence of the mysterious within the house, "within you," within a newly conceived domestic order. A "wise man" had told Levertov of the muse, assuring her that the goddess is not an external power "who comes and goes"; "having chosen," Levertov writes, "you remain in your human house," a presence that Levertov compares to "the light of the moon on flesh and hair," a presence that does not intrude upon but illuminates physical reality, as Ishtar is shown to do. At times it seems as if the muse has gone; in reality "you were not gone away / but hiding yourself in secret rooms."

> The house is no cottage, it seems,
>
> it has stairways, corridors, cellars,
> a tower perhaps,
> unknown to the host.

The domestic order within which the muse is housed is not a simple one, safely closed and sealed (a "cottage"); Levertov has already described the warmth and openness necessary to evoke the muse in the first place, and she now suggests a domestic order that has mysterious extensions downward into the dark earth and upward toward the sky. So, while the muse may seem to have vanished and the "host" may rail against her for leaving, "all the while // you are indwelling, / a gold ring lost in the house," the gold ring symbolizing both personal and marital wholeness, linking vision and body, like the image of "the light of the moon on flesh and hair." But just as it's not clear where the muse is, neither is it clear how to find her; once again, "the key's missing."

> Not even a wise man
> can say, do thus and thus, that presence
> will be restored.

The house (self, marriage, poem) *is* occupied by an obscure powerful presence, one that cannot be unlocked at will—but which does appear at those intense moments of communion when we taste and see the world, plucking its fruit.

The house is often occupied by male presences as well, usually in the form of guides whose wisdom is real but limited and which the poet must therefore incorporate and pass beyond. Sometimes, the poems merely represent simple idealizations, as in the loving, patient pastor in "A Cure of Souls." "Old Day the gardener," remembered from girlhood in "A Figure of Time," is more complex, looking like "Death himself, or Time, scythe in hand," but his scythe is really a pruning hook and his destructiveness— cutting back, clearing, weeding—is really life-enhancing; all the gardens "thrived in his care" and he becomes a figure of godlike omnipotence in whose care the poet would like to remain and whose artistic powers she would like to emulate. Such yearnings for protection *are* a form of "mourning or ghostwalking," but more often Levertov represents male guides who open up a vision for her, then depart, leaving her on her own, making the end of the poem a beginning. The "wise man" in "To the Muse" can assure her that the muse is indwelling, but he cannot give her the key to unlock the muse, just as the director in "The Film" offers her a vision in his movie, accompanies her home afterwards, but does not go in with her. When she enters the house, then, both "director" and mother are literally "gone," though aspects of them have been incorporated into her own vision. Similarly, a man and a boy in "The Novices" are drawn by "a clear-obscure summons they fear / and have no choice but to heed." When they arrive at a small clearing, they are met by a "wood-demon" who turns out to be "not bestial" or "fierce" but a "shabby," "shambling" bearlike figure, both "gentle and rough." "To leave the open fields / and enter the forest, // that was the rite," he tells them. "Knowing there was mystery, they could go." In "The Instant" it had been the mother who served as guide, to revelation of a serene, distant, godlike masculine power represented by Mount Snowdon. But in these poems the situation is reversed: a male figure presides over a revelation of dark mysterious powers that are within the poet and which she thinks of as distinctively female. In this sense, too, Levertov is, in O *Taste and See,* recalled to her own nature.

Levertov's desire to establish both continuity with and yet independence from the past applies to her relations to literary predecessors too. In the early sixties some of those modernist poets who, as Stanley Kunitz lamented, "would never consent to die," finally did. In "September 1961" Levertov writes not exactly of the deaths but of the withdrawal into silence of Pound, Williams, and H.D., their preparation for death beautifully described as "a painful privacy // learning to live without words."

> This is the year the old ones,
> the old great ones
> leave us alone on the road.

As they withdraw "the light of their presence," darkness closes in, leaving the younger poets feeling lost, confused, anxious, leaving them with the painful obligation of learning to live with words. But "we have the words in our pockets, / obscure directions"—a sentence we can read as saying that we have both words and obscure directions and that we have words that *are* obscure directions, an ambiguity that shows one of the ways in which Levertov embodies "obscure directions" in her own words. The description of the words as "in our pockets" makes them sound like raisins brought along on a hike; along with "grief, mercy," "tangerine, weather," *"language"* is taken in, absorbed, transformed "into *our* flesh *our* / deaths." Moreover, the very obscurity of the directions and the sense of language itself as mystery allow both for continuity and for plenty of space for difference from the previous generation. The darkening landscape in which the young poets are left—a long road surrounded by "deep woods"—is one that similarly combines direction and obscurity, linearity and digression. Near the end of "September 1961" Levertov writes:

> One can't reach
>
> the sea on this endless
> road to the sea unless
> one turns aside at the end, it seems,
>
> follows
> the owl that silently glides above it
> aslant, back and forth,
>
> and away into deep woods.

"The road leads to the sea," Levertov declared earlier in the poem. What the sea represents, however, is never made clear: it may be death awaiting us at the end of the road of life; it may be eternity; it may be vigorous, primitive life, as the poem's final image ("we think the night wind carries / a smell of the sea") suggests. Throughout the poem the end of the journey remains indefinite; so does the route. We are told that the road is "endless," yet two lines later an "end" is assumed. The only way to reach the sea, moreover, is by turning aside into the woods—"it *seems*." The endless journey toward a mysterious end is not a simple linear one; nor is the reader's movement through the poem, which often turns aside before continuing forward. The act of turning off the road is described through the image of the owl, an image that catches the poet's imagination and which, in a seeming digression, she "turns aside" to "follow"; by doing so, she comes to the image of the "deep woods," which balances and completes the image of the road. Again and again the writing allows the reader to experience "obscure directions," and the poet relates to her reader as her guides had to her—as someone who initiates into mysteries, then withdraws. "Knowing there was mystery, they could go," as do the young poets in "September 1961."

The images of the house in "To the Muse" and the road in "September 1961" reveal Levertov's manner of constantly accepting, and then dissolving, boundaries. In "The Novel" she develops an analogy between the lives of two characters in a work of fiction and the creative life of its author. These characters "live (when they live) in fear // of blinding, of burning, of choking under a / mushroom cloud in the year of the roach." Like their author, they feel "cramped" and would like to take "a thick black / magic marker," strike out all restricting circumstances, and attain "the eternity / of today." The hemmed-in Allen Ginsberg breaks out by means of apocalyptic transcendence—pure magic; but in Levertov selfhood is earned within the limits—physical, temporal, domestic—of secular life, an acceptance that makes possible those moments when we "halt, stretch, a vision / breaks in on the cramped grimace, / inscape of transformation." Only within the house or along the road can we experience the magical extensions of the real: the poetics of magical realism. Levertov gives us not transcendent but immanent vision.

Her poems, in fact, are strongest when they combine linearity with mystery, definition with obscurity. When she goes wrong, it's because she doubts herself or her reader and so floods the poem with light; darkness is destroyed, not experienced. Sometimes, particularly at the ends of poems, mystery is lost in directives and/or explanations. While hosing down "The Garden Wall," Levertov suddenly uncovers "a hazy red, a / grain gold, a mauve / of small shadows, sprung / from the quiet dry brown—"; but Levertov, nervous about significance, converts her particular experience into a general point about discovery: "archetype / of the world always a step / beyond the world, that can't / be looked for, only / as the eye wanders, / found." These lines also illustrate a propensity in Levertov and in Black Mountain poetry generally: to write too many poems about the writing of poetry, so that the poet spends too much time fussing over procedures, too little time deploying them. Elsewhere, Levertov uses familiar (or archetypal) symbolism without sufficient grounding, so that the tropes seem imposed. They have not, in terms of Levertov's own poetic, been taken *in* and given substance. "To the Muse," with its figures of the house, the garden, the hearth, the cave, and the tower, is such a poem; "Claritas" is another. "The All-Day Bird, the artist, / whitethroated sparrow," the poem begins, immediately appropriating the bird for one of Levertov's favorite themes, the poetic process. It is no surprise, then, that in the poem's closing section—

> Sun
> light.
> Light
> light light light.

—all specific reality, all precise distinctions, all "*shadow of a difference,*" disappear in a celebration of pure radiance.

In "The Runes," a prose poem that closes O *Taste and See,* Levertov writes, "In city, in suburb, in forest, no way to stretch out the arms—so if you would grow, go straight up or deep down." Trees fascinate Levertov, perhaps because they go both straight up *and* deep down. Her poems are most successful when they are at least "half in darkness" (*OTS,* 6)—a quality that can be found in "Shalom," a poem that comes immediately after "Claritas" as if to balance its simple ascent. "A man growing old is going / down the dark stairs," Levertov begins.

> He has been speaking of the Soul
> tattooed with the Law.
> Of dreams
> burnt in the bone.

Another of those guides who appears, then withdraws, the old man has been speaking of wisdom, of yearnings, and of sufferings, so ancient they are part of his (and our) very nature, soul and body. As he passes downward he looks up "to the friends who lean / out of light and wine / over the well of stairs." Outwardly comfortable, they are inwardly uneasy, asking his "pardon / for the dark they can't help" because they, like the director's wife in "The Film" ("The darkness / should not be revealed," she insists), they themselves fear the darkness. But at this point the poem makes a series of striking temporal and metaphorical leaps, obscure jumps that transform end to beginning, darkness to light:

> Starladen Babylon
> buzzes in his blood, an ancient
> pulse. The rivers
> run out of Eden.
> Before Adam
> Adam blazes.

The poem seems to spiral backwards in time, from present to Babylon to Eden and "before" even that. In reality, however, time is not a linear sequence, and human experience constantly returns upon itself, branching in new ways. The moment is elusive—"what is passing // is here," she writes in "The Coming Fall"—but within it, here, are both recurrence and new experience. The moment, then, contains the Eden from which Levertov had thought she was banished in *The Double Image,* the magical world to which she now returns; *O Taste and See* takes us "back into life, back to the gods" (*OTS*, 65). In the figure of the aging man, seemingly a victim of time, the search for the light (as in "starladen Babylon") persists, passionate, buzzing in his blood, an ancient pulse. He carries forward an archetypal search. But as words like "tattooed" and "burnt" suggest, it is in descending the stairs, living inside the elusive and often agonizing reality of time—rather than limiting ourselves to the "light and wine" of a comfortable existence—that a full, passionate search becomes possible. Moreover, it is not in the arrival at some final end that illumination lies; rather, it is the burning intensity with which the search itself is conducted that makes the old man blaze even as he descends to the darkness. When we reach the line "Before Adam," we expect the next line to assume a simple temporal sequence and name someone, something, that came earlier than Adam; instead, "Adam blazes" asserts that Adam, being eternal, lives now, in the old man. His descent toward death can be compared with Adam's exile from Eden; both are radiant in their acceptance of, entry into, a life that includes pain and death. In the mythology of *O Taste and See,* the descent of the old man, like the "fall" of Adam, is a fortunate one, as we have already seen in the title poem. "Shalom" closes, then, with the old man's acceptance of the dark passages in human experience:

> "It's alright," answers
> the man going down,
> "it's alright—there are many
> avenues, many corridors of the soul
> that are dark also.
> Shalom."

Images of a light discovered in darkness, as in "Shalom," recur throughout *O Taste and See;* there is the light of the moon at night (25), the bright movie screen in a dark theater (18–19), the "field / of sparks" moving "in darkness" (15), "golden pollen" falling from "dark trees" (13), and "dark" figures "outlined" by the setting sun in "a fur of gold," "a blur defining them" (38–39). The muse herself is a light, a "gold ring," that is hidden, obscure. Such images define a kind of wholeness, the poet's striving to take into the poem "*all* that lives." As the contrast between "Claritas" and "Shalom" suggests, however, she most often realizes this wholeness when she goes "deep down" rather than "straight up."

Sometimes, as we have seen, Levertov's endings make significance all too explicit, so that the poem becomes more an act of will than of discovery. At other times, however, her endings tactfully draw a boundary around experience at the same time that they open fresh perspectives that extend the poem "beyond the end." The last line of "The Film"—"So be it"—marks the completion of the movie's effect on the poet's mind and so the beginning of a new sense of reality. "September 1961" ends: "we don't / stop walking, we know / there is far to go, sometimes // we think the night wind carries / a smell of the sea. . . ." Images of the road and the sea circle the reader back to the beginning of the poem, but with the mood now changed from anxiety to tenacity, fortified by occasional but indefinite hints ("we *think*") that they are headed in the right direction, and the ellipsis at the very end both suspends the mystery of their quest and defines it as an ongoing one, just as the series of present participles at the end of "O Taste and See" characterizes the process of taking the world in as a continuous one. Often, Levertov's poems will end with a dark orphic utterance ("A silence / of waking at night into speech," 23) or, more often, with a very suggestive concrete image that, at first, seems to follow out of nothing that has come before in the poem. The end of "The Coming Fall" provides an instance: "—a wisdom, // a shiver, a delight / that what is passing // is here, as if / a snake went by, green in the / gray leaves." Earlier in the poem Levertov had resisted the change of season; at the end she moves into the flow of time, her lively awareness of its full nature expressed in the quick turns from "shiver" to "delight," from "what is passing" to "is here," in the similar balancing of green snake and gray leaves. Though at first it seems a surprising turn of thought, the image of the snake follows out from what has come before; but it also has rich suggestions that take us off in new directions. It is hard to read of snakes and not to think of the Garden of Eden, and once we do, we read the poem's title "The Coming Fall" in a new sense. We may then see the "human figures dark on the hill / outlined" by the "last sunlight" as Adam and Eve about to leave the Garden, and, in fact, we may see the whole landscape of the poem as at once literal and suggestive of a postlapsarian Eden. Yet in this landscape of "somber beauty" (80) snakes are not symbols of evil; they are simply animals that make us "shiver" with fear or delight. "The Coming Fall" marks an invigorating change, one that takes us back into life, and just as autumn begins as well as ends something, the end of the poem provides an image that both achieves closure and evokes new beginnings. At its close, the Levertov poem simultaneously returns upon itself and branches a new way.

But one of Levertov's most impressive achievements in O Taste and See is in her questioning of her own poetic aims and achievements in "Say the Word," a short story that, beneath its simple, almost flat surface, yields complex implications. The story takes place at an old farmhouse where the main character's husband and son are clearing the land of alders—"not wholesale but with judgment—to *reveal the form of the land* and give back some of the space years of neglect had stolen" (emphasis added). When the woman spontaneously mentions that a poplar which is blocking her view of some distant mountains "needs cutting," the two men eagerly take up the task. She loves mountains, strong silent presences with "dignity" and "distance," but as soon as she has "said the word," she becomes uneasy about cutting down the tree. At the end, when the poplar has been cleared, the man and boy are triumphant, while she feels "loneliness and confusion"—until she looks up to see "the last of daylight, and against it the far mountains were ranged, a wistful blue, remote and austere."

"Say the Word" affirms Levertov's preference for a landscape that is half wild, half domesticated, for a space that is open yet enclosed by distant mountains. One day the family picnics at a nearby abandoned farm where the overgrowth has "begun to close it in, block the horizon" and create a "melancholy" feeling. In contrast, their pruning and cutting reveal "the form of the land" on their own farm, where the atmosphere is one of "lightness and calm." Yet the story focuses most on the central character's fears that she is cruelly imposing her own wishes on the landscape. Is she revealing the "true form" of the place or thrusting one upon it? Unlike Olson and Ginsberg, Levertov does not project coercion outward onto a mythic abstraction like Moloch, but instead explores such propensities, and the possibility of controlling them, within herself. As a result, she comes to the realistic recognition that being in the world involves changing and even violating it—"not wholesale but with judgment." We may respond that it is not easy to say where good judgment ends and wholesale imposition begins, but that's exactly Levertov's point: the difficulty of exercising individual judgment when we no longer have the support of some external value system. Both the title of the story and its preoccupation with pruning, with cutting away, to uncover a hidden form suggest that Levertov is also thinking about the difficulties of writing, of forming experiences into wholes that will not just manifest an anxious craving for mastery. In Levertov, making and judging are not, a priori, coercive and inauthentic activities, as they are in much contemporary writing. She affirms a possible reciprocity—"an interpenetration, both ways." So at the end of "Say the Word" she is elated when the "remote and austere" mountains are suddenly revealed; she questions, explores doubts, but does not finally reject her poetics of discovery.

As in *The Double Image,* the vision of Eden provides a unifying myth in *O Taste and See,* as we might expect in a book so preoccupied with origins; but Levertov now deals with this theme with an emotional toughness and literary inventiveness that allow her to *realize* it in a way it had not been realized in her earlier work. Of course, the very presence of a unifying myth confirms, again, that Levertov possesses a vision that exists prior to and in fact enables her particular acts of "discovery." But Levertov's representation of the theme makes her poems seem, at best, convincing artistic illusions of such moments of discovery. For one thing, Eden enters these poems not as a mythical narrative but as a series of glimpses, as if in spontaneous moments of vision. Sometimes the allusions to Eden are explicit, as in "The Old Adam," "Another Spring," "The Stonecarver's Poem," and "Shalom." At other times, they are implied, as in the garden in "The Figure of Time," the snake in "The Coming Fall," or in the title poem. Moreover, Levertov does not repeat but actively takes in and revises the Judeo-Christian version of the myth. The poems "Sparks" and "O Taste and See" explicitly reverse biblical injunctions, which Levertov sees as fearfully preoccupied with ends rather than beginnings. "The threat / of the world's end is the old threat," she says in "Sparks," and in a playful rewriting of the medieval lyric, "Who Is at My Window," she calls the fear of both death and life "the old song." "The Old Adam" is a man who pines nostalgically over "a photo of someone else's childhood, / a garden in another country"; he wants to repeat an idealized past that was never his in the first place, a particularly ironic form of "mourning or ghost-walking." Neither outside time nor fully in it, the old Adam, like J. Alfred Prufrock but unlike the vigorous old man in "Shalom," merely grows old with a "floating / sense of loss." If fear is "the old song," mourning is "the lost way."

Against the old man's craving for repetition, Levertov posits an Eden in the here and now, the prospect of "living in the orchard and being // hungry, and plucking / the fruit." But the Eden that remains as a perpetual possibility for Levertov is no simple idealization; it coexists with pain, "the ache of marriage," a sense of "what is passing," temporality and death itself. According to "Another Spring," "Death in us goes on // testing the wild / chance of living / as Adam chanced it." Adam ate the forbidden fruit in spite of the threat of death as punishment; he risked death in order to extend his experience. His fall was fortunate, then, because with it Adam entered time, a mortal body, in which, as we've seen, "Adam blazes." "I could replace / God for awhile," Levertov writes, somewhat pretentiously, in "Earth Psalm"; she could reject him "to worship *mortal*," who is, she says, "the summoned / god who has speech," the muse who dwells in "our flesh our / deaths." The magical world is immanent in the real world. "Paradise," says Levertov in "Kingdoms of Heaven," lies "within you"; death, in "Another Spring," "goes on in us." In the poems of *O Taste and See,* Levertov again and again says the words that incarnate her double image of life, its fears and its promises, that she had sought but missed in her first book.

The epigraph is taken from "Great Possessions," *The Poet in the World* (New York, 1973), 95. Subsequent references are made to *PW* in the text; other abbreviations used are *DI, The Double Image* (London, 1946); *HN, Here and Now* (San Francisco, 1956); *OI, Overland to the Islands* (Highlands, N.C., 1958); *WE, With Eyes at the Back of Our Heads* (New York, 1960); *JL, The Jacob's Ladder* (New York, 1961); *OTS, O Taste and See* (New York, 1964).

1. *Black Mountain: An Exploration in Community* (Garden City, N.Y., 1973), 355.

2. "Poets of the Given Ground," *The Nation* 14 October 1961, 251.

3. Quoted in Duberman, *Black Mountain,* 414.

4. Levertov's notion of presence is discussed by Thomas A. Duddy, "To Celebrate: A Reading of Denise Levertov," *Criticism* 10 (Spring 1968): 138–52. See also Charles Altieri, *Enlarging the Temple: New Directions in Poetry during the 1960s* (Lewisburg, Pa., 1980), 225–44; Altieri is mainly interested in showing the limitations of an aesthetic of presence when Levertov "tries to adapt her poetic to pressing social concerns caused by the war in Vietnam" (226). For a book-length study of Levertov, see Linda W. Wagner, *Denise Levertov* (New York, 1967).

5. For an account of this movement and a sampling of its work, see *The New British Poets,* ed. Kenneth Rexroth (Verona, Italy, 1949), especially vii–xxxviii; see also Levertov's "Herbert Read: A Memoir," *Malahat Review* 9 (January 1969): 10–13.

6. *Paterson* (New York, 1958), 3.

7. Donald M. Allen, ed., *The New American Poetry* (New York: Grove Press; London: Evergreen Books, 1960), 441.

8. Walter Sutton, "A Conversation with Denise Levertov," *Minnesota Review* 5 (October–December 1965): 324.

9. Ibid.

10. *Stony Brook* 1/2 (Fall 1968): 168. Twelve letters from Williams to Levertov are printed in this issue. The letters are in the Williams collection at Yale.

11. Ibid., 164.

12. "Land's End," *Gryphon* 3 (Spring 1951): 11.

13. Sutton, "A Conversation with Denise Levertov," 326.

14. I treat *Here and Now* and *Overland to the Islands* as a single collection; Levertov let Lawrence Ferlinghetti select which, out of a large number of poems, were to be included in *Here and Now* (see Levertov correspondence in the City Lights collection in the Bancroft Library, University of California, Berkeley), and many of the poems he rejected appeared in *Overland,* so that the two books in no way reflect a chronological order of composition.

15. Sutton, "A Conversation with Denise Levertov," 335.

16. Ibid.

17. Allen, *New American Poetry,* 434.

18. *Black Mountain Review* 3 (Fall 1955): 19–22.

19. William Meyen and Anthony Piccione, "A Conversation with Denise Levertov," *Ironwood* 4 (n.d.), 26.

20. The first section of Duncan's H.D. book to be published appeared in *Coyote's Journal* 5/6 (1966): 8–31. But this and other chapters are dated as written in the very early sixties, and I am assuming that Levertov was in close enough contact with Duncan at this time to know—either by reading the unpublished chapter or by conversation—Duncan's views on H.D.

21. *Trilogy* (New York, 1973), 48.

22. "The Work of Denise Levertov," *Sixties* 9 (1965): 55.

ALBERT GELPI

Two Notes on Denise Levertov and the Romantic Tradition

Denise Levertov is often linked with the Black Mountain College poets and she has called Robert Duncan and Robert Creeley the finest poets of her generation. She shares with Duncan a religious sense of experience, as the individual penetrates to the design which holds him in its encirclement. The difference lies in the fact that Denise Levertov tends to look out, whereas Duncan looks within for the design. I cannot, of course, make too pat a distinction, for, as Coleridge observed, perception comes precisely in the identification of subject and object. However, since these two poets are so often named together, I want to make a distinction: a characteristic difference in emphasis or (more accurately) in the direction from which the interaction of subject and object comes to be considered. Duncan's language maintains a certain contact with nature as the mind's mirror, and for Levertov the rhythms of experience (and speech) find their validation in the rhythms of consciousness. But often in Duncan the blurred outlines and hazy insubstantiality stem from the fact that the subject and the object are both internal, double aspects of himself, whereas in Levertov the physicality of the imagery indicates that the focus of the poem is generally on the concrete reality as it is assimilated by consciousness.

Duncan has never written a poem like "The Breathing" or "The Ripple":

> On white linen the silk
> of gray shadows
> threefold, over-
> lapping, a
> tau cross.

Reprinted from *Southern Review* 3 (Autumn 1967): 1024–35, and from Albert Gelpi, *The Tenth Muse: The Psyche of the American Poet* (Cambridge: Harvard University Press, 1975).

Glass jug and
tumblers rise from
that which they
cast.

And luminous
in each
overcast of
cylindrical shade,
image
of water, a brightness
not gold, not silver,
rippling
as if with laughter.

In Denise Levertov nature is not absorbed by the centripetal
force of mind. She deliberately maintains the tension of the meet-
ing of mind and nature. In this sense hers is a sacramental notion
of life; experience is a communion with objects which are in
themselves signs of their own secret mystery. The two dicta of
Blake from which Duncan makes his poem are: "Mental things
alone are real" and "The Authors are in Eternity." In contrast
Denise Levertov says:

The world is
not with us enough.
O taste and see

the subway Bible poster said,
meaning *The Lord,* meaning
if anything all that lives
to the imagination's tongue,

all of which we "savor, chew, swallow, transform / into our
flesh." The world is typic: the least thing can yield an infinite
relevance to the responsive eye. This is the other side of Blake,
which sees the world in a grain of sand. Miss Levertov makes the
point explicit in "The Ground-Mist" and "The Garden Wall."
When the spray from the hose brings out the subtle colors in the
brick of the hitherto unnoticed wall, it becomes:

archetype
of the world always a step

beyond the world, that can't
be looked for, only
as the eye wanders,
found.

It is this active openness, mighty in its receptivity, that makes Denise Levertov suggest in "The Prayer" that not Apollo but Dionysus answered her plea. But the fact is that both gods have answered her prayer. She has said that "poets are instruments on which the power of poetry plays" but added immediately that "they are also *makers,* craftsmen. It is given to the seer to see, but it is then his responsibility to communicate what he sees, that they who cannot see may see." Consequently, if "content determines form," then "content is only discovered *in* form. Like everything living, it is a mystery." In *Poetry* (September, 1965) she published "Some Notes on Organic Form," which are remarkably concrete in describing that elusive notion in the genesis and gestation of the poem. The ground of all the particular observations is the sense that organic poetry "is based on an intuition of an order, a form beyond forms, in which forms partake, and of which man's creative works are analogies, resemblances, natural allegories." Still, she insists sharply, organic form does not mean formlessness or diffuseness like (in her distinction) free verse; it means not a dissipation of energy but a concentration of energy. For if the poetic form is to correspond truly to the natural form, language must be made (partly by conscious craftsmanship) to evolve into the hard and clear definition of the particular and unique situation.

In "Claritas" "the All-Day Bird, the artist," strives "to make his notes / ever more precise." Robert Duncan wrote "Answering" as a response to this poem; his bird sings out in "a burst / of confidence" "a song I did not sing." He stresses the artist's spontaneous outcry "as if the heart's full / responsibility / were in the rise of words"; "for joy / breaks thru / insensible to our human want." But the All-Day Bird, gripped by joy, argues that it is the pressure of his skill as singer which shapes the song "closer / to what he knows." His effort is to discriminate

the *shadow of a difference*
falling between
note and note,
a *hair's breadth*
defining them.

So when dawn breaks on his world, his eye and tongue seek out the clarity of

> Sun
> light.
>   Light
>   light light light.

During the past ten years Denise Levertov has earned a deserved and increasing number of admirers among both the Dionysians and the Apollonians, the formalists and the experimentalists, the academics and the beats, the way-in and the way-out. This powerful position helps to explain why she has emerged so distinctly from the other poets of her generation, and it is her combination of integrity and energy and technical control that allows her to hold her pivotal place at the spinning center of contemporary American poetry.

After its publication in *Poetry,* "Some Notes on Organic Form" was included in a volume of her essays, *The Poet in the World*. Her remarks are instructive not just because she cites Emerson (along with Coleridge, Frank Lloyd Wright, and Robert Duncan) but because she attempts to define with greater precision than had been done heretofore this notion which is basic to the Romantic vision but which was followed out more fully by Emerson and the "open form" poets after him: Whitman in the next generation; Pound and Williams fifty years later; and in the second half of the twentieth century, Beat poets like Ginsberg, Kerouac, and Le Roi Jones, poets of the San Francisco Renaissance like Robert Duncan and William Everson, and Projectivists like Charles Olson, Robert Creeley, and Levertov herself. With Pound and Williams and Olson, she worries about the amorphous expansiveness of Whitman and, by implication, his closest followers, and seeks to keep organic form from being equated with Whitmanian free verse. But the importance of Levertov's essay is that it draws together a century and a half of thinking about organic form and thereby describes what many critics of American poetry, including Hyatt Waggoner, have seen as the original and native strain in the American tradition. She traces out how an organic poem is written and what its sources and shape are. She cannot give rules and prescriptions, since the form of each poem is unique to the recreation of the experience—in fact is the recre-

ation of the experience—but her comments outline the process
of gestation:

> A partial definition, then, of organic poetry might be that it is
> a method of apperception, i.e., of recognizing what we per-
> ceive, and is based on an intuition of an order, a form beyond
> forms, in which forms partake, and of which man's creative
> works are analogies, resemblances, natural allegories. Such
> poetry is exploratory.

The source is "an experience, a sequence or constellation of per-
ceptions" through which the poet "is *brought to speech.*" Contem-
plation and meditation are intermediate steps between experi-
ence and speech:

> To contemplate comes from "*templum,* temple, a place, a
> space for observation, marked out by the augur." It means,
> not simply to observe, to regard, but to do these things in the
> presence of a god. And to meditate is "to keep the mind in a
> state of contemplation"; its synonym is "to muse," and to
> muse comes from a word meaning "to stand with open
> mouth"—not so comical if we think of "inspiration"—to
> breathe in.

(We find ourselves, Emerson says, "not in a critical speculation
but in a holy place.") The pressures which meditation in this
sense brings to bear on the components of the experience "culmi-
nate in a moment of vision, of crystallization, in which some
inkling of the correspondence between those elements occurs;
and it occurs as words." Thereafter the realization leads the poet
"through the world of the poem, its unique inscape revealing
itself as it goes." If the poem is truly organic, rhyme, repetition,
sound effects all result from connections and associations as per-
ception takes on word-sounds, and the phrasing, cadence, line
length, and groupings of lines result from the beat or pulsation
or movement in the psyche as the unconscious rises to conscious-
ness. The "intuitive interaction" of all one's faculties reproduces
experience in a new form as a structure of words or, as Emerson
said, "*alter idem,* in a manner totally new." One need only con-
trast Levertov's early poems, written in England, with those
after she came to America and became an American poet to feel
the dramatic shift which the Emersonian tradition, translated
more immediately through Ezra Pound and William Carlos Wil-
liams, made in the substance and technique of her verse.

RUDOLPH L. NELSON

Edge of the Transcendent
The Poetry of Levertov and Duncan

> *Sometimes, after staying in a village parlor till the family had all retired, I have*
> *returned to the woods, and, partly with a view to the next day's dinner, spent the*
> *hours of midnight fishing from a boat by moonlight, serenaded by owls and foxes,*
> *and hearing, from time to time, the creaking note of some unknown bird close at*
> *hand. These experiences were very memorable and valuable to me, anchored in*
> *forty feet of water, and twenty or thirty rods from the shore, surrounded sometimes*
> *by thousands of small perch and shiners, dimpling the surface with their tails in the*
> *moonlight, and communicating by a long flaxen line with mysterious nocturnal*
> *fishes which had their dwelling forty feet below, or sometimes dragging sixty feet of*
> *line about the pond as I drifted in the gentle night breeze, now and then feeling a*
> *slight vibration along it, indicative of some life prowling about its extremity, of*
> *dull uncertain blundering purpose there, and slow to make up its mind. At length*
> *you slowly raise, pulling hand over hand, some horned pout squeaking and squirm-*
> *ing to the upper air. It was very queer, especially in dark nights, when your*
> *thoughts had wandered to vast and cosmogonal themes in other spheres, to feel this*
> *faint jerk, which came to interrupt your dreams and link you to Nature again. It*
> *seemed as if I might next cast my line upward into the air, as well as downward*
> *into this element, which was scarcely more dense. Thus I caught two fishes as it*
> *were with one hook.*
>
> —Thoreau, *Walden*

Denise Levertov and Robert Duncan are invariably classed to-
gether as members of "the Olson group," poets influenced by
the projective verse theories of Charles Olson. M. L. Rosenthal
sees this group producing "a serious body of non-traditional
verse" and foreshadowing "the more dynamic directions of the
future." Stephen Stepanchev adds that the Olson poets share also
in common a poetry rooted in American experience and reflect-
ing the American idiom. Duncan himself says that since 1951 his
work has been classed in his own mind with "a larger work" that
appeared in the writings of Olson, Levertov, and Creeley. Al-
though Linda Wagner, in her recent book, *Denise Levertov*
(1967), maintains that "the Olson group" is tied together only
very loosely by personal association and certain theoretical be-
liefs held in common, it seems clear that Levertov and Duncan
are more closely related to each other, both personally and profes-

Reprinted from *Southwest Review* 54, no. 2 (Spring 1969): 188–202.

sionally, than are the members of the group as a whole. The fact of their personal friendship is essentially irrelevant to a comparison of their poetry, but the similarity of their views and their estimate of each other's poetry are not.

Duncan, although only four years older than Levertov, had been producing his mature poetry for many years before Levertov, in 1956, published her first book of American poems (her first book, *The Double Image,* had been published in England in 1946); so it is not surprising that Duncan does not claim Levertov as one of the poets who has helped shape his own style. He does credit one of her poems, "The Shifting," with first releasing his "sense of a new generation in poetry" in 1952. He has expressed great admiration for her work. In a prefatory note to her *Overland to the Islands* (1958), he says that her poems bring him again and again

> to the most intense thing, to that crossing of the inner and the outer reality, where we have our wholeness of feeling in the universe. She catches it as only the craftsman devoted to the language can catch it that has her genius there so that the thrill of adrenaline comes at the nape of the neck. . . . In the dance of word and phrase to express feeling, in the interior music of vowels, in subtlety of changing tempo within the form, in the whole supple control in freedom, she excels.

Levertov has not only been lavish in her praise of Duncan's poetry, but has also cited him as one of the major forces in the evolution of her own poetic style. As Linda Wagner puts it, "Of all poets contemporary with her, she most respects Duncan." In a biographical note in Donald M. Allen's anthology, *The New American Poetry* (1960), she mentions "conversations and correspondence with Robert Duncan" as one of the major influences on her. In the essay "Some Notes on Organic Form," which appeared in *Poetry* (September, 1965), she indicates one specific thing she learned from Duncan; namely, that one must leave "rifts" in the poem, "gaps between perception and perception which must be leapt across if they are to be crossed at all." In a poetry seminar at Brown University in November, 1967, she included Duncan with Yeats, Wallace Stevens, and William Carlos Williams as four poets whose work she goes back to constantly for creative inspiration.

But with all the identical classifications, the common poetic convictions, the personal relationships, the mutual esteem, one comes away from the poetry of Levertov and Duncan with the distinct impression that their differences are more crucial than their similarities. Both comparisons and contrasts can be clarified by looking at their poetry as organic in form, as religious in content, and as resident in that borderland between the temporal and the eternal, the common and the mysterious—poetry at the threshold between the mundane known and the transcendent knowable.

The metaphor of the threshold or border or boundary dividing realms of experience is common in the writings of both poets. In fact, one could call it a dominating metaphor of their poetic imaginations. Duncan gives the figure its most explicit statement when he refers to the locus of the poet's attention at "the threshold that is called both *here-and-now* and *eternity*," where "identity is shared in resonance between the person and the cosmos." Less explicit but more evocative are references from his poems. In "The Song of the Borderguard," it is the poet who stands guard at "the beautiful boundaries of the empire"—"the borderlines of sense." In "The Structure of Rime VII," the poet is told: "The streams of the Earth seek passage through you, tree that you are, toward a foliage that breaks at the boundaries of known things."

Perspective changes at the threshold of the transcendent; in paying homage to "the old poets" Duncan says: "In time we see a tragedy, a loss of beauty / the glittering youth / of the god retains—but from this threshold / it is age / that is beautiful." One can sometimes hear a "god-step at the margins of thought." "Flickers of unlikely heat / at the edge of our belief bud forth." The poet is referred to as an Outrider who comes "to the threshold of the stars, to the door beyond which moves celestial terror." "Often I am permitted to return to a meadow," the poet says, "as if it were a given property of the mind / that certain bounds hold against chaos." There are those who wish to cut off access to the fields of poetic vision: "In the caves of blue within the blue the grandmothers bound, on the brink of freedom, to close the too many doors from which the rain falls."

Finally, in his play on theosophical themes, "Adam's Way," Duncan dramatizes the encounter of the pure and innocent Adam and Eve with the temptation of Samael. He tells them: "God has removed you from your own ground / into a silly magic of Eternity—it's but a word—in which you are nothing and you rejoice." Adam and Eve give up their natural and holy love for the selfish love which Samael shows to them, a life which he admits is not the Tree of Life but instead what he calls "the Tree of the Other Side, of what is more." Samael kisses Eve, "awakening in her the grievous knowledge of the denial of love in which he dwells." Duncan implicitly acknowledges, as we all must, that he has partaken of the fruit of the Tree of the Other Side, that he does not dwell in the eternity of perfect love and innocence. But in his poetry he is trying always to break through into the transcendent realm.

In Levertov's work too we confront the image of the threshold or boundary. In his headnote to *Overland to the Islands,* Duncan placed Levertov's work in a sort of borderland: "that crossing of the inner and the outer reality, where we have our wholeness of feeling in the universe." That borderland becomes more readily identifiable as the same territory Duncan is exploring when we look at some of the relevant images in Levertov's poems. In the poem entitled "Threshold," a particular visual impression of form from the natural world excites the mind and raises the question of how that form can be captured in the pulsebeat of poetry. When she asks what stone hands turn "to uncover / feather of broken / oracle—" we become aware that the threshold leads to some sort of transcendental insight, a state which she labels "wonder." Much the same thought is expressed in "The Illustration," in which she speaks of learning "to affirm / Truth's light at strange turns of the mind's road, / wrong turns that lead / over the border into wonder." Another poem from *The Jacob's Ladder* refers to the gist of an insight "not quite caught, but filtered / through some outpost of dreaming sense." In an earlier poem, this borderland, identified as "the edge," is the source of the poem as true revelation, although it may not be the poem the poet expected to find there. And of course the Jacob's ladder image is borrowed from the Hasidic literature, where it represents a means of access between earth and heaven, the human and the divine. Even the colors on a brick wall, when properly perceived, can provide an entrance to the world of wonder: "archetype / of the world always a step / beyond the world, that can't / be looked for, only / as the eye wanders, / found." In the closest thing to a detailed statement of her poetics, "Some Notes on Organic Form," Levertov has referred to poetry as containing rifts, gaps between perceptions, which often span different realms of experience and understanding.

The X factor, the magic, is when we come upon those rifts and make those leaps. A religious devotion to the truth, to the splendor of the authentic, involves the writer in a process rewarding in itself; but when that devotion brings us to un-dreamed abysses and we find ourselves sailing slowly over them and landing on the other side—that's ecstasy.

This is one thing, then, that Denise Levertov and Robert Duncan have in common. For both of them, poetry is a dynamic means of exploration beyond what we already know into a realm of wonder or eternity which at this point we shall call transcendent. Whether Levertov's concept of the transcendent is the same as Duncan's is a key question. Clues to the answer may be found in the theories of organic form espoused by the two poets and practiced in their art.

The common denominator in all theories of organic form in poetry is the conviction that the form of a poem must emerge from the subject matter itself rather than from arbitrary predeter-mined structures and styles. Emerson's "ask the fact for the form" is usually cited as an authoritative precedent. With many contemporary poets, organic form simply means the freedom to be experimental in technique; it has no implications beyond style. With Duncan and Levertov, organic form goes much deeper; it has implications which can be called broadly theologi-cal. According to Levertov, organic form is "a method of apperception, i.e., of recognizing what we perceive, and is based on an intuition of an order, a form beyond forms, in which forms partake, and of which man's creative works are analogies, resemblances, natural allegories."

So far, this seems more philosophical, in a Platonic sense, than theological. But how is the poet to go about his task? A poem is demanded of him by the experience of a moment in life. To fulfill the demand, he contemplates, which means, says Levertov, "not simply to observe, to regard, but to do these things in the presence of a god." It demands an act of religious dedication to be able to see beneath the external characteristics and discern the form at the heart of creation. In "The Novices" a man and a boy go deep into the woods, "knowing some rite [is] to be performed." When they have shown their willingness to give themselves to nature in this way (much as Ike McCaslin did in Faulkner's *The Bear*), the gentle but awesome spirit of the forest appears and reveals his will—the rite was merely to enter the forest; now they are to look around them and see nature in a new way, "intricate branch and bark, / stars of moss and the old scars left by dead men's saws." As the spirit recedes among the forms, "the twists and shadows they saw now, listening / to the hum of the world's wood."

Duncan contributed to Howard Nemerov's book *Poets on Poetry* (1966) an essay entitled "Toward an Open Universe" in which is perhaps his clearest statement on organic form. The poet seeks to discover the divine order in things, "to penetrate to that most real where there is no form that is not content, no content that is not form." It is form which stirs the poet. Finding proper form for his poetic vision is certainly not a matter of adhering to established traditions; it hardly seems even to be consciously chosen. The poet follows his consciousness of "orders in the play of form and meanings toward poetic form." "We have only to listen and to cooperate with the music we hear." There is clearly a supernatural factor in this process. "There is not only the immanence of God, His indwelling, but there is also the imminence of God, His impending occurrence."

As one of Duncan's primary poetic subjects is poetry itself, one is not surprised to see the same convictions appear in his poems. In one of a series called "The Structure of Rime," he voices this apostrophe: "O Lasting Sentence, sentence after sentence I make in your image. In the feet that measure the dance of my pages I hear cosmic intoxications of the man I will be." In "Four Pictures of the Real Universe," he concludes: "Were it not for the orders of music hidden / we should be claimed by the preponderant void." In another poem from *The Opening of the Field* he says: "Poems come up from a ground so / to illustrate the ground, approximate / a lingering of eternal image, a need / known only in its being found ready."

While it would be unwarranted to use these statements on organic form as evidence that either Duncan or Levertov is supporting classical arguments for the existence of God on teleological grounds, it is undeniably clear that both of them conceive of an orderly and purposeful universe. It is clear as well that neither is a philosophical naturalist; neither shies away from the dimension of mystery and wonder in existence.

Beyond this significant similarity, however, the criterion of organic form reveals also a key difference between these two poets. Robert Duncan has used the freedom of organic form to write poetry that is considerably more experimental and esoteric than the poetry of Denise Levertov. I am not at this point making a value judgment on complexity and simplicity. Nor do I mean to imply that free form is the only poetic medium in which one can be obscure. But the notion of organic form is naturally more hospitable to the esoteric. Much of Duncan's poetry is not accessible to even the educated reader without considerable effort. Some critics and fellow poets as well have judged his work to be discouragingly dense. Perhaps the most severe attack has come from D. R. Slavitt in a review of *Roots and Branches* which appeared in *Book Week* (14 March 1965):

> He writes a toned-down imitation of Ezra Pound, full of private allusions to his chums and their books, undigested clots of autobiography, puerile incantations, improbable allusions, and insufferable arrogance in its privacy. What is not obscure is slovenly, and does not give much incentive to go back and puzzle out the rest.

Perhaps these comments reveal more about the reviewer than about Duncan's poetry. But Louis Simpson, writing in the *Hudson Review* (Autumn 1961) and finding in Duncan an "extraordinarily lyrical talent," criticizes him for the fragments of in-group talk and theory that litter his poems "as though their lodgment in his mind were enough to make them poetic." Of *Roots and Branches* James Dickey said in the *American Scholar* (Autumn 1965): "One brings away from it only a sense of complicated inconsequence, of dilettantism and serene self-deception, of pretentiousness, of a writer perhaps natively gifted who has sold himself the wrong bill of goods." X. J. Kennedy, while generally very favorably inclined, feels the need of advising the reader of his *New York Times* review to use a bit of "blind faith" which will enable him to surmount a few private allusions, mysterious gaps in syntax, and quirky spellings. It need hardly be said, of course, that some critics have lavished praise on Duncan and acknowledged no problem on the grounds of obscurity. Perhaps the most favorable responses have come from Hayden Carruth and Kenneth Rexroth, both writing in the *Nation*.

Duncan himself, however, seems to be conscious of a distance between himself and his readers. In a biographical note in *The New American Poetry,* he explains exactly how the poet Helen Adam has been an influence on him. Admitting her genius, he was able to

> shake off at last the modern proprieties—originality, style, currency of language, sensibility and integrity. I have a great appetite for approval from whatever source, and only the example of this poet who cares nothing for opinions but all

for the life of the imagination, for the marvellous that is the grain of living poetry, saves me at times.

In short, being true to one's own vision of poetic form may alienate a poet from his audience. In "Pages from a Notebook," after commenting that since Freud "we are aware that unwittingly we achieve our form," Duncan refers to readers of poetry as "our hunters." Then he changes the image and refers to the poem as "an occult document, a body awaiting vivisection, analysis, X-rays." And yet, his is not a reader-be-damned attitude.

> Yes, though I contrive the mind's measure
> and wrest doctrine from old lore,
> it's to win particular hearts,
> to stir an abiding affection for this music,
> as if a host of readers will join the Beloved
>
> ready to dance with me, it's for the
>   unthinking
> ready thing I'm writing these poems.

Duncan wants sympathetic readers, but he demands that they come on his own terms.

It is not, then, that he is turning the liberty of open form into license for deliberately perverse obscurity. It is rather that Duncan conceives of poetry (as have many before him) as an attempt somehow to say the unsayable. If one is feeling a bit testy, he might say with James Dickey: "As he keeps telling us, he is a mystic, which of course allows him to say anything in any order." If one is feeling more charitable, he might say instead that Duncan's poetry "makes sense" when it is seen as the serious attempt of a mystical personality to capture in words the emotional subjectivity of an ineffable experience. When one crosses the threshold into the transcendental, one is faced inevitably with the problem of communication. As Duncan sees it, there is an obscurity in the nature of things.

> There is a wholeness of what we are that we will never know; we are always, as the line or the phrase or the word is, the moment of that wholeness—an event; but it, the wholeness of what we are, goes back into an obscurity and extends to and into an obscurity. The obscurity is part too of the work, of the form, if it be whole.

But I do not think we should let Duncan off the hook quite this easily. It seems to me that there is a seriously limiting factor in his theory and his poetry which stands out in bolder relief when the contrast with Levertov is pursued. Duncan seems to create a radical discontinuity between the world of poetic vision and the world of everyday reality—what Wallace Stevens called the quotidian. As Duncan put it in his statement on poetics for the Allen anthology:

> A child can be an artist, he can be a poet. But can a child be a banker? It is in such an affair as running a bank or managing a store or directing a war that adulthood counts, an experienced mind. It is in the world of these pursuits that "experience" counts. One, two, three, times and divided by. The secret of genius lies in this: that here experience is not made to count. Where experience knows nothing of counting, it creates only itself out of itself.

In terms of the dominating metaphor of the threshold, Duncan has created a clear dichotomy in the universal dwelling place— between genius and experience, the one and the many, eternity and the here and now. It is at this point that a significant difference appears between the poetry of Duncan and Levertov.

Earlier I said that I was making no value judgment on simplicity and complexity. But now such a judgment must be made. We may grant that the world contains people who tend to simplify complex problems and people who counteract oversimplification by revealing the complexity of life—and that we need both kinds. We may grant that the history of human thought seems to be a pendulum swing between these tendencies. We may grant Thoreau's point in *Walden* (however overstated) that "it is a ridiculous demand which England and America make, that you shall speak so that they can understand you. Neither men nor toadstools grow so." And we may grant that Robert Duncan's complex vision is essentially mystical and ultimately ineffable. But when we contrast him with a poet whose poetic vision also crosses the threshold into transcendental wonder, who does not oversimplify the complexity of existence, but whose poetry, with all its profundity, must be classed for the most part as accessible to the understanding of the common reader, then I think we have grounds for concluding that Denise Levertov emerges as the superior poet. The key to that superiority is that in the Levertov universe there is no radical discontinuity between the worlds of poetic vision and everyday reality. In her vision the threshold between eternity and the here and now does not seem to be so well-defined a boundary as it is in Duncan's. And while Duncan stresses the poet's transcendental vision almost exclusively, Levertov remains solidly anchored in the common life and enables the reader to see mystery within the here and now.

Ralph Mills, Jr., in a perceptive article in *Tri-Quarterly* (Winter 1962) on Levertov's work, says that "she plumbs the depths of the proximate." "The quotidian reality we ignore or try to escape Denise Levertov revels in, carves and hammers into tight, precise lyrics." In doing so, "What she noticed so shrewdly was that the ordinary is extraordinarily mysterious." There are evidences all through Levertov's poetry that justify Mills's generalization. The title of one of her books is *Here and Now.* The title poem of *O Taste and See* begins: "The world is / not with us enough." In a poem entitled "Seems Like We Must Be Somewhere Else," she says, "If we're here let's be here now." In "The Goddess," she does not experience the Muse's power until she is thrown out of Lie Castle and tastes on her lips the mud of the ground outside. She quotes approvingly as a headnote to the poem "Joy" some words of Thoreau: "You must love the crust of the earth on which you dwell. You must be able to extract nutriment out of a sandheap. You must have so good an appetite as this, else you will live in vain." She finds metaphors from nature that reinforce this truth. The earth worm, "by passage / of himself / constructing," pays "homage to / earth, aerates / the ground of his living." As with the bee, "Beespittle, droppings, hairs / of beefur: all become honey," so in our lives the "honey of the human" emerges from the experiences of the common life. Borrowing a Joycean term, Robert Pack, writing in *Saturday Review* (8 December 1962), says that her best poems move "toward epiphanies, the intense rendering of a moment." He calls her poetry mystical and commends her for her freedom from the kind of self-consciousness that is prevalent in contemporary mysticism. The reason for this, he says, is that she begins not with dogma, but with perception. "Her sense of the invisible spirit of things is rooted in what she sees, and through precise description, through intimation and evocation, she leads the reader to the brink of mystery without trying to push him into the abyss."

Levertov, in her ability never to lose touch with the stuff of the common life even when her poetic vision leads her across the threshold into the realm of mystery, reminds one of Thoreau fishing at midnight on Walden Pond. Close to nature as he was, he found himself thinking transcendental thoughts. But then some horned pout would pull at his line. "It was very queer, especially in dark nights, when your thoughts had wandered to vast and cosmogonal themes in other spheres, to feel this faint jerk, which came to interrupt your dreams and link you to Nature again." Levertov keeps her own grip and ours firmly on the line. In searching out "the authentic," she even takes the poetic risk of making an observation "rising from the toilet seat." Even if she had not said this, we would have known intuitively that the poetic world of Denise Levertov contains toilet seats. We are not quite sure whether Robert Duncan's does or not. Levertov's Jacob's ladder from earth to heaven has solidly built steps with sharp angles that scrape the knees and console the groping feet. We are told to "taste and see" not only tangerines and weather, but "all that lives / to the imagination's tongue." And this includes the emotional experiences of life—grief, mercy—even our own deaths. It is Thoreau's "faint jerk" that is missing from Duncan's poetry. He loses hold of the line that stretches from the private world of his mystical vision to the here and now.

One could argue that Denise Levertov's concept of the transcendent is not the same as Robert Duncan's. It could be maintained that although both of them operate at the threshold, in Duncan's poetic world the other side is clearly a divine realm, whereas the other side of Levertov's world is merely the dimension of mystery within the human. It is quite true that Duncan uses "God-talk" freely and equally true that Levertov tends to avoid the language of traditional transcendence. On the few occasions when she does use it, it is clear that she is not making conventional metaphysical statements. For example, when she quotes the subway poster slogan, "O taste and see," she adds that it obviously is intended to mean the Lord. But then she gives her own interpretation: "meaning / if anything all that lives / to the imagination's tongue," the full range of our human experiences.

In other words, if theological statements are to have any meaning at all, they must be understood in anthropological terms. Mills seems to take this tack in dealing with her poetry. While he acknowledges, in a poem like "The Instant," the presence of "a spiritual revelation of a nearly ineffable sort," he contrasts Levertov's handling of such an illumination with the way the tradition of post-Symbolist literature (by this he means Eliot, Pound,

Yeats, Auden) would objectify it "into the order of a larger metaphorical universe." In Levertov's poetry, the experience stands alone, is viewed in its own terms. Then Mills likens her form of illumination to that of Blake and Rilke, "though with them it gives foundation to a whole mythological scheme."

Mills is correct, I think, in finally differentiating the Levertov vision from the Blakean. It is a distinction similar, though not identical, to the one I have been attempting to draw between Levertov and Duncan. But in correctly stressing Levertov's poetry of the immediate, Mills has not sufficiently clarified the dimensions of her "spiritual revelation."

I believe we are dealing with two different kinds of genuine transcendence here. Theologically, transcendence is much less of a problem for Duncan. Though it is certainly true that he does not "believe" in any orthodox creedal sense (he writes that "if Christ, heaven or hell are real, in the sense that Christian belief demands, then we are all damnd"), he has no trouble whatsoever in the concept of the supernatural, making room in his world for fairies as well as Christs. He speaks in *Roots and Branches* of two returns of his mother's presence after her death. Levertov's calculated avoidance in her poetry of the language of traditional transcendence is evidence that she, much more than Duncan, is a product not only of the real world of immediate sights and sounds but of the equally real world of twentieth-century science, philosophy, and theology.

In her avoidance of "God-talk" which is less and less meaningful to the modern mind, while at the same time she steadfastly refuses to capitulate to a naturalistic view of the universe and probes into the wonder and mystery of existence, Denise Levertov has produced a body of poetry particularly congenial to the outlook of contemporary radical theology.

The recent popularizing of "death of God" theology obscures the fact that the traditional concept of a transcendent God has not been a viable option to many thoughtful people for a hundred years or more. The Altizers, Hamiltons, and Van Burens have simply called attention to the fact that such intellectual soul-searching has been going on within the province of theology itself. Without getting involved in any bizarre notions that a God who was once alive has somehow recently died, we can take seriously the redefinition of transcendence that has been going on as a result chiefly, though not exclusively, of the works of Paul Tillich and Dietrich Bonhoeffer. In *Honest to God,* John A. T. Robinson summarizes these insights:

Statements about God are acknowledgements of the transcendent, unconditional element in all our relationships, and supremely in our relationships with other persons. Theological statements are indeed affirmations about human existence—but they are affirmations about the ultimate ground and depth of that existence.

There are depths of revelation, intimations of eternity, judgements of the holy and the sacred, awarenesses of the unconditional, the numinous and the ecstatic, which cannot be explained in purely naturalistic categories without being reduced to something else. . . . The question of God is the question *whether this depth of being is a reality or an illusion,* not whether *a* Being exists beyond the bright blue sky, or anywhere else.

It is in this sense that Denise Levertov is a poet at the threshold of the transcendent. In the poem "Who Is at My Window" a blind cuckoo sings a song of fear about the future. The poet responds: "I want to move deeper into today; / he keeps me from that work. / Today and eternity are nothing to him." Note that today and eternity are classed together, both being distinguished from the fear the bird directs toward the future. Clearly one reaches eternity by going deeper into today. Levertov often uses religious imagery to celebrate human life: a city "avenue's / endless nave echoes notes of / liturgical red." She sings a psalm praising the hair on man's body. When she gains insight into herself, the world stirs "with unheard litanies." Respect for the transcendent within the here and now involves not only the realization of the full dimensions of one's own humanity, a major theme in her poetry, but respect for the humanity of others. Her echoing of the biblical truth that "we are members one of another" takes on special impact, rising as it does from a consideration of the grotesque yet haunting figure of Adolf Eichmann on trial.

What then is the transcendent for Levertov? In "The Well" she stands on a bridge and in her mind's eye sees the Muse glide across the dark lake—"and I know / no interpretation of these mysteries." But her heart leaps in wonder as the doors of the world are opened to her. And like Thoreau, who saw the water of Walden Pond as connected underground with the sacred water of the Ganges, she looks into her river and realizes "that the humble / tributary of Roding is / one with Alpheus, the god who as a river / flowed through the salt sea to his love's well." This is as close as Levertov comes to defining the transcendent.

God *is* mystery, the depths, wonder. That is all we know on earth and all we need to know. In "The Novices," the man and boy were enabled to see with new eyes when they enacted the rite of going deep into the woods. Our earlier discussion left out one important detail in the poem. Knowing that some rite was to be performed, before the spirit of the woods came to them, they found a chain running at an angle into the earth from an oak tree, "and they pit themselves to uproot it, / dogged and frightened, to pull the iron / out of the earth's heart." Then the wood-demon appeared and told them they need not perform any rite of obscure violence. They were not even to ask what the chain was. "Knowing there was mystery, they could go."

I began by referring to Levertov and Duncan as poets on the threshold of the transcendent. For Duncan the image can stand unchanged. It does not seem appropriate, however, to say that Levertov crosses the border into transcendence in a horizontal sense, as if she were leaving the country of immediate experience for some special mystical realm. Rather, one might say, borrowing the Tillichian notion of depth, that Denise Levertov probes beneath the threshold of the here and now and finds the transcendent within the stuff of immediate experience.

DIANA SURMAN COLLECOTT

Inside and Outside in the Poetry of Denise Levertov

I

"We awake in the same moment to ourselves and to things."
This sentence from Jacques Maritain was chosen by the Objectiv-
ist poet George Oppen as an epigraph to his book *The Materials*.[1]
Its presence there accents a paradox central to some of the most
interesting American writing today. "Objectivism" is a term
very loosely used at present, and I can think of no better way of
giving it definition, than by recalling Louis Zukofsky's gloss on
the word "Objective" in the special number of *Poetry* Chicago he
edited in 1930. First he takes a definition from Optics; "An
Objective—the lens bringing the rays from an object to a focus."
Then he offers its "Use extended to poetry": "Desire for that
which is objectively perfect."[2] The Objectivist movement initi-
ated by Zukofsky in the thirties was a programmatic formula-
tion of the poetic theory of Ezra Pound and the poetic practice of
William Carlos Williams over the previous twenty years. In par-
ticular, it derived from Pound's effort, through the Imagist move-
ment, to replace what he called "the obscure reveries / Of the
inward gaze" with a poetry concentrated on outward things.
Hardness, edge, were the qualities that recommended the work
of H.D. and Marianne Moore to him; he praised in their poems
"the arid clarity . . . of *le tempérament de l'Américaine*."[3]

Yet neither Pound nor Zukofsky was so ignorant as to empha-
size the outward eye to the exclusion of what goes on inside the
seeing mind. Indeed, Zukofsky claims that, among the Objectiv-
ists: "Writing occurs which is the detail, not the mirage, of see-
ing, of thinking with the things as they exist. . . . Shapes sug-
gest themselves, and the mind senses and receives awareness"
(*Prepositions*, 20). It is implied here that the eye is the focal point
in a two-way process. This vivid commerce between inside and
outside is a distinctive feature of the poets of the Black Mountain

Reprinted from *Critical Quarterly* 22, no. 1 (Spring 1980): 57–70.

school, who have assimilated the discoveries of the Objectivists and their predecessors in the American avant-garde. Consider Robert Creeley's

> I keep to myself such
> measures as I care for,
> daily the rocks
> accumulate position.[4]

Here, interpenetration between the inner world of the poet and the outer world of objects, establishes a mode of writing which Denise Levertov has made hers also.

II

Denise Levertov is an American by adoption. She was born near London, of Russian and Welsh parentage, in 1923. In 1948 she married the American writer Mitchell Goodman, and went to live in the United States. By then, she had already published a first book of verse in England; Kenneth Rexroth has described her, at her debut in the Britain of Dylan Thomas, as "the baby of the New Romanticism."[5] These early poems were accomplished precisely insofar as they were "obscure reveries / Of the inward gaze": weighted with symbolism, they have a dreamlike immobility. One is reminded of Charles Olson's claim that Williams, following in the footsteps of Whitman, taught American poets to *walk*.[6] No "new measure" had reached British writers at that time. Hence Levertov recalls: "Marrying an American and coming to live here while still young was very stimulating to me as a writer, for it necessitated the finding of new rhythms in which to write, in accordance with new rhythms of life and speech."[7] After first finding affinities with academic writers such as Richard Wilbur, Levertov began the search for new rhythms in the milieu of the Black Mountain poets. With Rexroth's encouragement, she submitted herself to a fresh apprenticeship with the work of Williams; she wrote of this, around 1960: "I feel the stylistic influence of William Carlos Williams, while perhaps too evident in my work of a few years ago, was a very necessary and healthful one, without which I could not have developed from a British Romantic with almost Victorian background, to an American poet of any vitality" (*The New American Poetry*, 441). "Vitality" strikes a keynote here. It reminds us of Robert Duncan's contention that the essential difference between American and British poetry in our era is that the first is *active,* it moves. "In American poetry," he writes, "the striding syllables show an aesthetic based on energies."[8] For Denise Levertov, the main transmitter of this aesthetic was Charles Olson's essay "Projective Verse"—an essay, incidentally, which Williams thought so summative of his life's work, that he included it intact as a chapter of his *Autobiography.* The most influential formulation of this essay is not Olson's own, but a statement attributed to Edward Dahlberg: "one perception must immediately and directly lead to a further perception."[9] Thus, a couple of decades after Zukofsky's "Objective," the new school of poets insisted afresh on the *act* of perception, or rather on a series of acts which would shape the poem after their kind.

III

One poem of Levertov's which exemplifies these new influences, and her own discovery of "new rhythms" is the title piece of *Overland to the Islands,* the volume published by Jonathan Williams in 1958.

> Let's go—much as that dog goes,
> intently haphazard. The
> Mexican light on a day that
> "smells like autumn in Connecticut"
> makes iris ripples on his
> black gleaming fur—and that too
> is as one would desire—a radiance
> consorting with the dance.
>   Under his feet
> rocks and mud, his imagination, sniffing,
> engaged in its perceptions—dancing
> edgeways, there's nothing
> the dog disdains on his way,
> nevertheless he
> keeps moving, changing
> pace and approach but
> not direction—"every step an arrival."[10]

This poem is "about" movement. It begins with the casual invitation "Let's go" and then introduces the dog, as an example of movement; thereafter, poet, poem and reader move with him, "intently haphazard"; one could almost say that the dog *is* the projective movement of the poem: his interest leads us from one perception to the next. Levertov has no inhibition about presenting the dog, "his imagination, sniffing, / engaged in its perceptions," as a model for the poet; but nor does she attempt to press this conclusion upon us. She does not stop to do this, as she too "keeps moving."

Anyone familiar with the poetry of Carlos Williams will feel at home here. In such poems as "Pastoral" or "The poor" or "By the road to the contagious hospital," Williams is equally undemanding in relation to his environment, equally unwilling to press a comparison; he is content to record, and move on. The very dog of Levertov's poem is known to us from the opening lines of *Paterson* Book I, where Williams declares his intent "To make a start, / out of particulars," and slyly presents himself as "Sniffing the trees, / just another dog / among a lot of dogs."[11] Even the mannerisms in Levertov's poem—the quotation in the fourth line, the parenthesis by which she succeeds in all but keeping herself out of the poem ("and that too / is as one would desire")—are redolent of the master.

In a comment on "Overland to the Islands" Levertov says: "The last phrase, 'every step an arrival,' is quoted from Rilke, and here, unconsciously, I was evidently trying to unify for myself my sense of the pilgrim way with my new American, objectivist-influenced, pragmatic, and sensuous longing for the Here and Now."[12] Later, Levertov identifies what she calls here "the pilgrim way" as "a personal fiction." It is certainly a *supreme* fiction, in Stevens's sense, since when she describes life as a pilgrimage, she is interested in the pursuit of a reality beyond that of the everyday, the "Here and now." Yet Levertov's very sure-footedness in the *Here and Now* (the title, incidentally, of her first American collection) makes her refuse to leave behind the contingent world in pursuit of a transcendent reality. Thus the common dog, with its iridescently "gleaming fur" can act as an avatar to her, but thus also, the "rocks and mud" beneath its feet are essential to its imaginative progress.

IV

Denise Levertov's belief that one's inner discoveries should move hand in hand with one's outward perceptions has been the main impulse of her experiments in writing and her discussions of poetics. "Some Notes on Organic Form," dated 1965, is one of her earliest published statements on a re-thought Romanticism. In it, she emphasizes the concept that "there *is* a form in all things (and in our experience) which the poet can discover and reveal" (*The Poet in the World,* 7).

This essentially Platonic version of the artist's task is perhaps the last thing that one would expect from a confessedly "American, objectivist-influenced, pragmatic" writer. It leads Levertov to revive Hopkins's terms *inscape* and *instress,* and to add: "In thinking of the process of poetry as I know it, I extend the use of these words, which he seems to have used mainly in reference to sensory phenomena, to include intellectual and emotional experience as well" (*The Poet in the World,* 7). In another essay, she goes further than this and argues that, just as "the *being* of things has inscape" so too does the poet's own being, and that the act of transmitting to others the inscape of things, is also the act of awakening one's own being (*The Poet in the World,* 17).

It is by such steps that we arrive at that flow between inside and outside that Williams characterized as "an interpenetration, both ways." In the opening of *Paterson* Book II, "Sunday in the park," Williams presents such interpenetration in overtly sexual terms; "Dr. Paterson" is speaking:

> Outside
>   outside myself
>   there is a world,
> he rumbled, subject to my incursions
> —a world
>   (to me) at rest,
>   which I approach
> concretely—
>
>
>   The scene's the Park
>   upon the rock,
>   female to the city
>
>
> —upon whose body Paterson instructs his thoughts
> (concretely)
>
>   (*Paterson,* 57)

Here Paterson's role in relation to the rest of the world is obviously masculine: the objective world is "subject" to him; some lines further on, he "starts, possessive, through the trees"; yet within a page, he is describing himself as not merely possessive but "passive-possessive," and he seems to present this as a proper condition for the poet.

There are, in Levertov's writings, an almost equal number of descriptions of the poetic process as a passive and so-to-say "female" condition, as there are equations for a more aggressive and "male" activity. She appears to have taken to heart Williams's advice, in a letter he wrote her, that a poet must be "in essence a woman as well as a man."[13] Indeed, she comments from her own experience, with unusual honesty: "Perhaps I don't know myself very well, for at times I see myself as having boundless energy and a savage will, and at other times as someone easily tired and so impressionable as to be, like Keats, weighed down almost unbearably by the identities around me" (*The Poet in the World,* 216).

V

This combination of receptivity and creative energy appears to be essential not only to Denise Levertov's identity as a poet, but also to her sense of herself. In a comparatively recent poem, she records her delight at an interpretation of her name in its Hebrew meanings. *D* or daleth means 'door"; hence we get:

> entrance, exit,
> way through of
> giving and receiving,
> which are one[14]

"Giving and receiving" are capable of becoming "one" in an American poetic which can incorporate somatic awareness—the body's sense of itself, as well as of the objects around it—in the disposition of words on the page.

Levertov has clearly cultivated such awareness at a subtle level. She speaks of *waiting* for the poem "in that intense passivity, that passive intensity, that passionate patience that Keats named Negative Capability" (*The Poet in the World,* 29). Reading her poetry and prose we realize that she writes best from that state of restful alertness in which, Wordsworth claimed, "we see into the heart of things." Hence "vision," "inscape," "revelation" are key words in her criticism, and she frequently cites such writers as Coleridge, Emerson, Rilke, in trying to identify the special value of such insights to poetic composition. One such passage, from Carlyle, is worth quoting, as it seems to express her own experience: "A musical thought is one spoken by a mind that has penetrated to the inmost heart of the thing; detected the inmost mystery of it, namely the melody that lies hidden in it; the inward harmony of coherence which is its soul, whereby it exists, and has a right to be, here in this world" ("Prospectus," *Sartor Resartus;* cited in *The Poet in the World,* 17). "To write is to listen" says Levertov, on analogy with Picasso's "To draw is to shut your eyes and sing" (*The Poet in the World,* 229). Carlyle, Picasso, Levertov, all imply that the value they seek in art is *inside* as well as *outside,* that the song is "there" ready to be transcribed by him who hears it, that the composition exists already only to be seen by the artist.

VI

For Levertov, this knowledge does not undermine the outward senses, but substantiates them. Poetry requires, she says, the "utmost attentiveness," and the eye has a crucial part to play in bringing her poems into being. In "Pleasures," for instance, seeing is a means of discovering the hidden properties of ordinary objects:

> I like to find
> what's not found
> at once, but lies
>
> within something of another nature,
> in repose, distinct.

The rest of the poem gives specific instances of this kind of discovery of the unknown within the known:

> Gull feathers of glass, hidden
>
> in white pulp: the bones of squid
> which I pull out and lay
> blade by blade on the draining board—
>
> > tapered as if for swiftness, to pierce
> > the heart, but fragile, substance
> > belying design.[15]

Such lines are themselves acts of attention: their breaks indicate her careful scrutiny ("lay / blade by blade"); they record her reading of nature's book. We are reminded irresistibly of Thoreau, one of the American authors to whom Levertov constantly returns, and of Emerson, whose "Ask the fact for the form" was almost a slogan to the writers of the Black Mountain school.

Creeley, in fact, coined the expression "Form is never more than extention of content." Levertov amends this to read "Form is never more than a *revelation* of content" (*The Poet in the World,* 13). Thus the composition of the poem is itself regarded as a vehicle for revelation; indeed, Levertov argues that the very spaces on the page help the mind to fresh insights into the nature of things.

VII

If poetry is to become a simple act of transcription from nature, the poet must abandon his traditional role of supremacy over things. These writers believe that meaning is preexistent in things: it does not depend on structures of thought and feeling imposed by the poet. Thus simple contingency offers a means to transcend itself, and Levertov can write: "A poetry that merely describes, and that features the trivial egotism of the writer (an egotism that obstructs any profound self-explorations) is not liberated from contingency" (*The Poet in the World,* 95). In castigating egotism here, Levertov echoes, perhaps, Olson's account of the modern poet's necessary relation to the world, for which he invents the term "Objectism." "Objectism [he writes in "Projective Verse"] is the getting rid of the lyrical interference of the individual as ego, of the 'subject' and his soul, that peculiar presumption by which western man has interposed himself between what he is as a creature of nature . . . and those other creations of nature which we may, with no derogation, call objects" (*The Poetics of the New American Poetry,* 156). Olson's prime example of "Objectism" is W. C. Williams. Williams once described in a letter to Marianne Moore a youthful experience in which, he said, "everything became a unit and at the same time a part of myself." "As a reward for this anonymity," Williams concluded, "I feel as much a part of things as trees or stones."[16]

Joseph Hillis Miller is surely right to see this "anonymity," this abandonment of the separate ego, as an abandonment also of that separation between the inner world of the subject and the outer world of objects which is a debased inheritance from Romanticism. "In Williams' poetry [Miller writes] there is no description of private inner experience. There is also no description of objects which are external to the poet's mind. Nothing is external to his mind. His mind overlaps with things; things overlap with his mind."[17] Thus Williams may be placed at an extreme remove from the young T. S. Eliot who found in the philosophy of F. H. Bradley a congenial account of the prison of subjectivity: "My external sensations are no less private to myself than are my thoughts or my feelings. In either case my experience falls within my own circle, a circle closed on the outside. . . . In brief, regarded as an existence which appears in a soul, the whole world for each is peculiar and private to that soul."[18] This ontological distinction between Williams and Eliot informs the modes of their writing and the attitudes they have to their readers. Where Eliot claims the artist's prerogative to preselect experience for the reader, Williams complains that "there is a constant barrier between the reader and his consciousness of immediate contact with the world."[19] He thus takes his stand with Whitman, who told his reader in "Song of Myself":

> You shall not look through my eyes either, not take things from
>   me,
> You shall listen to all sides and filter them for yourself.

For Levertov, as for Whitman and Williams, experience is a continuum. Geoffrey Thurley recognizes this, when he says of her work: "In place of the refined poetess sitting isloated among the teacups, socially aligned with her visitors but privately alienated from them, we encounter . . . the poet–housewife/mother . . . whose living-space coincides with [her] aesthetic space. The old separation of the *avant garde,* in which the private world of poetic experience excluded the actual grubby world of social living, is replaced by a unified continuum."[20]

VIII

In Levertov, as in Williams, there is no blurring of the edge between self and objects, but it is not a cutting edge: she is as free as he is of the angst that has dogged Romantic writers up to our own day. Hence the attitude with which she approaches the world is essentially one of wonder, of delight. Her poems bear out Williams's dictum that "There is a long history in each one of us that comes as not only a reawakening but a repossession when confronted by this world."[21]

For Levertov, writing is a way of recording such acts of "reawakening," of "repossession"; it is radiant with *recognition*. She exclaims in "Matins,"

> That's it,
> that's joy, it's always
> a recognition, the known
> appearing fully itself, and
> more itself than one knew.
>
> (*The Jacob's Ladder,* 57)

The perpetual problem of a poetry of recognitions is that it may only rarely get beyond exclamation. This poem, for instance, is punctuated by ejaculations of "the authentic!", and simply offers us fragments of experience that have struck the poet as in some way "authentic." Such writing remains obstinately Imagist, and lays itself open to the criticism of an early American review of Imagism, that "poem after poem of this sort is full of the simple wonder of a child picking up pebbles on the beach."[22] However, if we can accept such naïveté as, in itself, "authentic," then we can begin to appreciate that it does not simply negate all our previous expectations of poetry, but offers a distinctively new mode.

IX

In order to describe this mode, I find myself falling back on Roman Jakobson's well-known distinction between the metaphoric and metonymic poles of discourse.[23] You will recall that Jakobson associates metaphor, the assertion of similarity, with poetry, and with Romantic modes of experience. Metaphor and simile record the Romantic poet's efforts to identify *likeness* in the world about him, to impose his meanings on it, to span the felt distance between subject and object. Metonymy, on the other hand, rests on *contiguity;* it is enough for things to be associated in space for them to be placed together in discourse. Thus Jakobson identifies metonymy as the pole towards which prose, and in particular the literature of Realism, tends.

We can see then that Henry James, who argues that "life is all inclusion and confusion; art is all discrimination and selection," would be inclined to metaphor and symbolism, by Jakobson's definition; whereas Balzac, who expressed his intent to "set forth in order the facts" is metonymic or Realist—if we may assume that, for him, the order in which the facts naturally occur is a sufficient order. Williams must undoubtedly be categorized with Balzac, since he overtly refuses the egotist's or artist's privilege of discrimination, in favor of transcription. "What is there to select?" he asks, "It *is*."[24]

Williams explicitly rejected metaphor and simile early in his poetic career. Here is a significant passage from the Prologue to *Kora in Hell* (1917):

> Although it is a quality of the imagination that it seeks to *place together* those things which have a common relationship, yet the coining of similes is a pastime of a very low order . . . Much more keen is that power which discovers in things those inimitable particles of dissimilarity to all other things which are the peculiar perfections of the thing in question . . . This *loose linking* of one thing with another has the effects of a destructive power little to be guessed at . . . All is confusion, yet it comes from a hidden desire for the dance. (*Imaginations*, 18–20; emphases added)

This is a charter for the metonymic writer. It lies behind all Williams's efforts to establish a new mode of writing, in the face of Eliot's tremendous success as a symbolist poet. Confronted by that success, he wrote in *Spring and All:* "how easy to slip / into the old mode, how hard to cling / to the advance" (*Imaginations*, 103). The "old mode" is the mode of symbolism, of metaphor; the "advance," as Williams saw it, was the move beyond Romantic dualism into the metonymic mode.

The alternative to metaphor, in Williams's view, was a stress on particulars—hence the well-known slogan "No ideas but in things"; and hence, too, the injunction of *Paterson* Book III:

> —of this, make it of *this,* this
> this, this, this, this.
>
> (*Paterson*, 168)

Multiplicity, the listing of things without violating their particular existence, becomes a deliberate strategy, and is responsible for the shape of Williams's poems on the page. "By the brokenness of his composition," he wrote, "the poet makes himself master of a certain weapon which he could possess himself of in no other way" (*Imaginations*, 16).

The first poem of *Spring and All* demonstrates this strategy in its local detail:

> All along the road the reddish
> purplish, forked, upstanding, twiggy
> stuff of bushes and small trees . . .

It stops short of personification even though "sluggish / dazed spring approaches"; the poem continues:

> They enter the new world naked
> cold, uncertain of all
> save that they enter.
>
> (Imaginations, 95)

The reader may extrapolate from these lines a metaphor for the immigrant's bleak prospect of America, or for the baby's arrival in the world, but he is not *entitled* to do so by the mode of the poem.

This is a major difficulty for English students coming to Williams from a training in reading Eliot's poetry or indeed any poetry in the European metaphoric tradition—and in that we must include such writers as Wallace Stevens and Robert Frost. Because Williams is a metonymic poet, his work often seems, to the uninitiated, close to prose. His own development, indeed, involved a rejection of Keats's idiom in favor of the kind of Whitmanesque jottings that Allen Ginsberg has referred to as "prose-seeds."[25] Metonymy was the natural medium in which he could set down the contiguous pattern of his perceptions. Hence the necessity to his work, and to that of the writers who followed him, of typographic freedom, of open form, which allows the "prose-seeds" to establish their own growth.

X

This is the context of Levertov's belief that "form is never more than a *revelation* of content," and of her own poetic practice. In her writing, as in Williams's, there is no *depth,* no measurable distance between what is said and what is meant. In this, both differ from the most well-intentioned of the Transcendentalists. Tony Tanner has pointed out the strain inherent in Thoreau's attempts to "move from the surface detail to the Universal benevolent One which underlay it," the evidence in his writing of "an effort of penetration, a will to seduce the larger meaning out of the small particular."[26]

Levertov seems, like Williams, to have achieved a concatena-

tion of the "surface detail" with the "larger meaning." Her po-
etry may be said to be *all surface*. I have attempted to show that
this is not a matter of style alone, but of the poet's state of
awareness. Thus she writes:

> life is in me, a love for
> what happens, for
> the surfaces that are their own
> interior life.[27]

In passages such as this, it seems to me that Williams's phrase
"passive-possessive" gets its full complement of meaning. Love
is a precondition of Levertov's relaxed relationship with herself
and with things. This persists in *The Sorrow Dance* at the very
threshold of her poems against the Vietnam War. My last exam-
ple, "Joy," is from this volume. It has an epigraph from Thoreau,
which robustly insists:

> You must love the crust of the earth on
> which you dwell. You must be able to
> extract nutriment out of a sandheap.
> You must have so good an appetite as
> this, else you will live in vain.

Joy, the, "well . . . *joyfulness* of
joy"—"many years
I had not known it," the woman of eighty
said, "only remembered, till now."

Traherne
in dark fields.
              On Tremont Street,
on the Common, a raw dusk, Emerson
"glad to the brink of fear."
              It is objective,

stands founded, a roofed gateway;
we cloud-wander

away from it, stumble
again towards it not seeing it,

enter cast-down, discover ourselves
"in joy" as "in love."[28]

In this poem, the very scraps of discourse are like the crusts from which Thoreau's nutriment must be extracted. Here the contiguity is not of things, but of "prose-seeds," disparate recognitions. The poet allows them to lie, like found objects, on the page, and to offer a sense of revelation analogous to her own.

It is in this sense that the poem *moves:* that is, it moves *us,* just as the original experience moved the poet. It also moves, as "Overland to the Islands" moved, towards a final discovery. In Levertov's words, "The metric movement, the measure, is the direct expression of the movement of perception" (*The Poet in the World,* 11). Here the measure enacts the meaning as "we cloud-wander / / away from it" and "stumble / again towards it." The poem approaches its meaning in just such an oblique manner—via the words and experience of others, to a direct statement ("It is objective") which recalls the signal "It is alive" of Williams's "At the Ball Game." Like Williams, Levertov seems intent on using the brokenness of things as a vehicle for wholeness, and she does indeed offer an analogy for this wholeness, close to the center of the poem: "stands founded, a roofed gateway." Again, I restrain myself from the term "metaphor," since it seems to me that the gateway is *there,* just as the experience is there, to be entered—an entry which is not simply into the full value of the world outside, but also the full value of the world within oneself. This is what the poem ultimately "discovers" to us: we

> discover ourselves
> "in joy" as "in love."

NOTES

The first time a work is mentioned, details of publication are given in a note. In subsequent citations, titles and page references are given parenthetically in the text. The British editions of Denise Levertov's books, published by Jonathan Cape, are at present out of print.

1. Oppen, *The Materials* (New York: New Directions/San Francisco Review, 1962).

2. Zukofsky, 'An Objective' (1930); reprinted in *Prepositions* (London: Rapp and Carroll, 1967), 20.

3. Pound, "A List of Books" (1918); reprinted in W. Cookson, ed., *Ezra Pound: Selected Prose 1909–65* (London: Faber & Faber, 1973), 394.

4. Creeley, *Poems 1950–65* (London: Calder and Boyars, 1966), 190.

5. Rexroth, *Assays* (New York: New Directions, 1961), 189.

6. Olson, "Paterson (Book Five)," *Evergreen Review* 2, no. 9 (Summer 1959): 220–21.

7. Levertov, "Biographical Note" in Donald M. Allen, ed., *The New American Poetry* (New York/London: Grove Press/Evergreen Books, 1960), 441.

8. Duncan, "Notes on Poetics Regarding Olson's *Maximus,*" *Black Mountain Review,* 1956; reprinted in Donald Allen and Warren Tallman, eds., *The Poetics of the New American Poetry* (New York: Grove Press, 1973), 187–88.

9. Olson, "Projective Verse" (*Poetry New York,* 1950); reprinted in Allen and Tallman, *Poetics of the New American Poetry,* 149.

10. Levertov, "Overland to the Islands"; reprinted in *The Jacob's Ladder* (New York: New Directions, 1961), 73.

11. Williams, *Paterson* (New York: New Directions, 1963), n.p.

12. Levertov, "The Sense of Pilgrimage" (1967), *The Poet in the World* (New York: New Directions, 1973), 69.

13. Williams, letter of 23 August 1954; in "Letters to Denise Levertov," *Stonybrook* 1/2 (1968): 163–4.

14. Levertov, "To Kevin O'Leary, Wherever He Is," *Footprints* (New York: New Directions, 1972), 26.

15. Levertov, *With Eyes at the Back of Our Heads* (New York: New Directions, 1960), 17–18.

16. Williams, letter of May 1934, in John Thirlwall, ed., *The Selected Letters of William Carlos Williams* (New York: McDowell, Obolensky, 1957), 147.

17. Introduction to J. Hillis Miller, ed., *William Carlos Williams: A Collection of Critical Essays* (Englewood Cliffs, N.J.: Prentice-Hall, 1966), 7.

18. Bradley, *Appearance and Reality,* cited in Eliot's Notes on *The Waste Land, The Collected Poems of T. S. Eliot 1909–35* (London: Faber and Faber, 1936), 84.

19. Williams, *Spring and All* (1923); reprinted in Webster Schott, ed., *Imaginations* (New York: New Directions, 1970), 88.

20. Thurley, *The American Moment* (London: Edward Arnold, 1977), 119.

21. *The Autobiography of William Carlos Williams* (New York: Random House, 1951), 19.

22. Lewis Worthington Smith, "The New Naïveté," *Atlantic Monthly,* 1916; cited by Glynn Hughes, *Imagism and the Imagists* (London: Oxford University Press. 1931), 67.

23. Jakobson, *Fundamentals of Language,* rev. ed. (The Hague/Paris: Mouton, 1975), 90–96.

24. Williams, introduction to Byron Vazakas, *Transfigured Night* (New York: Macmillan, 1946), xi.

25. Ginsberg, 'Notes for *Howl* and Other Poems' (1959), reprinted in Allen, *New American Poetry,* 414–15. See also *Autobiography of William Carlos Williams,* 53.

26. Tanner, "Pigment and Ether: A Comment on the American Mind," *BAAS Bulletin* 7 (1963):40–45.

27. Levertov, "Entr'acte" from "Staying alive," *To Stay Alive* (New York: New Directions, 1971), 66.

28. Levertov, "Joy," *The Sorrow Dance* (New York: New Directions, 1967), 33.

CHARLES ALTIERI

Denise Levertov and the Limits of the Aesthetics of Presence

My major concern so far has been to illustrate what I consider significant achievements by postmodern poets in the sixties. It seems fair now to claim that the poets studied are all accomplished craftsmen, able to make language and structure dramatize and intensify their imaginative explorations of immanent values. And, more important, in articulating these values, the poets manage to continue the Romantic enterprise of locating visionary and aesthetic aspects of imaginary activity firmly within basic existential concerns. In a time when many writers were tempted to rest content with claims for autotelic formal achievements or assertions about the imagination as a source for free play or disorder in a repressive culture, these poets have managed to ally poetry with the work of philosophers altering the culture's perspectives on the nature of thinking itself. Instead of posing explanations for phenomena or elaborating abstract mythic or conceptual systems, they turn to constructing and reflecting upon the kinds of attitudes and stances that can place man in relationship to experience where old questions seem irrelevant and the power of basic ties to both culture and nature stands clear. The poets—especially O'Hara, Snyder, Creeley, and Merwin—each give resonance and imaginative life to Heideggerean claims that poetry is the taking up of sites in which being, or the numinous familiar, discloses itself and testifies to the powers of the attentive mind.

If, however, I attend only to craft or to the power of particular imaginative stances, I run the risk of oversimplifying the poetry and the poetics of postmodernism. The craft and the attitudes ultimately derive from specific philosophical assumptions, and one can fully understand the poetry only if one recognizes the problems and the possibilities inherent in these assumptions. Po-

Reprinted from Charles Altieri, *Enlarging the Temple: New Directions in Poetry during the 1960's* (Lewisburg, Pa.: Bucknell University Press, 1980), 225–44. Copyright © 1980 by Bucknell University.

etry does not usually present and defend ideas in a way amenable to assessing their truth, but one can, perhaps must, nonetheless, discuss the *adequacy* of its philosophical assumptions. If one is to take poets seriously, both as representatives of their culture and as participants in a dialogue about what it means to be fully human at a given time, one must ask how completely and complexly their assumptions register and account for perennial and specific problems. One must discuss whether their perspectives can respond to the multiple tensions between mind and world, individual and society, and the person and his own desires, which are constant features of both cultural heritage and daily existence.

When one puts pressure on postmodern poetics by asking questions about philosophical adequacy, one immediately confronts a powerful contradiction: considered as metaphysical or religious meditation, the poetry of the sixties seems to me highly sophisticated; it takes into account all the obvious secular objections to traditional religious thought and actually continues and extends the inquiries of philosophers as diverse as Heidegger, Whitehead, and Wittgenstein. This very success, however, makes it disappointing that the poetry fails so miserably in handling social and ethical issues. One cannot avoid asking why this is the case, and when he does he finds that at least one poet, Denise Levertov, has preceded his questions. (In this respect, at least, poets continue to be Pound's "antennae of the race.") Miss Levertov has been one of the major voices of the new poetry in the 1960s, and while not very original, she is often quite a good poet devoted to developing concrete moments in which the numinous emerges out of the quotidian. Yet what interests me most about her work, what I shall now develop, is her experience of the inadequacy of the aesthetics of presence when in *The Sorrow Dance* (1967) and subsequent volumes she tries to adapt her poetic to pressing social concerns caused by the war in Vietnam. Miss Levertov presents a very compelling critique of that aesthetic, but even more telling is her own lack of poetic power and authority when she tries to adapt the principles that had shaped her work to social questions. In effect, her later work testifies to the most basic intellectual weaknesses of the contemporary aesthetic and presents a challenge that I hope will be met by poets in the seventies.

Let me first briefly sketch her earlier objectivist celebrations of presence as plenitude. As she summarizes her poetic career, the informing myth or "plot behind the plot" is the desire to com-

127

bine and reconcile "the spirit of Here and Now" learned from Williams "with the Romantic spirit of quest, of longing to wander towards other worlds" inherited from her father's interest in traditions of mystical thought:

> I find my main theme again in the title poem of *Overland to the Islands:* "Lets go," it begins, "much as that dog goes / intently haphazard"; and ends, "there's nothing / the dog disdains on his way, / nevertheless he / keeps moving, changing / pace and approach but / not direction—every step an arrival." The last phrase, "every step an arrival," is quoted from Rilke, and here, unconsciously, I was evidently trying to unify for myself my sense of the pilgrim way with my new American, objectivist influenced, pragmatic and sensuous longing for the Here and Now; a living-in-the-present that I would later find further incitement to in Thoreau's notebooks.[1]

To unify these strands in her work Miss Levertov gathers into her poetry elements of all three approaches to presence explored in chapter 2. From Olson, and more directly from Duncan and Creeley, she takes her objectivist ideals: verse must capture the energies of the attentive consciousness open to the event of arriving each step along the way. But like Creeley, her tone and dramatic context differ radically from Olson's bardic voice and generalizing perspective. Both poets keep the less hero-oriented dimensions of Olson's aesthetic, but use them in specific domestic contests that share O'Hara's emphases on the local, the casual, and the contingent. Finally, in her desire to correlate objectivist ideals with the mystical attitudes that sustain the "pilgrim way," her pursuit of presence leads to meditations on the deep image[2] and the development of techniques to render a "slip inward," or in her case a slip beyond, to a sense of the infinite depth and mystery at the horizon of what is sharply seen.

Her most characteristic image for reconciling the sense of continual arrival in a satisfying present with the "pilgrim way" is the image of ripeness, as exemplified by the last stanza of "Under the Tree":

> let the oranges
> ripen, ripen above you,
> you are living too, one
> among the dark multitude—
>
> (*WEBH,* 46)

Presence as plenitude here is very different from Olson's energy of spring or Snyder's "Communionism," or even his movement into the "back country of the mind." Rather this stanza concentrates a slow process of satisfaction (the repeated "ripen") blending into a sense of transcendent union. The poem dwells lovingly on "one," a word at once requiring a strong pause and, because it is enjambed, a quick transition into the "dark multitude." Ripeness then functions in several ways. As a physical image it renders a sense of the scene as self-contained plenitude. But ripeness is of its very nature a transitional state; it testifies to the fact that individual perfection is not essentially an end in itself but a means for becoming a functioning and satisfying element in the total process. The tree puts forth fruit in order to nourish the seed and create new life. Moreover, from man's perspective the ripe fruit calls out to be eaten, and thus is another way to sustain life. Psychologically a similar ripening process takes place for the speaker. The stanza's initial imperative, "let," summarizes the poem's moral movement. The speaker is willing to accept process as process and to dwell with attention on the fullness of the "Here and Now." Like the fruit, she is at once fully there and gradually preparing for a new relationship to the total life process, a relationship embodied in the shift in attention from the trees to herself and then to the climatic sense of oneness. (In many of Miss Levertov's poems this movement from ripeness to union takes explicit sexual form.) Finally the sense of oneness leads in the last line to the "slip beyond" into a metaphysical vision of shared process at a deeper level of awareness. "Dark multitude" is unfortunately vague and abstract, but in a sense these qualities are necessary to get the intended feeling of the whole physical scene being carried into a level of experience where the mind itself sees its place in an all-embracing process.

How different from this satisfying enclosed space and relaxed accepting attitude is the opening poem of *Relearning the Alphabet:*

> Dreamed the thong of my sandal broke.
> Nothing to hold it to my foot.
> How shall I walk?
> Barefoot?
> The sharp stones, the dirt. I would
> hobble.
> And—
> Where was I going?

Where was I going I can't
go to now, unless hurting?
Where am I standing, if I'm
to stand still now?

(*RLA*, 3)

Every step is no longer an arrival as she replaces confident asser-
tion with a series of questions that set the dominant tone of the
volume. This poet of place and attention now can neither stand
peacefully nor follow a purposive path. Moreover, accustomed
to merging her ego into a field of actions, she now feels that field
breaking up into a public self merely playing roles and a genuine
"I" that grows so deeply private one must fear for its continued
presence:

Between chores—
                    hulling strawberries,
                    answering letters—
or between poems,

returning to the mirror
to see if I'm there.

(*RLA*, 59)

Even touching and tasting, two of her most recurrent acts of
celebration, now only alienate the sensitive spirit from the things
of this world:

At any moment the heart
breaks for nothing—

poor folk got up in their best,
rich ones trying, trying to please—

each touch and a new fissure appears,
such a network, I think of an old
china pie-plate
left too long in the oven.

(*RLA*, 19)

Black beans, white sunlight.
These have sufficed.

> Approval of mothers, of brothers,
> of strangers—a plunge of the hands
> in sifted flour, over the wrists.
> It gives pleasure.
> . . . .
> But hunger: a hunger there is
> refuses. Refuses the earth.
>
> (*RLA,* 51)

No orange will compensate for the fact that the present moment is now inextricable from the continual awareness of the senseless suffering and death created by the war in Vietnam. The psychological counterpart to this hunger is the doubt about her previous poetic stance that permeates *Relearning the Alphabet:*

> What do I know?
>> Swing of the
>> birch catkins,
>> drift of
>> watergrass,
>> tufts of
>> green on the
>> trees,
>> (flowers, not leaves,
>> bearing intricately
>> little winged seeds
>> to fly in fall)
>> and whoever
>> I meet now,
>> on the path.
> It's not enough.
>
> (*RLA,* 5–6)

What she knows can no longer suffice because she is now confronted with two problems her aesthetics of presence cannot handle. With the war so dominant a fact of experience, especially for the poet whose sensitivity now becomes a kind of curse, she perceives in the present at least as many inescapable reminders of suffering and pain as causes for awe and religious acceptance. Second, the war brings home the poet's helplessness. What mystery she does perceive in the present is too personal and too particular to help her either judge or transform the suffering. The "dark multitude" has shown itself as a mass of isolated individuals who share only confusion. In "The Cold Spring" she seeks to renew her sense of the numinous sources or origins that can sustain the way of poetic affirmation, but she finds instead that at the source of the spring feeding poetic inspiration, the life-giving waters are reddened and muddied by human violence. The eye now is only a physical instrument recording ambiguities and can give no direction, no structure, to the I: "Reduced to an eye / I forget what / I / was" (*RLA*, 9).

"Advent 1966" is Levertov's most powerful statement of the changed landscape where the sensitive eye, which once served to unite the "I" with the numinous scene, now sees only a demonic version of incarnation. And this reversal of traditional possibilities for satisfying mythic transformations is paralleled by the fact that now the intense literal reality of the flames from napalm no longer allows the shift to mythic dimensions of fire so easily and movingly rendered in "Eros at Temple Stream" (*OTS*, 55):

> because of this my strong sight,
> my clear caressive sight, my poet's sight I was given
> that it might stir me to song,
> is blurred.
> > There is a cataract filming over
> my inner eyes. Or else a monstrous insect
> has entered my head, and looks out
> from my sockets with multiple vision,
>
> seeing not the unique Holy Infant
> burning sublimely, an imagination of redemption,
> furnace in which souls are wrought into new life,
> but, as off a beltline, more, more senseless figures aflame.
>
> And this insect (who is not there—
> it is my own eyes do my seeing, the insect
> is not there, what I see is there)
> will not permit me to look elsewhere,
>
> or if I look, to see except dulled and unfocused
> the delicate, firm, whole flesh of the still unburned.

> > > > > (*RLA*, 4)

Relearning the Alphabet has a place in the modern tradition of volumes of poetry revaluing a whole poetic career and tentatively exploring new directions. Like Yeats, Eliot, and Stevens before her, she knows what she has to do, but she has considerably less at her disposal to help her realize the new goals. Her task is twofold—to awaken the sensitivity of those supporting the war so they might see its evils (see *RLA*, 13, 27), and to formulate an ethic and an aesthetic that might help restructure the consciousness of society. The poetry of numinous presence must grow more discursive in order to propound values at once more explicitly ethical than those of immanence and more general than those bound to the now muddied objective contexts of specific moments of perception. The poetics of presence must be complemented by models allowing society "to equate human with humane" (*RLA*, 104) in order to help people accept the "task" of becoming " 'more ourselves' / in the making" (*SD*, 82).

Where, however, is she to find within her sense of poetry and the poet's role, style and themes adequate to the task she sees as necessary? Where will she find an ethical basis for creating models of humane behavior? To what value structures can the poet turn when for most of her life she has rejected humanism and the early moderns' use of tradition and creative imagination as the basis of her ideals? While she recognizes that the aesthetics of presence no longer suffices, she has only its implicit ethical ideals to work with. That aesthetic is built on visions of immanence whose only ethical corollary is the command to let be and to recognize the fullness of what lies before one. Such an ideal might provide the goal for a transformed society, but it will not give much help in determining or propounding the means for creating such a society. Moreover, that aesthetic is intensely antisymbolist (see *SD*, 40) and can provide little guidance when the poet feels that she must deal with symbolic generalizations and must transform moments of vision into the basis of discursively presented structures of value. With so much cut away in order to reach the numinous present, what has the contemporary poet left with which to build an ethical vision based on his insights?

I am now entering aspects of the crisis presented in *Relearning the Alphabet* that are no longer under Miss Levertov's self-conscious control. She wants to raise questions in order to provide at least tentative answers, but the poems giving answers only make one realize that the crisis is a deeper one than she seems to think. She tries to work out a solution by turning to the notebook form, for here she can remain faithful to the now-confused present while replacing the dramatic poem of sharply realized perceptions with one loose enough to allow moral reflections. In this form she can discuss moral issues without pretending to a structured moral vision and can allow moments of moral conviction to emerge from her intense suffering and inner contradictions. If the poet cannot adequately judge her age intellectually, she can provide personal witness of what it is doing to its sensitive and reflective spirits. Moreover, unwilling and perhaps unable to construct heroic models of resistance that may be mere fictions, she can in the notebook form capture as models of humane behavior whatever acts strike her, without endangering the power of the acts themselves by either interpreting them or excessively dramatizing them. Personal example is perhaps the only ethical model for social action that makes coherent sense within an aesthetics of presence because it simply shifts attention from the numinous qualities of natural scenes to the qualities of human actors in social situations.

In theory, then, the notebook form makes a certain amount of sense, given Miss Levertov's plight. But it simply does not work, and perhaps could not work to achieve what she desires. The notebook style at best can serve as a historical document dramatizing the problems of a sensitive consciousness at given moments. But it has little reconstructive value because it provides no checks—either formal or in demands for lyric intensity—against the temptations—so strong when one is driven by moral outrage—to easy rhetoric and slack generalizations. Moreover, the form exerts very little authority: it seems only the cries of a passive victim. Here perhaps the "wise passiveness" cultivated by the poetics of presence shows its ultimate weakness. It is, of course, not easy for the poet, so lacking in real social power, to assert authority, but there are, if she will ally herself with them, moral and artistic traditions that demand and support resistance to the kind of forces oppressing Levertov. But before I get into theoretical questions about the limitations of all modern political poetry, I shall look closely at the undeniable weaknesses in Miss Levertov's efforts. Then one can hardly doubt that there are better philosophical and aesthetic foundations for public poetry, and one can see how deeply her own work is victimized by the very problems she describes in the aesthetics of presence. (That description, I might add, is a considerable achievement.)

The following lines are the climactic narrative section of Miss Levertov's "From a Notebook: October '68–May '69":

> O happiness
> in the sun! Is it
> that simple, then,

to live?
—crazy rhythm of
scooping up barehanded
(all the shovels already in use)
careless of filth and broken glass
—scooping up garbage together
poets and dreamers studying
joy together, clearing
refuse off the neglected, newly recognized,
humbly waiting ground, place, locus, of what could be our
New World even now, our revolution, one and one and
one and one together, black children swinging, green
guitars, that energy, that music, no one
telling anyone what to do,
everyone doing,

each leaf of
the new grass near us
a new testament . . .

Out to the dump:
acres of garbage glitter and stink in wild sunlight, gulls
float and scream in the brilliant sky,
polluted waters bob and dazzle, we laugh, our arms ache,
we work together
shoving and kicking and scraping to empty our truckload
over the bank
even though we know
the irony of adding to the Bay fill, the System has us there—
but we love each other and return to the Park.

Thursday, May 15th
At 6 a.m. the ominous zooming, war-sound, of helicopters
breaks into our sleep.

To the Park:
ringed with police.
Bulldozers have moved in.
Barely awake, the people—
those who had made for each other
a green place—
begin to gather at the corners.

Their tears fall on sidewalk cement.
The fence goes up, twice a man's height.

Everyone knows (yet no one yet
believes it) what all shall know
this day, and the days that follow:
now, the clubs, the gas,
bayonets, bullets. The War
comes home to us . . .

(*RLA,* 106–7)

The details are flat, often sentimental, asserting rather than mani-
festing value (for example, "black children swinging, green /
guitars, [what other colors could they be?] that energy, that mu-
sic" or the sentimental polarity of tears and cement). And loose
propagandistic phrases like "the people" and "The War / comes
home to us" neither create fresh insights nor bear up under intel-
lectual analysis. More telling is the pathetic quest to make asser-
tions of value in generalizations that seem simplistic. "Happiness
/ in the sun" might be a simple moment of life, but it is not an
adequate model for basing so general a conclusion as, "Is it / that
simple, then, / to live." No, for our culture it is not, whether one
accepts its vision of authentic life or whether one wants to
change it in any meaningful way. And the symbolic equation of
the grass revealed in its freshness when the garbage is removed
with "a new testament" has a certain momentary validity, but it
is too slight an event on which to hang so portentous and inclu-
sive a symbolic referent.[3] Here human action restores a simple
natural dynamism, but that is a far cry from receiving the vision,
structure, and ground of a new law as implied by the metaphor.
No wonder she does not develop this but quickly changes her
perspective. Where she arrives, though, is even more problem-
atic. Miss Levertov has a quick mind; she recognizes the irony of
removing garbage only to add to the Bay-fill destroying the San
Francisco harbor, and she records this both to dramatize the self-
irony a revolutionary can maintain and to stave off her critics.
But her clever way of dismissing the irony will not do. In fact, it
makes childish and questionable the love she is trying to cele-
brate. It is precisely that easy praise of human virtues and the
tendency to assert it in order to cover up political contradictions
that has made the new calls to revolution suspect and under-
mined the authority of those poets celebrating it.

What bothers me most in this passage, though, is the way it
exemplifies problems I suspect are endemic to a poetics of imma-
nence. That aesthetic, in the pursuit of an unmediated sense of
Being and in its attempts to make ontologically real harmonies

perceived between aesthetic and natural processes, tends in social questions to confuse art and life and to misuse poetic categories of thought. Miss Levertov, as I have shown, explicitly denies a symbolic way of thinking in her pursuit of objects; numinous experiences require primarily attentive participation and not artificial interpretive acts of the reflective mind. Not terribly conscious or analytic, then, about what symbols she does use, she is likely to misuse the poet's synthesizing power by constructing problematic analogies like that between the uncovered grass and the New Testament. After encountering repeated instances of this kind of faulty thinking, the reader is likely to grow skeptical, and to replace a sympathetic openness to her work with an analytic attitude—scrutinizing language he should trust the poet has scrutinized so that he can simply respond to it.

A more elaborate misuse of aesthetic categories takes place here when she facilely extends the particular experience of cooperation at People's Park into a universal model for the new society to be created by the revolution. It takes very little skepticism to note that this group is politically homogeneous and gathered together for a short time to achieve a particular purpose that has obvious mythical values underlying it. Such a model is far removed from the problems encountered in creating or maintaining a political society, particularly in cultures that value freedom and difference. A political society must unify groups with a variety of sensibilities, interests, and priorities, and it must do so with structures capable of enduring through time and of defining laws and modes of compromise. The poetic imagination is mythic and tends to confuse imaginative visions of shared ends and unified societies with complex social conditions requiring that, since it is almost impossible to have people agree on ends, people come up with ways of getting them at least to share certain rules of behavior in the pursuit of individual ends.[4]

This social denial of the complexity and differences constitutive of modern societies is reinforced by a characteristic postmodern view of the nature of evil. The aesthetics of presence is essentially monistic, conceiving evil as basically only a privation, a failure to perceive correctly or to align one's consciousness with the latent harmonious orders of a given scene. The dream is that proper action will follow naturally from a correct understanding, or, more radically, a correct positioning in which the understanding receives its "sentences" from the situation. But however appealing the metaphysics of this vision might be, the realm of politics is largely constituted by the need to correlate different visions and priorities. When faced with practical choices, one can hardly escape the fundamental dualist conceptions of the differences between people's perceptions and, when perceptions agree, differences between the priorities accorded to what is perceived. Poetry, one might say, is primarily a meditative mode of consciousness that seeks to bring minds into accord with one another by dramatizing a given perspective. But politics is a mode of action, where the distribution of goods and powers requires reconciling different perspectives. It is not enough to see how others might see: people need to find forms of agreement that do not require sharing the same particular perspectives and priorities. Poetry unifies perspectives within provisional dramatic points of view; society must seek abstract agreements acceptable to dramatic positions widely separated in time, space, and quality.[5]

Given these conditions, one must recognize the fact that no poetry is likely to have much direct impact on the social order. Still, as high modernism makes clear, in style if not in content, political poetry need not be embarrassingly simplistic. This form of poetry can profoundly engage one's sympathies, if not political allegiances. To do so, however, political poetry, and perhaps the more general category of ethical as opposed to perceptual poetry, must first of all recognize the enormous gulf between values found in meditating on nature and those explicitly developed by reflection on public themes and problems. With respect to public poetry, then, modernism is far more effective than the postmodern alternative because of the modernist reliance on tradition and the mythmaking or reconstructive imagination. First, tradition provides both a set of recurrent public and ethical problems that have been central to political debate and a series of roles and allusions that can give dignity and depth to the poet's social stance. Indeed the more fully one includes history in his work, as Yeats does for example in "Nineteen Hundred and Nineteen" and "Meditations in Time of Civil War," the more he perforce admits the complexity of political questions and achieves for himself a stance that can claim authority and universality for both its suffering and its ideals. Second, the very tension between ideals and the recalcitrance of history forces the poet to recognize the complexity of human motives and the enormous gulf, in both society and in the self, between the imagination and empirical reality.

Ideals make dualists of us all, but they need not force us to despair. The third advantage of the modernist poetic, in fact, stems directly from this gulf. For in order to reconcile desires bred by the traditions of imaginative literature with the realities societies produce in the name of these ideals, poets had to distinguish between social values and a deeper ground for values carried by the tradition but never realized.[6] This social condition generates in turn an ethical distinction between empirical or social and ideal or best selves, and it gives the poets a powerful set of analogies between remaking the self imaginatively and reconstituting social order. In the poetry, then, social conflicts need not remain abstract nor invite self-righteous judgment. Social order becomes the parallel to the poet's remaking himself in terms of ideal images, and his struggles to establish poetic orders at once repeat and give authority to his pursuit of social order— an order dependent on correlating psychological and social materials. By making the self an analogue for redeemed society, these poets were easily tempted by elitist and authoritarian models of order, and they had their own problems in successfully distinguishing between art and politics. But because they were so aware of the ideal (not necessarily "fictive") status of their visions, their poetry maintained a sense of the difficulties and possible self-delusions involved in relating art and life, poetic tradition and political realities. And, more important, because they distinguished between perception and making or reconstructing viable social myths and images, their public poetry retained a sense of drama and conflict. They could create personae who could do more than pathetically record their hopes and confusions in the form of private notebooks. They felt that they could speak to society, not simply be overheard by it lamenting impersonal, demonic forces, and hence they articulated dignified forms of public speech as a last noble, if hopeless, model for the poet's active relationship to his society.

More than Levertov's work is at stake in this contrast, and the problems in developing an adequate postmodern public poetry are largely symptoms of psychological problems inherent in the aesthetics of presence. The quest for immanent plenitude, for example, leads readily toward quiescent passivity. Snyder and Levertov make it clear that too strong a sense of evil as mere privation and too much reliance on strategies of perception or imaginative stances as the mode for overcoming that privation leave the self helpless or pathetic in relation to social forces. Moreover, by locating most or all significant values in moments of vision, the poet has great difficulty constructing specific ethical values or moral images that are more applicable and more general than specific epistemological poses. The pursuit of immanence simply does not bring into play important rational faculties of the mind, nor does it focus the poet's attention on historical and traditional forces that might both define the contemporary situation and provide values and images from the past one can use to judge and transcend it.

The postmodern ideal is that the poet's sense of cosmic order and his awakened sensitivity will play the role once played by tradition and by moral universals. However, both moments of vision and individual sensitivity can be terribly evanescent. One can see, for example, in the work of Creeley and O'Hara that as soon as one requires specific personal and secular meanings from this poetic, he finds himself tormented by pressures to have each moment of experience provide in intensity what it cannot give on the level of ideals or principles. There is simply no conceptual level to the experiences the poets cultivate capable of providing them with a sense of consistent identity. In addition, it is difficult to avoid fears of solipsism if one's sense of objective orders in reality and one's ties to other consciousnesses depend upon a series of intense moments of numinous awareness. Finally, this stress on the present makes the poets painfully frustrated by those dead moments in which the energies of place and psyche are not manifest. Merwin's two basic fears—that what offers itself as presence may be mere illusion and that negation may be the only valid plenitude—offer in abstract form the logical alternatives to Snyder's and Duncan's plenitude—an alternative constantly possible within the vision of value as presence free of moral and social contents.

It will not suffice, however, to dwell on these possible problems inherent in the aesthetics of presence. Critics should probably be aware of the spiritual tensions a poetic can create for poets, and even for the literate culture that adopts their values, but they should also remember that, for the modern mind at least, tensions and problems are the stuff poetic dreams are made of. The critic must remain open to the power of poems rendering these problems, and he must recognize that the poets themselves are not only aware of them but working to transcend them in their poetry. Indeed the primary value of reflecting upon the limits of a general poetic may well be the focus it provides on what that poetic has helped the poets achieve. For without the constant pressures I have been describing, the many varieties of presence as plenitude and the general project of rethinking the contemporary metaphysical situation would seem quite trivial and unnecessary. The poems gain in authority and power from the tensions in theme, psyche, and culture the poet manages to articulate as their ground.

One ought finally to keep in mind that if the contrast with modernism serves to clarify the limits of the poetry of the sixties, it also helps in another way to illustrate the significance of its achievement.[7] For in their attempts to articulate the creative powers of the imagination, even the greatest of the modernists blinded themselves to two primary needs in any society. They were unable to imagine culture except in ideal and mythic terms, and most of them could provide alternatives to what they saw as a vulgar positivist and philistine society only by returning to what now seem outmoded and indefensible forms of organicist social and metaphysical thought. The postmoderns would have performed a significant cultural role if they merely tried to right the balance. I hope I have shown that they have given their readers considerably more than that.

Whatever they have given cannot be enough. This is simply the fact of the spiritual condition in which we find ourselves. But they have made it possible for us to view our own experiences from the position that R. D. Laing calls *ontological security*. If they do not either reconcile us to society or lead us to want or to see how to change it, they do help reconcile us to the more general and perhaps more significant situations in which it is man's constant task to find ways of affirming his own existence. Postmodern poetry builds a temple out of nature, not a city, but that can be a considerable achievement even for those whose ultimate dream is some version of a redeemed society. History shows that man's efforts to build temples have little effect on the specific practices characterizing life in the city. Yet history also shows that without the temple, however it may be constructed, life in the city seems at best vulgar and callous, at worst a demonic force driving man back on the woeful inadequacy of endless introspection. When Lowell left Rome for Paris, the archetypal secular city, he found only the second alternative—forcing him to a more and more enervated self-consciousness and a desperate quest to locate all value in domestic experience. The other alternative, implicit in many poets and working for adequate expression in Miss Levertov's "Relearning the Alphabet," requires that one first seek ontological security and then gradually try to extend the terms of that security as the elements of a moral alphabet that one can begin applying to social issues.[8] Once identity has a fixed base, it is possible to endure the contradictions, restraints, and tentative projection of ideals that constitute the public moral life. As Hegel put it, the temple must exist before men can create in it the statue or image of the ideal man that will serve as the center for communal self-definition. Only then, he argues, can the subjective arts emerge to express the many ways that image can be reflected in the political and social organization of the community. While the other contemporary arts, in the throes of what John Barth has called "Exhaustion," continue to reinterpret the subjective aspects of a dying social order, the best postmodern poets are at work articulating the shape of a new temple that may provide the locus for a new image of man.

NOTES

1. The three quotations here are from Miss Levertov's "A Personal Approach," in *Parable, Myth, and Language,* ed. Tony Stoneburner (Cambridge, Mass.: Church Society For College Work, 1967), 19, 28, 23. In the text I use the following abbreviations for her work: "A Personal Approach," *PA;* "The Origins of a Poem," *Michigan Quarterly Review* 7 (1968): 233, 238, *OP;* "An Argument," *Floating Bear* 2 (1961), n.p., *FB; With Eyes at the Back of Our Heads* (New York: New Directions, 1960), *WEBH; The Jacob's Ladder* (New York: New Directions, 1961), *JL: O Taste and See* (New York: New Directions, 1964), *OTS: The Sorrow Dance* (New York: New Directions, 1967), *SD; Relearning the Alphabet* (New York: New Directions, 1970), *RLA; To Stay Alive* (New York: New Directions, 1971), *SA.* For a fuller treatment of her application of the aesthetics of presence, see Thomas A. Duddy, "To Celebrate: A Reading of Denise Levertov," *Criticism* 10 (1968): 138–52.

2. Her essay in *Floating Bear* (see n. 1) argues with Robert Kelley's definition of the *deep image* and proposes Miss Levertov's own view of the way to mystery in poetry. See also *OP.*

3. It is interesting to read Miss Levertov's poems on People's Park in the light of Northrop Frye's mythic reading of that event on the archetype of the expulsion from Eden. See Frye's "The Critical Path: An Essay on the Social Context of Literary Criticism," *Daedalus* 99 (1970): 336–37. Where Levertov participates in the myth, Frye sees beyond it, at least to the extent of understanding why the event appeals so to the imagination. Miss Levertov rarely asks why she responds the way she does. This is one indication of the intellectual shortcomings in her work.

4. I am here summarizing the argument of Alasdair MacIntyre, *Secularization and Moral Change* (New York: Oxford University Press, 1967), 24–35.

5. Miss Levertov's discussion of evil is typical of contemporary poets, most of whom believe evil is not a fact of experience but a condition created by faulty ways of perceiving reality:

What I have up to now been suggesting as the task of the poet may seem of an Emersonian idealism (though perhaps Emerson has been misread on this point) that refuses to look man's capacity for evil square in the eyes. Now as perhaps never before, when we are so acutely conscious of being ruled by evil men, and that in our time man's inhumanity to man has swollen to proportions of perhaps unexampled monstrosity, such a refusal would be no less than idiotic. . . . But Young's final injunction, in the passage just quoted, is what, for me, holds the clue to what must make the poet's humanity humane. Reverence thyself is necessarily an aspect of Schweitzer's doctrine of Reverence for Life, the recognition of oneself as life that wants to live among other forms of life that want to live. This recognition is indissoluble, reciprocal, and dual. There can be no self respect without respect for others, no love and reverence for others without love and reverence for oneself; and no recognition of others is possible without the imagination. The imagination of what it is to be those other forms of life that want to live is the only way to recognition; and it is that imaginative recognition that brings compassion to birth. Man's capacity for evil, then, is less a positive capacity, for all its horrendous activity, than a failure to develop man's most human function, the imagination, to its fullness, and consequently a failure to develop compassion. (*OP,* 237)

6. I have worked out the ethical vision of literature involved here in my essay "Northrop Frye and the Problem of Spiritual Authority," *PMLA* 87 (1972): 964–75.

7. Quentin Anderson, *The Imperial Self: An Essay in American Literary and Cultural History* (New York: Knopf, 1971), has attacked the contemporaries for continuing certain spiritual traits first pronounced in Emerson and Whitman, particularly their negation of history, their desire to link the individual ego to the cosmos by expanding consciousness, and their negating fixed communal and social roles or demands for action in favor of the quest to "incorporate" the universal into the self. My criticism obviously shares certain themes of his, but he falls into the trap I am trying to avoid: for him if literature is not social and devoted to reconciling the individual to society, it is meretricious. Such emphases not only deny the importance of ontological questions, they even rule out the mediating role literature can play in shaping the ideals that lead one to work for social changes, even if the specific working out of these ideals in theory and practice is better accomplished in nonliterary ways.

8. Let me offer here in note form what probably should be an appendix on one important ethical scheme only implicit in most of the poetry but articulated in Miss Levertov's poem "Relearning the Alphabet" as one possible response to the crisis the volume presents. (Since she has not followed it up, it apparently did not satisfy her.) I refer to the possibility of basing ethical values not on myths or images of heroic

perfection but on principles inherent in the language and in the pre-reflexive aspects of culture that man lives in as he does in nature. Philosophers influenced by Wittgenstein and J. L. Austin, like Stuart Hampshire and Stanley Cavell, are working on the problem, but Levertov's poem is especially significant for me because it typifies how in my case it was the poets and not the philosophers who marked out this line of inquiry.

One best approaches this possible ethical ideal by returning to the contrast between symbolist and immanentist models. One of the impulses giving authority to philosophies of immanence is a sense that neither cultural traditions nor humanistic theories of imaginative models of human excellence to be imitated have had any effect in altering the increasing insensitivity and inhumanity of society. The temptation, then, for Wordsworth and Nietzsche as well as for the contemporaries, is to turn away entirely from the idea of morality as based on self-conscious attempts to justify behavior in relation to rational, traditional, or ideal grounds. If change is to be possible it will come not from cultural forces but from natural ones capable of defining and influencing humane behavior. Nature, however, is a set of phenomena at once too general and too specific to ground discussions of ethical value—too general because it encompasses every form of behavior and cannot without submitting itself once again to rational argument define behavior adequate for man's specific form of life, and too specific because each moment of natural experience is different and requires intellectual structures if the moments are to be sorted and tranformed into principles.

This helps explain, I think, why Miss Levertov's critique of her own aesthetics of presence is so compelling and why that aesthetic cannot be extended, as she tries, to ethical principles. But one is left with the question of whether there are no alternatives between ideal cultural models and amorphous natural ones. George Lukács, in *Theory of the Novel,* trans. Anna Bostock (London: Merlin Press, 1971), 63–64, 144–53, makes the key distinction that allows for a middle term between these extremes. In discussing Tolstoy's attempt to resist the problems of subjectivity and of the radical deformation of his culture by seeking a ground of values in natural laws and processes, he distinguishes this too amorphous nature from a second nature. This second nature is not the high culture but the complex of social meanings that the ordinary man relies on to define, without self-conscious reflection, the meaning of his fundamental actions and the rules he follows in moral actions. I am slightly transforming Lukács into the perspective of the philosophers mentioned above, but their point is also his—that a morality can be self-consciously based not on imaginative ideals but on what is called "the constitutive rules" implicit in the basic institutions underlying virtually any social life. (See here in particular John Searle, *Speech Acts* [Cambridge: Cambridge University Press, 1969], 131–49, 175–98.) This second nature is in effect the broader and more specific ground needed: it locates within the familiar and the natural (at least in so much as the prereflexive and humanly universal can be treated as "natural") widely accepted yet not actualized moral principles.

Now to "Relearning the Alphabet." In the midst of the volume's erring ways, Miss Levertov sees at moments one possible alternative to her feeling that nature as she has known it only intensifies her present confusions:

> O language, virtue
> of man, touchstone
> worn down by what
> gross fiction . . .
> . . . .
> O language, mother of thought,
> are you rejecting us as we reject you?
>
> (*RLA*, 21–22)

> Without a terrain in which, to which, I belong,
> language itself is my one home, my Jerusalem. . . .
>
> (*RLA*, 97)

Language can provide the sense of origins and the secure basis for defining virtue no longer to be realized in the objectivist vision, for ordinary language is not created by the fictive imagination but has developed as a moral "touchstone" through mankind's continual arbitration of good and evil. Language is the repository of fundamental moral instincts, marking and valuing those distinctions and qualities which the culture has found basic to its fundamental human interests as it tries to define its experiences. The poem "Relearning the Alphabet" dramatizes how man can return to those simple moral terms as the ground of a new view of natural, antisymbolist morality. The alphabet is a syntax of moral values and their possible relations with one another. The poem's opening lines exemplify the way this syntax functions and state the poem's intention:

> A
>
> Joy—a beginning.   Anguish, ardor.
> To relearn the ah! of knowing in unthinking
> joy: the beloved stranger lives.
> Sweep up anguish as with a wing-tip,
> brushing the ashes back to the fire's core.
>
> (*RLA*, 110)

The simplicity of this alphabet is important—both because the revived morality must be a morality of the "people," not of heroic imaginative men, and because it is opposed to the technological sophistication and complex computational models that support the destruction of Vietnam's simple pastoral culture. Erotic fire can once again be redeemed, now as the desire for cleansing destruction and as the universal archetypal desire to restore Koré (the phrase "fire's core" is Duncan's) from Hell into the praise of radiant life.

Earlier poems in the volume, as shown above, provide the questions this poem tries to answer, and they also help define the importance of the alphabet structure in which its wisdom is embodied. The note of questioning and doubt requires for its resolution some kind of structure so that in the process of a poem the experience of wandering can be countered by the faith that there is a ground and basis of judgment to which one can return "to dig down, to reexamine" (*RLA*, 102). Lost in the structureless ephemera of her notebook form where one can only record doubts and desires, not satisfy them, Miss Levertov cries out, "A beginning / Where shall we / begin? / Can't go / further" (*RLA*, 105). Later the poem envisions the possibility of that beginning when it sees the conditions needed for change: "*Change is now / change is now / things that seem to be solid are not*" (*RLA*, 108). But to realize that change, one must see how "Maybe what seems / evanescent is solid" (*RLA*, 109). What is evanescent, I take it, is the recurrence of life (fire's core) and of the moral qualities that justify man's faith in that life. To make that faith solid one needs a structure. And the excellence of "Relearning the Alphabet" is that it not only provides an abstract structure but in its formal patterns forces one to experience the abstractions as the concrete structure of experience. Thus as one reads the poem, he finds himself occasionally lost or wandering, but once he recognizes that each section will end by returning to moral terms employing the particular letter of its title, he finds himself both continually satisfied by these returns and surprised by the cleverness of the poet and the plenitude of moral possibilities she uncovers by her fidelity to her form. The section on the letters I, J, for example, begins with a painful stumbling that recalls earlier poems but surprises the reader by the multiple terms of its resolution:

> Into the world of continuance, to find
> I-who-I-am again, who wanted
> to enter a life not mine,
>   to leap a wide, deep, swift river.
> . . . .
>   I go stumbling
>   (head turned)
>   back to my origins:
> (if that's where I'm going)
>   to joy, my Jerusalem.
>   (*RLA*, 112)

In a similar way the poem's concluding section takes on the difficult task of finding moral terms and images using the *z* sound and surprises the reader with its range of terms—in the process further enkindling the blaze of moral vision and providing precisely that beginning again desired by *Notebook* if absence is to be transformed once more into presence:

> *Sweep up*
> *anguish as with a wing-tip:*
>
> the blaze addresses
> a different darkness:
> absence has not become
> the transformed presence the will
> looked for,
> but other: the present,
>
> that which was poised already in the ah! of praise.
>
> (*RLA*, 120)

This blend of the aleatory with underlying structures is crucial here because it captures the qualities of moral life on this outwardly pre-reflexive level of experience. Man is not aware of the laws or of their secure ground. Yet when man needs them, they are there if only he can stop dreaming of other more romantic and potentially more merely fictive possibilities. Here perhaps, as one comes to reflect on the plenitude of simple principles capable of satisfying both formal and moral needs, one can find a place where he can reconcile optimism of will with optimism of intelligence. Growing confidence in the poem's form might also testify to a possible confidence in ordinary experience. Here, in the language in which that experience is expressed and carried out, is one possible source for keeping the humane in humanity. Socially this entails making people conscious of how much of their lives are defined in simple strategies of contemporary poetics—the rejection of high tradition, the necessary angel, and the last Romantic hero in favor of careful intense attention to the natural and the familiar.

PART THREE *Politics*

PAUL A. LACEY

The Poetry of Political Anguish

When she spoke at Earlham College recently, Denise Levertov read a piece she called "Perhaps No Poem, But All I Can Say and I Cannot Be Silent." In the question period, when a student asked her why she gave the piece that title, she answered that, though she felt what she was saying intensely, she was not yet sure that the piece had the form and control which a poem required. That form she related to the inwardness of a poem. It has to be not merely addressed to a person or problem *out there,* it must come from *in here,* the inner being of the poet, and it must address something *in here.* In "Origins of a Poem" she speaks of the need for the poet to maintain dialogue with the heart, or with the reader within. "Every art needs two—one who makes it and one who needs it." For Levertov, both are the poet.

In her latest book, *Candles in Babylon,* she includes "A Speech: for Antidraft Rally, D.C., March 22, 1980" and a note which says that this *is* a speech, not properly classifiable as a poem but not prose, either. She includes it because draft counselors and high school teachers have requested it. In each of these cases, Levertov has offered a work significant for its intensity of comment on a political or social problem; and in each case, without apologizing for either the form or the content of the piece, she has wanted to distinguish it from poetry. Behind this problem of classification lies the issue of the connections between poetry and politics, an issue which Levertov addresses extensively in both her collections of essays, *The Poet in the World* (1973) and *Light Up the Cave* (1981).

Few poets of our time have devoted more intellectual energy to exploring the nature of poetic form—the way poems happen, the nature of inspiration, ways to "invite the muse," the discipline behind open forms, how one discovers the shape a particular content must assume, the significance of line breaks, and the like. A substantial part of her two collections of essays is devoted to such shoptalk about the poet's craft. At the same time, few

Reprinted from *Sagetrieb* 4, no. 1 (Spring 1985): 61–71.

poets have devoted more intellectual energy to exploring how political themes and commitments might find appropriate expression in poetry. She pursues these questions in her essays, but even more powerfully and intensely in the poetry itself.

In literary history there has not always been a question how politics and poetry connected. From classical times the main tradition of Western literary criticism asserted that poetry ought both to delight and instruct, to be sweet *and* useful. Such criticism subsumed political, religious, social or philosophical content under the description of genres. A poem, such as the *Iliad* or the *Aeneid,* which recounts a people's history as an explanation of its future destiny, is an *epic.* A poem, such as Pope's "Essay on Man" or Mandeville's "Fable of the Bees," which offers a philosophical or religious account of human nature so as to recommend a particular social or economic order, is *didactic.* The possibility of a political stance is presupposed in the poet's choice of genre. It is an aspect of how the poem is to be *useful* or *instructive.* To speak of a political epic or a didactic political poem is redundant. As long as critical theory addressed questions of form and content separately and conceived of form as the decoration of content, there was not much reason to worry about whether politics and poetry belong together.

Essentially two things have to happen before the relation of politics and literature becomes a controversial issue. First, political process must develop to the point where party politics emerge. That is to say, factions develop in opposition to one another in a framework where competition for the power to govern takes the form of influence with a ruler or an electorate. "Politics" as we understand it does not emerge as a subject of discussion until it is *partisan* politics; before that it is simply patriotism, if it has any name. When the *partisan* nature of political views becomes obvious, the relation of politics to literature becomes a matter of debate. The English Civil War, the Commonwealth period and the Restoration give us compelling examples of intense political activity among writers and of their self-awareness of their writing as a form of political activity. We need only think of Milton's sonnets to illustrate the point.

Second, to put the matter in the terms used by Meyer Abrams in *The Mirror and the Lamp,* before the relation of politics and literature becomes controversial, literary criticism must shift away from *imitative* or *pragmatic* theories of literature to *expressive* ones. With the beginnings of Romanticism, then, there begins the debate about the connection of politics and literature—not merely because the great English Romantic writers responded to the French Revolution and the Napoleonic era but because their most characteristic form came to be the lyric. And as the lyric came to be valued as the most *expressive* and therefore the most genuine of poetic forms, the didactic came to be correspondingly distrusted, so that Shelley, one of the most politically engaged of English poets, would say in his Preface to *Prometheus Unbound,* "Didactic poetry is my abhorrence."

First, *politics* becomes *partisan politics*—taking sides; later on, poets give a political dimension to their alienation from society by their sympathy for revolutionary or other extreme political positions; both these developments are going on at the same time that the most intensely personal, self-expressive forms are becoming accepted as the norm for what poetry ought to be. Politics and poetry come to a parting of the ways: "Out of our quarrel with others we make rhetoric," says William Butler Yeats, "out of our quarrel with ourselves, poetry." Rhetoric is the stuff of partisanship, of propaganda, of persuasion and instruction in what is already known, of politics. Poetry is the quarrel with the self, the exploration of what the poet believes and the discovery of what he knows. Rhetoric is didactic; poetry is lyrical.

In Denise Levertov all the elements of the controversy meet. She is the inheritor of this literary tradition. She believes that poetry creates "autonomous existences out of words and silences" by finding the organic form which reveals the inner meaning of experience. Poetry aspires to the autonomy of Song, but its musicality arises from "fidelity to experience." The fully realized poem is a world in itself. "Because it creates autonomous structures . . . poetry is, in process and in being, intrinsically affirmative." In finding the form which is the revelation of content, the poet makes clear to herself "and thereby to others, the temporal and eternal questions." The poet finds the right form *out there* by internalizing those temporal and eternal problems, holding dialogue with the heart. "What the poet is called on to clarify is not answers but the existence and nature of questions."

But precisely because poetry is what it is, all aspects of human experience can rightly find a place in poetry. The temporal and eternal questions can have a political content as well as any other kind of content. "For the poet, . . . there is no such thing as an isolated study of literature."

To allow that political themes may be appropriate to poetry does not solve the problems of form, however, for the lyric is still the most commonly expected poetic genre in our time. The political poem, Levertov says in "On the Edge of Darkness: What is Political Poetry?" (1975) is "ostensibly lyric;" it consists of short poems written in the poet's own voice, "markedly, candidly, speaking in the poet's unmediated character, . . . written from a personal rather than a fictive, and a subjective rather than objective, standpoint." Yet the political poem must deal with social observations, descriptions of events, expressions of opinions such as the lyric has not typically addressed. "The poetry of political anguish is at its best both didactic and lyrical."

As Levertov has made these ideas clear in her prose, she has been struggling to realize their meaning in her poetry. She has become ever more skillful in achieving the goals she sets for the political poem, "to affect our senses and engage our aesthetic response just as much as one with whose content . . . we can have no argument." But that achievement has been hard-won, starting with *The Sorrow Dance* (1967) and *Relearning the Alphabet* (1970), the two books in which her "poetry of political anguish" first appeared. The accomplishments of both those books was high, but a number of poems felt obsessive, fragmented, unfinished. In *Relearning the Alphabet,* particularly, works seemed imperfectly realized. Both "An Interim" and "From a Notebook: October '68–May '69" seemed to be works in progress rather than finished poems.

To Stay Alive (1971), her most significant exploration of political themes in her poetry, gave her a base on which all her subsequent political poetry rests. In that book she succeeded in enunciating for herself a politically revolutionary position through the medium of poetry which remains open-ended and exploratory. She expresses her commitment to partisan political questions, but in ways which clarify "not answers but the existence and nature of questions." How she accomplishes this will emerge from a close examination of the reorganizing and completion of the long poem sequence called "Staying Alive."

To Stay Alive is made up of two sections of poems, "Preludes" and "Staying Alive," containing poems drawn from four different sections of the two previous books. The ordering of the poems has changed substantially, and the final poem sequence has almost tripled in length. In her preface Levertov says that the justification for bringing these poems together is esthetic: "It assembles separated parts of a whole." As "a record of one person's inner/outer experience in America during the 60's and the beginning of the 70's," the book presents a search for integrity in both political utterance and poetic form. For Levertov, however, the only valid test of the book is esthetic: whether it creates that sense of wholeness, that intensity of inner experience and reflection upon it which alone satisfies the "reader within."

"Staying Alive," the long multisectioned, multiform poem which makes up three-quarters of the book, is the test case for how Levertov successfully brings politics and poetry together into an esthetic whole. In it she has set herself the hardest imaginable task, for in what seems like a sprawling, loosely associational form "Prologue—An Interim," and four "Parts," the first three each followed by an "Entr'acte"—she draws on political and personal events from late December 1967 through November 1970, criss-crosses America, Italy, Yugoslavia and England, circles back in time from childhood to young adulthood to the present, and intersperses prose journal entries, excerpts from newspaper reports, political leaflets, popular song lyrics, passages from letters, quotations from Rilke, Gandhi, Brecht and Camus and echoes of poems by Keats, Hopkins and Swinburne.

But the poem is neither loosely sprawling nor merely associational. Its strategy is what it has always been for Levertov, to move from Reverence for Life to Attention to Life, from Attention to Seeing and Hearing, which leads to Discovery and Revelation of Form, and from Form to Song, which is how she describes the process in "Origins of a Poem" in 1968. For her, knowing and making are inseparable. "Staying Alive," however, begins in *interim,* in-between-time—the immediate occasion for which is the impending draft-resistance trial of Mitchell Goodman—when everything appears temporary and provisional. Alienation from American society has its counterpart in increasing doubt about the poet's past: where the present lacks meaning, neither a usable past nor a desirable future are easily discovered. The poet's "clear caressive sight" is blurred; language, "virtue of man" erodes, rejects us as we reject it. The thread of connection which ran from Reverence for Life to Form and Song has been broken; no fabric stands whole. Consequently, a new fabric must be made, every strand twisted, pulled and tested.

The poem cannot be woven until the unweaving has occurred. We find our way through it by following the broken threads, by discovering how they are reconnected, and by finding the new, whole threads which draw the pattern together.

The first pattern, then, is disjunction. Life or death. The dwindling of the soul or the immensity of sky and sea. "Peace as grandeur. Energy / serene and noble." The self-immolation of "the great savage saints of outrage." The coral island of language, eroded by war; the witness of resisters who "make from outrage / islands of compassion others could build on." Restoration has begun, but devastation still dominates the poem, as it dominates the society in which the poet lives. That disjunction continues in "Part I (October '68–May '69)," which explores the stark choice of "Revolution or Death." That phrase acts on us as though the throb of train wheels repeated it. Working into that rhythm are those suggested by *Which side are you on?*—the old labor song—and the first question at Passover, "What makes this night different from all other nights?" Everything speaks of choice: choosing a side, being of the chosen people, choosing life with the young because "Death is Mayor Daley." Death is also *Unlived life / of which one can die.*" This exploration of choice proceeds on several levels: the political and the social are the most obvious, but the personal is even more influential, signaled by the weaving of nineteenth-century poems about death into the pattern of the poem's reflections. At stake is not only how the world might be revolutionized but how the poet can grow into the second half of her life.

Death is not merely "the obscene sellout." It is also lovely and soothing, as the phrases from Keats and Swinburne remind us. Over against the longing for death, we have the image of the pulsing brain:

> The will to live
>
> pulses.   Radiant emanations
> of living tissue, visible only
> to some photo-eye we know
> sees true because mind's dream-eye,
> inward gage, confirms it.
>   Confirmation,
> a sacrament.

"Part I" circles its subjects, exemplifying in its method what it "discovers" as its conclusion: that revolution must not be merely circular and life not merely linear, but that both must radiate from a center. This revolution becomes "prismatic radiance pulsing from live tissue," the photographic image of the living human brain. Objects, events, memories cluster around an unknown, shifting center which gives them "a character that throughout all transformations / reveals them connatural." "Revolution or death" speaks simultaneously of the political and the psychic life.

Time, place and language serve as images for what is happening to the poet. Her roots are in the nineteenth century, so she is out of touch with those—the young—she most wants to know. She chooses revolution, but fears that her words do not reach into it. "Language itself is my one home, my Jerusalem," but in this age of refugees she too has been uprooted.

> My diction marks me
> untrue to my time;
> change it, I'd be
> untrue to myself.

"Entr'acte" is indeed an interval between acts. It is, first of all, a return to a beloved landscape, to a former way of living, and to the pleasures of the body. In "Life at War" she writes:

> Yes, this is the knowledge that jostles for space
> in our bodies along with all we
> go on knowing of joy, or love. . . .

and that remains a characteristic way for her to represent what has most meaning for her. For Levertov, deep knowledge has to be known *in the body,* literally incorporated. Even memory is bodily knowledge for her. "What pain! What sharp stabs of recall! What revelations." This interval, like the earlier interim, offers a time of renewal and re-collection:

> Again to hold—"capture" they say—
> moments and their processions in palm
> of mind's hand.

The recursive nature of "Staying Alive" is further emphasized in "Part II," where there is no "going beyond" but a digging down and reexamination of already started themes: the meaning of revolution; the inadequacy of language—revolution is "the wrong word"—the incomplete images and gestures which offer "A beginning" for living a life. She finds hints of the new life in the witness of Mitchell Goodman, A. J. Muste, other pacifist and resister friends, and in the making of the People's Park in Berkeley. In the clearing of that land she has seen "poets and dreamers studying / joy together" making the "place, locus, of what could be our / New World even now, our revolution."

Even as "The War / comes home to us" the poem has begun

to enrich the images on which a life can grow. Time becomes not a sequence but a radiating from a center, "pulsations, as from living cells." Place becomes valorized anew, in a People's Park. Revolution becomes like a force of nature, a tree rising out of a flood, a sea full of swimmers, islands—like the islands of compassion—which "step out of the waves on rock feet."

The second "Entr'acte" takes us back again to bodily knowledge of the cost of revolution, "the grim odds we're / up against." What the body knows is the nausea of tear gas, feeling a kind of death which is also "a kind of joy" as the mind remains "clear in its despair." In "the interim" the poet fled to the sea to repossess her soul; in the first "Entr'acte" she went back to a Maine home in winter to "capture" moments in memory; now in the clarity of anguish "Nothing / will do but / to taste the bitter / taste."

With "Part III" the poet returns to Europe after ten and England after twenty years. This marks another turn inward and a new recovery of resources. "What gentleness, what kindness / of the *private life* I left, unknowing, // and gained instead the tragic, fearful / knowledge of *present history*." The reader cannot tell how to balance the loss and gain represented here: so much of "Staying Alive" is a lament for what has happened to the inner life, yet it is impossible to believe that the poet would prefer to have remained ignorant of the "tragic, fearful knowledge" of our times. When she returns to the "writhing lava" of America, it may be with "fierce hope" or no hope, but she will continue to struggle. The poet's spiritual condition becomes clearer to her in a friend's account of a dream of being entrapped in a tunnel with great dogs barking at either end. This image from the unconscious mirrors the poet's own feeling of being unable to move forward but needing to dig down and reexamine. The dreamer remains the victim of her dream until she brings imagination to her aid: "The dogs / will not go away. / They must be transformed." She imagines herself sitting quietly in the middle of the tunnel, using the "fiery stillness" of her being to transform the images of fear into something else. The dream therapy acts as a parable for the poet, whose friend shares what she has learned with her: "Get down into your well, // it's your well // go deep into it // into your own depth as into a poem." At the end of "Part III," the poem has turned from *places* to the process of making a place for oneself, from images of terror and emptiness to what Jung calls "symbols of transformation."

The third "Entr'acte" returns to the image of the pulse, which appears so significantly in earlier parts of the poem—in the radiant pulsations of the living brain, the pulsing rhythm of "revolution or death," the pulsation of time from a center—and makes it the primary symbol of how to stay alive. It is a sign of bodily wisdom, echoing Keats's "axioms in philosophy are not axioms until they are proved on our pulses," and it is a sign of attunement to "the great pulse."

> Peace could be
>
> > that grandeur, that dwelling
> > in majestic presence, attuned
> > to the great pulse.

Now the poet further deepens the meaning of the image by bringing together two dominant themes of the poem, *revolution* and *poetry,* and describing each as a throbbing pulse. Revolution is a "flame-pulse" which sustains life; poetry is "living water" which refreshes the parched soul. Fire and water are contraries; if they are pitted against one another, both will be destroyed. They are also two of the four elements, the primary building blocks of creation; brought together they help make a life. Revolution and poetry, if they are pitted against each other, will each perish.

> > But when their rhythms
> > mesh
> > then though the pain of living
> > never lets up
>
> > the singing begins.

"Part IV" begins "I went back." Going back is the dominant theme of this final section of the poem, and with it Levertov gathers up and reconciles the conflicts which have provided the dialectic of "Staying Alive." She has gone back to her past in England, to recover some of the gentleness and kindness of that life; she has gone back to America, her literal home, filled with the "objects of dailiness" which pull her there; she has gone back to her memories of her sister; she has gone back to the wild zigzagging pace of airplane life, "the push and shove of events," but no longer as "a defective migrant," for she knows where she longs to be; most important, she has gone back down into the depth of her own well, the inner place where all those experiences can find a resolution and a home.

From *interim,* the time of waiting, the poet has returned to the dailiness of life, which has its rhythm of expansion and contraction, its pulse of happiness and sorrow. For the first time in this long poem, happiness explicitly emerges as a theme. The poet experiences it unalloyed in dancing, in looking at Zen paintings, in the momentary community of clearing People's Park and dodging police clubs and in the close fellowship with revolutionaries in Europe. What had been only threads of happiness, forgotten or unvalued in the long, grinding struggle against death, now appear as a strong, connecting strand in the pattern of her life. Happiness comes in those moments, but the capacity to be happy resides within the self.

Camus wrote:
"I discovered inside myself, even in the very midst of
winter, an invincible summer."

The choice is not simply between revolution *or* death; "Staying Alive" is punctuated by deaths. Some are natural deaths; some the political statements of Buddhist monks and "the great savage saints of outrage," Norman Morrison and Alice Herz; some are the inexplicable suicides, the gestures of ultimate, hopeless alienation. One dead friend ignored the world outside of herself; another was flooded by it. Each is a suicide.

There is no suicide in our time
unrelated to history, to whether
each before death had listened to the living, heard
the cry, "Dare to struggle,
dare to win."

The poet must come to her terms with each of these deaths, to grieve, to regret, to rage, to discover how she might incorporate into her own life the abiding values of these lost or wasted lives.

Life comes to the poet in moments, flashes, pulses—brief throbs of love, hate, rage or happiness. What we learn with her is not that happiness does not last but that it can return again. Meanwhile there is the kind of waiting which is restorative. The pulses of insight or experience can be taken into the dark well, the middle of the tunnel, stored there until they are transformed into sustaining energy.

Get my head together. Mesh. Knit
idiom with idiom in the
"push and shove of events."

"Staying Alive" took its start in broken connections and un-
raveling threads. The pulse of life was low and irregular. At its
conclusion, the knitting and meshing continue, but death has
broken some connections forever. Some have found death in the
revolution itself. Some have been unable to stay alive. New
connections are forming, however; language is regaining its in-
tegrity, through the acts of those whose word is good and
through the struggle of the poet to unite the two pulses of revolu-
tion and poetry so that the singing can begin. The fabric of
resistance communities has been tested and borne the strain. The
poet has come back to the places which restore her, where her
inner life finds a home.

Characteristically, what Levertov has accomplished in compre-
hending the revolution she has achieved in and through the mak-
ing of the poem. It is an exemplar of what she has called the
poetry of political anguish at its best, both didactic and lyrical. In
the pulling together of the poems in *To Stay Alive,* and particu-
larly in the completion of the fragmentary notebook poem in
"Staying Alive" Levertov has substantially enlarged her range as
a poet and helped revitalize political poetry in England. She has
learned how to weave together private experience and public
event so that both are available to the reader, to show us the
inner and outer lives in conflict and in reconciliation, to integrate
reportage and documentary into lyrical form and find a genuine
inscape. At the end of "Staying Alive" we have affirmation but
not final resolution. That is as it should be; we could trust no
other conclusion. The poem remains open-ended, like the life it
celebrates.

CARY NELSON

Levertov's Political Poetry

Denise Levertov's "Staying Alive" is equally problematic. The long poem sequence is decisively thwarted by the same historical imperative which brings it into existence. Levertov's whole career speaks to a mysticism whose verbal interest is continually risked by comparison to a real world more resistant to ecstatic ascent. All that justifies her personal expansiveness is the traditional American poetic myth—that our national madness is in essence the misdirected primal energy of the continent itself, and that the poet can symbolically redirect that force toward affirmation and growth. Until Vietnam, Levertov managed to handle her inheritance at a distance, overcoming discrete incidents of violence through integration into larger verbal rhythms, subjecting personal grief to purgation. She avoided encountering the larger myths of our history and kept her poetic territory elsewhere and self-enclosed. Her earlier poetry nurtures a vision exceedingly fragile, almost evanescent. The poems declare their own articulation to be a substantive human action, though the assertion is continually vulnerable. Yet with *To Stay Alive,* a perfectly commendable moral commitment to practical action *outside* poetry enters the poetry itself. Moreover, she demands that her visions prove equal to direct confrontation.

In several introductory poems reproduced from earlier volumes, she establishes, rather poignantly, the crisis that led her to a new and more provisional poetic form in "Staying Alive." The "Olga Poems" give witness to her entire career to that point; they are evidence that intimate, personal death can be made fruitful through verbal transformation. "A Note to Olga (1966)" hesitantly extends this claim to a social setting; at a political demonstration, her sister's death surprisingly proves a resource. The next four poems pit this vision of poetry "whose language imagines *mercy, lovingkindness*" against her experience of the war:

Reprinted from Cary Nelson, "Whitman in Vietnam: Poetry and History in Contemporary America," *Massachusetts Review* 16 (Winter 1975): 63–65.

the mucous membrane of our dreams
coated with it, the imagination
filmed over with the gray filth of it.

(13)

In our bodies, this knowledge "numb within us / caught in the chest" contends with a Whitmanesque faith that our "understanding manifests designs / fairer than the spider's most intricate web" (13).

Levertov's sense of the war's human cost for us is precise and telling, though her litany of its distant violence lies heavily on her tongue: "the scheduled breaking open of breasts whose milk / runs out over the entrails of still-alive babies" (14). Brutal and accurate as these lines may be, they are essentially clichés of violent war. We can hear in them a history of violence verbalized at a distance, perhaps even specific rhetoric like that of the English reaction to the German invasion of Belgium in the First World War. Moreover, our own physical security makes the language flat and unconvincing. We have no historical ground for sympathetic identification; such words will not come to us. Williams argues that our poetry must seek the Indian in our hearts, but he never truly finds that voice. To give voice to the land, to give voice to Vietnamese pain—these passionate quests are generated by internal needs, they are motivated by self-interest; at worst, they are ironically a kind of poetic colonialism, pathetic evidence that our history shapes and uses our poetry whatever our intentions. Levertov tries to remember "when peaceful clouds were reflected in the paddies" and of the Vietnamese says, "it was reported their singing resembled / the flight of moths in moonlight" (15). The first image is weak and vague; the second is almost patronizing, it suffers from the same untraversable difference she tries to indict with "it was reported." The irony is self-reflexive.

These poems are made of personal defeat. Levertov admits she cannot "see except dulled and unfocused / the delicate, firm, whole flesh of the still unburned" (16). She fears an insect has come to see through her eyes. The wellspring of her own humanism fails her; the lines opposing poetry and love to the war ring flat. We believe her despair and her revulsion, but her mystical language is hollowed out by the history which drives her to use vision as an opposing force. "Nothing we do," she confesses, "has the quickness, the sureness, / the deep intelligence living at peace would have" (14). The admission is admirable, but it dismantles the poetry, for she does not pursue her own depression far enough. If she were truly to drop "off a limb of / desperation"—not, as she writes, "plumb into peace for a day" (56), but into a poetry of numb self-extinction—she might then find a voice which could survive its times intact. Such a voice for Levertov would have an indestructible lightness that even Merwin (who never deceives himself about historical realities) cannot find.

The alternative she chooses in "Staying Alive" does not succeed. The poem's title is deliberately a more process-oriented version of the book's title, as if to warn us that no conclusive victory can follow. Yet such a victory is precisely the poem's goal; she would create a poetic world in which love is the greater power, but she cannot. The poem's openness to historical circumstances, its broad Whitmanesque inclusiveness, is essentially a challenge to do battle. She borrows the patchwork form suggested to her by Williams's *Paterson* including journals, letters, conversations, newspaper reports. Williams, however, managed with a delicate humor to lead us into believing that even the most thwarted political rhetoric could be maneuvered toward a communal poetic speech. Yet when Williams in 1924 wrote that we build "battleships *for peace*" he had a somewhat different historical situation to contend with; it had its own very bitter ironies, to be sure, once the idealism of the First World War was undone by the realities of trench warfare, but irony itself is no longer available as an uncompromised response. There is no workable irony, no nostalgia to be recovered, from the legacy of children disembowled and villages napalmed for peace. In the very complacency of its venality, the rhetoric of this war (whose language is the core of our self-knowledge) is an impossible adversary.

If conventional irony will not function effectively, neither will anger. The poetry always falls short of the rage we bring to it. Levertov herself knows that well enough. Indeed all her comments about the war's effect on language testify to her sense of the futility of the poetic enterprise. "I'm / alive to // tell the tale," she wrote in *Here and Now,* "but not honestly: // the words // change it." That recognition has to be confronted in these poems where the words are so much more necessary and yet so inadequate. As she suggests in *The Poet in the World* (16–19), poetry will not serve well simply to verbalize a prior conviction. Thus her anguish at Vietnamese suffering finds only conventions of violence as its outlet. The hidden subject of "Staying Alive" is this blocked and subverted expressiveness, the poet's despair that appropriate images of pain—so specific and telling as to be unforgettable—are unachievable. Anger in contemporary poetry is thus perhaps best rendered as an emotion no longer possible. The Vietnam poems most likely to survive are those that emphasize not moral outrage at the private suffering so easily visible in televised images but the very translucence and inaccessibility of those images.

Levertov herself moves toward that kind of treatment in *The Freeing of the Dust*, which includes her first fully successful Vietnam poems. "The Pilots," based on direct experiences in North Vietnam of the sort very few established American poets have had, records her touching reticence in questioning captured American pilots. Since her hostility cannot survive their actual presence, she is reticent about asking them if they knew "precisely / what they were doing, and did it anyway, and would do it again," if "they understood what these bombs / are designed to do / to human flesh." In no way does this reticence lessen the horror at what the bombs do, yet it does complicate the poet's ability to act and speak; it complicates them with a poignancy exactly right for Levertov's poetry. If "these men understood these acts," she writes, "then I must learn to distrust / my own preference for trusting people." In "Modes of Being," another poem in the same volume (98–99), Levertov uses a form that emphasizes the disjunction between her own consciousness and the history taking place in Vietnam. Four sections dealing with her own reactions are separated from but interspersed with three italicized passages about the prisons in South Vietnam:

> *Near Saigon,*
> *in a tiger-cage, a woman*
> *tries to straighten her*
>   *cramped spine*
> *and cannot.*

The flat narration establishes Levertov's respect for suffering that is, finally, not her own. Free herself to take pleasure in nature, she can neither forget nor fully maintain the connection with the unspeakable mutilations of the tiger cages:

> Joy
> is real, torture
> is real, we strain to hold

a bridge between them open,
and fail,
or all but fail.

Levertov ends the poem with a passage that recalls the imagery of the conclusion to Wright's "A Mad Fight Song for William S. Carpenter, 1966." Here, however, the almost hieratic description of an impossible bird testifies to an apotheosis we desire that cannot be:

> What wings, what mighty arch
> of feathered hollow bones, beyond
> span of albatross or eagle,
> mind and heart must grow
>   to touch, trembling,
> with outermost pinion tips,
> not in alternation but both at once,
> in one
> violent eternal instant
> that which is and
> that which is . . .

The connective tissue to bind together the various forms of event-fulness into one body will not be fleshed out in the body of the poem. Its verbal reach falls, a victim, however indirectly, of the same history in which a man in a tiger-cage *tries to stretch out his hand / and cannot.* The poem gestures toward a language of radical fusion it cannot find, it is unable to name the wingspread with which it would take flight. Then the poem testifies to the rude irony language can intrude, for it can at least be said that Levertov's history and that of the Vietnamese prisoners are each "that which is and / that which is . . ."; they are linked by language that certifies only what experience cannot absorb. The poem trails off in ellipses, irresolute in the presence of its own metaphors. In their own rather different ways, both "Staying Alive" and "Modes of Being" testify to the end of a poetics of open optimism. "Modes of Being," I think, succeeds because it accepts and indeed uses the forces that undercut its ambitions.

PATRICIA HAMPL

A Witness of Our Time

In recent years, I have tended to read Denise Levertov for the news, thinking of her, more than any other American poet, as a reporter or witness at the political front. Actually, a *soul* at the front; she has not been simply a reporter, for the pain of her poetic witness has been that she has felt herself implicated in the worst this country and this age has dropped down upon itself and upon the unprotected of the world. She has been the enemy of the killers, of Nixon and the death machines, of the death-designers who say, "Now we can aim straight into someone's kitchen." But, in common with a whole generation of young people in the sixties, she has also felt a terrible alliance of guilt with this death culture. A constant worry that being alive at all, being well and safe, is a shameful act in the face of the torn limbs and napalmed, jellied flesh of our Asian neighbors:

> Are we infected,
> viciously, being smart enough
> to write down these matters,
>   scribes of the unspeakable?

Levertov's poetic documentation of the protests against the war in Southeast Asia has been more impassioned, overwhelming, and continued than anyone else's. It seems to have overwhelmed her too. In *The Freeing of the Dust,* her eleventh and most recent collection, she seems amazed at how history has defined her:

> Burned faces, stretched horribly . . .
> No day for years I have not thought of them.

It is a history that has caused her to write many blunt, painfully blank, and desperate lines, poems without grace, full of confusion and sometimes misplaced anger—just to get it all on paper,

Reprinted from *Moons & Lion Tailes,* 2, no 1 (1976): 47–53.

just to be sure the awful facts were not lost. Her last three books (*To Stay Alive, Footprints,* and the current collection) have read like jounals of a terrible time, diaries written quickly and urgently with no looking back, no desire to "create."

The Freeing of the Dust is the strongest of the three. It is a brave book. Like the previous two volumes, it has the authenticity of a life lived passionately, a life in which things matter, a life deeply bonded to the world and the times we live in. But it also has the clear, fearless love of beauty, of the earth's gorgeousness that belongs to a survivor, to one who has seen terrible and dark things and cleaves to the joy of light with something more than pleasure.

One section of the book is devoted to poems about Levertov's trip to Hanoi in 1972. This section has the poems of devastation we have come to expect from her—or from anyone who writes about Vietnam ("Too Much to Hope," "Weeping Woman"). Also the poems of blank disgust and frustration and self-doubt ("May Our Right Hands Lose Their Cunning," "The Pilots"). But there is as well, as if given from the land itself, certainly not from the mind, something healing. In Vietnam, that devastated land, beauty and the effortless energy of the earth and of people at home on the earth come to her. "In Thai Binh (Peace) Province," a poem dedicated to Muriel Rukeyser and Jane Hart (her Hanoi traveling companions), she says:

> I've used up all my film on bombed hospitals,
> bombed village schools . . .
> So I'll use my dry burning eyes
> to photograph within me
> dark sails of the river boats,
> warm slant of afternoon light
> apricot on the brown, swift, wide river,
> village towers—church and pagoda—on the far shore,
> and a boy and small bird both
> perched, relaxed, on a quietly grazing
> buffalo.

"It is that life, unhurried, sure, persistent," she says, "I must bring home when I try to bring the war home. // Child, river, light." In Vietnam, of all places (but then—it makes sense), she finds the life of peace.

Just as the horror of the war, when she wrote about it in America, filled every part of life with a scarred and terrible face, now the actual life in Vietnam, the miraculous beauty and survival of its people, softens her, humbles her, and gives her back her sight again. Some taint of guilt or uncertainty about her *right* to her own store of joy seems to have been washed clean in this book—a book which definitely has not left Vietnam behind, though.

In *The Freeing of the Dust* a great sigh is released. Nothing is forgiven, nothing of the horror is forgotten, no despair canceled: the death machines and the killers are still there, and Levertov still names them. She admits to having murder fantasies about Nixon and Kissinger: "It is / to this extremity // the infection of their evil // thrusts us." She is still furious at the "genial poets, pink-faced earnest wits" who won't bother themselves with taking sides (in "Goodby to Tolerance").

But now she allows herself to be the singer and safekeeper of the shouts of joy and possibility as well. The book opens with a kind of overture: several poems from planes or buses, poems written in suspension. The first, "From a Plane," suggests the surprised attention she gives throughout the book to the growing world, the world in spite of itself:

> Always air
> looked down through, gives
> a reclamation of order, re-
> visioning solace: the great body
> not torn apart, though raked and raked
> by our claws—

Nothing is certain:

> the planet
> under the clouds—
> does it want us? Shall we be welcome,
> we of air, of metallic
> bitter rainbows,
> of aching wings?

But the very question, this deep loneliness for the planet, for health, for the beauty of things, gives energy and attentiveness to the other task of the poet: to see and to sing. So much is seen clearly in these poems, small moments deftly noted, the colors and shapes of things coming off the page sure and absolutely vivid, objects with voices:

> Glance up
> from the kitchen window;
> that tree word,
> still being said,
> over the stone wall.

Or:

> Colors

> come slowly
> up from behind the hilltop,
> looking for forms to fill for the day,
> dwellings.

Or a poem so full of red and white it seems photographed:

> Each day
> the cardinals call and call in the rain,
> each cadence scarlet
> among leafless buckeye,

> and passionately
> the redbuds, that can't wait
> like other blossoms. . . .

> Lumps of snow
> are melting in tulip-cups.

Section six is its own small book, the history of the end of Levertov's marriage of over twenty years and the beginning of a new life alone. It is strong, clear, not self-righteous, comradely even. This section brings to mind a difference between Levertov and other women poets of great strength like Adrienne Rich. Levertov is not a feminist poet in the way Rich is—ardently, polemically, at the center of her identity. Feminist poets, as a side effect of necessarily denouncing the patriarchy and its oppression, shifted the pain and guilt of Vietnam off their own backs to a certain extent and put it more decisively on men and male-made culture.

Rich, Robin Morgan, and Marge Piercy, to name several feminist poets, have written against the war, of course. But once feminism had entered their lives and changed their view of the world, the seering guilt about Vietnam was laid at the men's doorstep. It was their baby, their shame. White middle-class poets (women) "suddenly" had something to say about being oppressed themselves, and they spoke from this emergent stance as victims.

Levertov, while certainly not antifeminist (she includes machismo as one evil among others in "The Pilots"), did not share this experience, apparently, of new birth through feminism. The war was, and remains, the central fact for her. While many women poets found themselves in the position of accuser (and victim), Levertov maintained her identity as an outraged, frustrated voice, but as a citizen of the oppressive nation, rather than as a victim of it. This meant that she did not, could not, separate herself psychically from that paralyzing guilt that the war brought with it, at least to anyone who let the war's message sink in.

So her "survival" and the beauty and strength of so many of her poems feel like a representative survival of song itself and the survival of the eye and its innocence. In a wonderful long poem, "Conversation in Moscow," she talks about this: a Russian poet, charmed by her "idealism" but sad with the history of his guilty country, is amazed by her "youth and purity." She, in turn, is astonished to think she can represent youth or purity to anyone after the years of struggle and disillusionment. It is a moving poem, the despairing, vanquished poets of the two great killer cultures meeting over black tea (with, ironically, an interpretor between them). She realizes that even within her, even within Russia and America, the purity is there, side by side with the despair.

In "The Way It Is," too, she admits, in spite of the shattering of the past life by divorce and her country by war:

> Yet almost no day, too, with no
> happiness, no
> exaltation of larks uprising from the heart's
> peat-bog darkness.

"Joy is real," she says, "torture is real." As the Russian poet says shyly, in the Moscow poem: " 'The Poet / never must lose despair.' " Levertov says that they all understand this to mean:

> we mustn't, any of us, lose touch with the source,
> pretend it's not there, cover over
> the mineshaft of passion

                    despair somberly tolls its bell
                         from the depths of,

        and wildest joy
        sings out of too,
                    flashing
                         the scales of its laughing,
                              improbable music,

        grief and delight entwined in the dark down there.

The final line in the book is "I am tired of the 'fine art of
unhappiness,' " a line that releases the deeply held sigh at last,
the sigh of one who has looked long and steadily at our common
life, at what we have been capable of doing, and at its awful
consequences.

Denise Levertov is a poet who has been humbled by the desti-
tution she has felt in the face of desperate, powerful enemies,
even by the planet itself: "How gray and hard the brown feet of
the wretched of the earth / . . . How lively their conversation to-
gether / How much of death they know." It is this experience
that gives her book its greatest song.

DANIEL BERRIGAN, S.J.

Denise Levertov's Prose

The hallmark of Denise Levertov's prose is something so simple and elusive as clear-eyed common sense. In the nature of things, so esoteric a virtue has not been grandly rewarded. Common sense? Mainline writers, along with their multicorporate pushers, have stampeded toward the rainbow named Avarice; others have shown a sorrowful, even despairing obsession with the Confession That Bares All.

Levertov is aware of the implications here, destructive as they are of political understanding and writers' craft. And of life itself, as in writers who have constructed a game called despair; and played it, bullet to head.

She takes up such matters, despair, anomie, political indifference, matters which most writers today prefer to keep decently out of sight and mind. She analyzes despair and its practitioners, and those who justify it as a resource. And by a parallel right instinct, she avoids the rapacious rush to trivialize life, to bring it in line with a desperate and trivial culture.

She is that rara avis, a poet, a political writer, very much a woman. These are the poles of her art as of her existence. She stays close to essentials, and the resolve, in the best sense, has paid off. Her writing remains wonderfully contemporary, it walks with us, illumines the journey of conscience that began in civil rights days and continues on into the eighties and the antinuclear struggle.

She charts the essentials; how we grew, what mistakes we made, how we failed one another, what gains and losses percolated, boiled over. And perhaps, most important, how we've grown, and into what. (*We* being the phalanx of ages, backgrounds, hopes, tactics, that started marching in the fifties and continues till now.)

There is a measure of courage required to march and be arrested. And there is another sort of courage, intelligence, and

Reprinted from Daniel Berrigan, S.J., *Poetry, Drama, Prose* (Maryknoll, N.Y.: Orbis Books, 1988), 337–39. A review of *Light Up the Cave* (1981).

discipline implied in setting down a record of the march, the arrests, the meaning of it all. Their tone, excitement, verve! In the lives of most who take part, there is no comparable taste of the lost American art known as community.

Her essays thus hearten young and old alike; they are a diary of our neglected soul. Norman Mailer did something like this in the sixties; but since those heady days and nights, he, like most such marchers and writers, has turned to other matters. (I remember half seriously writing Mailer in 1980, announcing that we of the Plowshares Eight were prepared to name him the chronicler of our crime and punishment. He responded by sending a [small] check to the defense committee. Otherwise, no taker.)

Levertov is still marching, still recording the march. There are dazzling skills here; they start in the feet, rhythmically implanted in mother earth, and make their way, mysterious, tingling, into hands, fingers, pen. It begins with courage, a continuity of courage, a cold stream in the temperate larger stream of soul. Robert Frost's contrary stream, headlong in one direction when the rivers of a given time, and the voice of those rivers, would have us believe that "all is well."

"All is well" was the siren voice of the seventies. That the word was a lie, a blockage of soul, a numbing that threatened to turn us shortly dead—this seemed to penetrate almost no one. Many writers were ensconced on campuses where moral insolvency and bonhomie went hand in hand. A very few made it big, with what came to be known as "blockbusters." (The term, one recalls, referred to the largest of the prenuclear bombs of World War II.) Others joined the urban working class, one met them driving cabs or doing short order cooking or cleaning or acting as security guards. A few came and went in academe, an adjunct job here and there, hewers of wood and drawers of water so to speak, untenured and unrehabilitated. They published where they could in little magazines and presses, counted themselves lucky to publish at all.

But at the same time, writers like Levertov kept to the themes, kept to the marches, kept being arrested. The big sleep was on, but some were awake through the seductive night. The questions kept them awake. Were humans, any humans, going to make it through the century? Would there be a next generation? Were we intent, as a people, on bringing down the world, and if so, by what authority, in whose name? Who was the enemy anyway? Why was all the mad intemperate talk (winnable nuclear war, limited nuclear war) coming from one side, ours; and all the talk of mitigation, dread, disarmament, coming from the "enemy"?

The questions, until recently, kept being ignored. So did the questioners, including the questioning writers like Levertov. I presume that this is her history, as it is of a few others. She tells of that comatose decade, the seventies, almost as though it hadn't existed. She marches, keeps something alive, is personally dispassionate. There was work to be done, that was all. It little mattered that the work was despised or ignored or neglected. It was simply there, as evil was, as the world was; as hope was. She is passionate only about the issues, life or death. In this she, so to speak, turns the cultural method on its head. That is to say, American writing in the seventies, both prose and poetry, was disproportionately passionate about the self, and correspondingly numb (passion not being in large supply) toward the public weal and woe. Thus was a natural balance thrown out of kilter.

In insisting on this balance, and thus restoring it, Levertov reminds me of Paul Goodman; in political sanity, in large scope and interest, in intellectual clarity—and especially in moral unabashedness. I think of her, as I recall him, unashamed to be old-fashioned and patriotic, calling the country to accounts, being (horrors!) "judgmental" toward morons and rogues in high places, linking her work to spirits like Thoreau, Emerson, Hawthorne, Melville, Mother Jones, John Brown, the Quaker chroniclers—and, in our lifetime, to the incomparable Martin Luther King and Dorothy Day. Moralists, poets, activists, pacifists, abolitionists, prolabor, propoor, prohuman, these formed her history, as ours, if we can but rise to it; living it, rising to it, testing its native decency against the manifest social indecency of war, piratical economics, hatred of the poor, racism, nouveau riche clowning, the mad mutual rhythms of waste and want.

I have not so much as mentioned the richness and scope of her literary criticism. *Multum in parvo;* the entire book is beyond praise. I think of how, in a sane time, such a book and those which preceded it, including poetry, short stories, literary essays, social criticism, would form a university course entitled something like: A Renaissance Woman of the Late Twentieth Century. But this is dreaming; it would mean crossing jealous frontiers, violating "expertise."

Meantime, for those who come on this book, there is much to ponder, much to learn. Since these essays were published, several of her themes have grown, imperceptibly and ominously, like stalactites aimed at the heart of things. The despair for in-stance, which she analyzes so acutely, a point of departure for a debased theory of "art at the extremes"—despair has spread, become the national mood, from sea to shining sea. Its articula-tions, symbols, justifications are all about, infect everything; grab and run economics, chic selfishness, parasitic evangelism. Not merely a few poets are cultivating it, but the public at large, its institutions, those who read, those who manage, the image makers. Fear at the heart; a heart of darkness, frivolity at the surface.

All this being our predicament, political responsibility, resis-tance, together with the recounting and pondering and exempli-fying—these can no longer be viewed as a choice in a range of choices. Our options, as they say, are no longer large. The eye narrows (the choices narrow), when we look (when we refuse to look) into the medusa mirror—the Mark 12A for example, a first-strike nuclear warhead, destroyed by eight of us in Septem-ber 1980. Or when in nightmare, there slides toward us head-on the monstrous piranha, a nuclear submarine named Trident. Its prey we know. Knowing, we may choose to do nothing; which is to say, to go discreetly or wildly mad, letting fear possess us and frivolity rule our days.

Or we may, along with admirable spirits like Denise Lever-tov, be driven sane; by community, by conscience, by treading the human crucible.

LORRIE SMITH

Songs of Experience
Denise Levertov's Political Poetry

Denise Levertov's large body of political poetry records the vicissitudes of a deeply ethical imagination grappling with the difficult public issues of the last twenty years. At forty-four, Levertov had published six volumes before her first Vietnam protest poems appeared in *The Sorrow Dance* (1967). The seven volumes since *The Sorrow Dance* all contain poems in response to contemporary political issues; in prose and at readings she is an outspoken activist.[1] Though she continues to write many nonpolitical poems and to gather politically topical poems in separate sections within volumes, Levertov's work since the late sixties is infused with the reciprocal beliefs that "only revolution can now save that earthly life, that miracle of being, which poetry conserves and celebrates"[2] and that by its very nature, poetry itself is "intrinsically revolutionary."[3]

The effort to fuse poetry and revolution is more vexed, however, than Levertov suggests in her numerous *ars poetica*. Her evolution as an engaged writer demonstrates the dilemmas facing those poets of her generation who changed in middle age and in midcareer to accommodate a growing political consciousness but whose radicalism is embodied, for the most part, in traditional forms and idioms. Levertov's grounding in what Charles Altieri calls an "immanentist" poetics[4] is initially shaken by the demands of radical activism, and she is faced with the need to speak didactically without sacrificing her earlier lyricism. This dilemma is primarily psychic for Levertov; except for some experimentation with long sequences, her forms and techniques remain essentially unchanged throughout her career. Levertov's maturation as a political poet shows in increasingly complex and refined renderings of the political implications of personal life, poetic practice, and, in her latest volumes, religious belief.

Reprinted from *Contemporary Literature* 27, no. 2 (Summer 1986): 213–32. Copyright © 1986 by the Board of Regents of the University of Wisconsin System.

Throughout her career, Levertov sustains a devotion to the formalist creed that "poetry is a way of constructing autonomous existences out of words and silences."[5] Her late-romantic poetics amalgamates Keats's Imagination and Negative Capability, Emerson's organic form, and Williams's mediation between "the spirit of here-and-now" and a "supernatural" realm of values. Her early poetry easily bridges the distance between the "inner" self and the "outer" world by uncovering the numinous in quotidian moments, and she negotiates these two poles with an inductive and organic movement: examining an object, event, or feeling to arrive at a larger revelation. She is, like Williams, a poet of the found object and fortuitous epiphany. "The World Outside" contains characteristic images of illumination and a near-mystical transformation of everyday materials. Through leaps of language, a shadow on "the kitchen wall" yields a "pilgrimage," pigeons "spiral" upwards in "celebration," "tenement windows" reflect a lustrous "blaze," and sunset over Hoboken flashes in a Wordsworthian "westering" glow:

On the kitchen wall a flash
of shadow:
            swift pilgrimage
of pigeons, a spiral
celebration of air, of sky-deserts.
And on tenement windows
a blaze
            of lustered watermelon:
stain of the sun
westering somewhere back of Hoboken.

(*JL*, 4)

Levertov's subjectivity is at home in the sensory world and easily interacts with it through the mediation of the creative, synthesizing imagination. Her prepolitical poems embrace a benign universe whose inherent order is available to the sufficiently perceptive and articulate poet. Though she inscribes the typical romantic obstacles to revelation in many poems—the flow of time, the otherness of nature and people, the clamor of everyday events, the inertia of what she calls, in a favorite quotation from Rilke, "unlived life, of which one can die"—she almost always overcomes them with a tone of celebration, often ending poems with an ecstatic exclamation at the luminous natural world. Neither the autonomy of "the world outside" nor the integrity of the artist's vision is compromised; each is enhanced and made available to the reader through the equally autonomous form of the achieved poem.[6]

Several critics, however, have noted an imbalance that Levertov will explore deeply before redressing it in her political poems. In an early review, Robert Pack qualifies his generally favorable assessment:

> She too often seems predisposed to see things as beautiful or holy. At such times she forces her mysticism. . . . Mystic vision without sufficient doubt or terror, without a firm grasp of unequivocal evil, easily becomes sentimental. To me, Levertov's world is not yet complete, for as yet I find in it no unredeemed pain, no aspect of reality that is unsupportable.[7]

Yet the potential for a more complete worldview is, in fact, inherent in her early poetry. As early as *The Jacob's Ladder* (1958), Levertov begins to expand her circumference to include specific social and political topics. "During the Eichmann Trial" establishes empathy as a basis for political commitment. Her effort to come to grips with evil, an impenetrable "other," leads to the realization that Eichmann is not a stereotyped monster but a "pitiful man whom none // pity, whom all / must pity if they look // into their own face" (*JL*, 61). In such lines, Levertov attempts to maintain dialogue with an almost incomprehensible "other" and to bind humanity within her poet's vision and language. But she does not allow pity to become forgiveness or pathos, and the poem ends with a depiction of Holocaust horrors and a realization that all are implicated and responsible, "each a mirror / for man's eyes" (*JL*, 67). By assuming personal guilt in a context of universal complicity, she is able to assimilate evil into a coherent moral vision without denying its ultimate "otherness." Evil is merely conceived, however, as an absence of compassion and a failure of imagination; its full counterweight is not yet measured.[8] Only with increasing experience and awareness will Levertov's scope expand to embrace doubt and terror as well as praise and wonder. Her confrontation of "unequivocal evil" in the world is contemporaneous with political awakening and activism during the Vietnam War, and her inclusion of explicit political issues in her poetry gives concrete shape to her earlier vague sense of social malaise.

Levertov's evolution as an engaged "poet in the world" naturally follows from her growing involvement in leftist politics. Though she was active in Ban the Bomb demonstrations during the fifties, her poems from this period rarely reflect political beliefs. But the Vietnam War and the social turmoil of the sixties compelled Levertov and many of her contemporaries to align themselves with younger radicals, question their aesthetic assumptions, and address political issues directly in poems and public readings. The trauma of the war violently disrupts Levertov's unifying vision and psychic integrity: "Reduced to an eye / I forget what / I / was" (*RA, 9*). Her focus on the numinous surfaces of the "Here and Now" (the title of her first American volume, 1957) proves inadequate for confronting a larger scope of political events, and with *The Sorrow Dance* she begins to question the value of a visionary poetics disengaged from political commitment. The war is an "other" she cannot assimilate because of its real but incomprehensible horror, its unreal sensationalism as portrayed by the media, and its actual distance in a foreign country. The private sanctity of the present moment becomes entangled with the more diffuse public reality of the Vietnam War. Images of blurred vision and distorted language are frequent in this period of traumatic disruption: she sees too well or not at all, is driven to both protest and silence. For a poet of Levertov's sensibility, such disjunctions are extremely distressing, for they threaten the whole foundation of her poetic enterprise.

While political activism provides a structure and an outlet for Levertov's deeply felt moral outrage, it also engenders new dilemmas: an awareness of history as it impinges on the present moment, of reality beyond her direct apprehension, and of unassimilable dualities at odds with her innate impulse to synthesize experience through poetic vision. The interpenetration of inner and outer that sustains psychic equilibrium in Levertov's first six books becomes polarized, after the war, in an almost Manichaean opposition of good (life as she has known it, human potential as she can envision it, poetic power as she has enacted it) and evil (the knowledge, simultaneously, of war, suffering, hypocrisy, oppression, and ultimate global obliteration). Thus Levertov's growth as a political poet involves the intensely personal working out of the very traditional confrontation of evil in the world, for her political awakening is equivalent to a fall into the world of experience outside her direct line of vision and beyond her control as a poet. The tension of trying to maintain integrity—to balance her fundamentally mystical imagination with a larger sphere of events and issues—is betrayed in recurrent patterns of unresolved polarity and paradox.

Initially outraged at the war and then despairing, Levertov gradually accommodates the disjunction between political anguish and poetic affirmation. Her poetry after *The Sorrow Dance* attempts to achieve equilibrium and earn transcendence in a world that thwarts this effort. Increasingly, her poetry is conceived as an active "counter-rhythm" to chaos and horror. Not until she learns to live with paradox, relinquishing the desire to reconcile good and evil, can Levertov move beyond defeat toward new, though diminished, forms of affirmation. Her deep yearning for synthesis gradually moderates into a sort of detente which eases the polarized tension between personal life and public contingency, lyric revelation and didactic statement. As she has recently written:

> What those of us whose lives are permeated by a sense of unremitting political emergency, and who are at the same time writers of poetry, most desire in our work, I think, is to attain to such osmosis of the personal and the public, of assertion and of song, that no one would be able to divide our poems into categories. The didactic would be lyrical, the lyrical would be didactic. That is, at any rate, my own probably unattainable goal.[9]

Though "inner" and "outer" are often painfully separate in Levertov's fallen world, they are also paradoxically united because one person suffers and records the dissonance. Her most successful political poems neither collapse the distinctions between these terms nor flatly oppose them, but sustain an equilibrium in which the integrity of each is preserved and enlarged by the other.

Levertov's first antiwar poems appear at the end of *The Sorrow Dance* in a section entitled "Life at War." The poem "Life at War" characteristically describes the knowledge of evil in bodily terms: the war feels to her like "lumps of raw dough // weighing down a child's stomach on baking day" (*SD*, 79). Likewise, these final poems weight the whole volume with their dark significance. Experience of good and knowledge of evil are split, irreconcilable, indigestible. A pattern of polarity emerges as the emblem of her recurring dilemma:

the knowledge that humankind,

delicate Man, whose flesh
responds to a caress, whose eyes
are flowers that perceive the stars,

whose music excels the music of birds,
whose laughter matches the laughter of dogs,
whose understanding manifests designs
fairer than the spider's most intricate web,

still turns without surprise, with mere regret
to the scheduled breaking open of breasts whose milk
runs out over the entrails of still-alive babies,
transformation of witnessing eyes to pulp-fragments,
implosion of skinned penises into carcass-gulleys.
. . . .
Yes, this is the knowledge that jostles for space
in our bodies along with all we
go on knowing of joy, of love.

(*SD*, 79–80)

Unable to find an appropriate balance between lyric and didactic in these first angry protest poems, Levertov sometimes borders on polemical cliché and sentimentality. But her technique of presenting precise, descriptive details is one she will use continually to "bring the war home" to her readers. Her ironic counterpointing of lyrical metaphors with military diction and graphic depiction gives force to her political critique, and the jarring disjunctions of language mirror Levertov's own disjointed consciousness. The extremity of images in "Life at War," necessary to shock both the reader and herself into full and visceral awareness, is tempered at the end with a more solemn resignation: "nothing we do has the quickness, the sureness, / the deep intelligence living at peace would have." Though she can desire peace, she makes no motion here to heal the split that her fall has caused. Doubt and anger supplant wonder and celebration, and it will take several volumes before Levertov can begin to regain her equilibrium.

Levertov republishes these first protest poems as a preface to her longer, more experimental poems in *Relearning the Alphabet,* which one critic accurately calls a "spiritual autobiography."[10]

After the crisis and despair of "Life at War," she needs to rethink her position and reform herself as a poet to make room for all the conflicting "knowledge that jostles for space." These needs provoke a quest for a poetics more adequate to the complexity of her newly politicized consciousness—specifically, new forms and language that will not abstract or aestheticize experience and that will encompass doubt and terror as well as beauty and holiness. Levertov continues to try to absorb the knowledge of war, but her efforts usually end in paralysis and defeat. In the emblematically titled "The Gulf," her imagination of an "other"—a black boy during the Detroit riots—only becomes "useless knowledge in my mind's eye" (*RA*, 16); the "gulf" between them, and between imagination and reality, remains unbridged. In "Biafra," she tries "to make room for more knowledge / in my bone-marrow" but can only trail off with an impotent "no hope: Don't know / what to do: Do nothing:" (*RA*, 18). Though she can still portray herself in another poem from this volume as "a woman foolish with desire" ("July, 1968," *RA*, 64), the optimistic hope that life goes on in this "dark time" is constantly threatened with despair. This painful state of limbo—and its concomitant state of inarticulateness for the poet—is evoked more fully in "A Cloak":

> And I walked naked
> from the beginning
>
> breathing in
> my life,
> breathing out
> poems,
>
> arrogant in innocence.
>
> But of the song-clouds my breath made
> in cold air
>
> a cloak has grown,
> white and,
>   where here a word
>   there another
> froze, glittering,
> stone-heavy.

> A mask I had not meant
> to wear, as if of frost,
> covers my face.
>> Eyes looking out,
> a longing silent at song's core.

>> *(RA, 44)*

This poem explicitly conceives of her transformation as a fall from "arrogant" innocence into a world of powerless speech and action. Levertov mourns the loss of poetic power that had once been as natural as "breathing in . . . breathing out."

The title poem of this volume, however, regathers energy to counter inertia, discovers new language to replace silent longing. The poem posits an experimental solution to the stasis and despair that attended Levertov's awakening consciousness of evil. She free-associates on the letters of the alphabet in order to re-awaken and transform poetic power. The conventional and (for a poet) comforting structure of the alphabet allows both freedom and progression ("All utterance / takes me step by hesitant step towards //—yes, to continuance" [*RA*, 118]). The poem's meditative process recalls her Hasidic-Anglican father's interest in Kabbalah and numerology and Williams's arbitrary but structured process in *Kora in Hell* of writing daily for a year.[11] Following the confusion and questioning of the fragmented work-in-progress, "From a Notebook," "Relearning the Alphabet" feels satisfying and heartening. Though the poem does not address specific political issues, its position as the finale of the volume automatically forces it to encompass and temporarily resolve the crises of consciousness and action in preceding poems.

The dominant tone of "Relearning the Alphabet" is optimistic, even playful, recapturing a child's pleasure in singing the ABC's and in mastering language. The poem begins with "Joy" and ends with "praise"—key words in Levertov's earlier poetry; images of transcendental light recur throughout the poem. The poem is radical in its quest for linguistic roots; the alphabet itself generates verbs that propel the poem's action: the letter *B* is for "being"; *C*, of course, for "seeing," *D* leads to a new genesis for "Denise": "In the beginning was delight" (another pun, as well as the obvious Biblical echo). The fervent desire to recover the mode of celebration that supported her innocent poetic vision is not entirely nostalgic or unqualified, however. The poem records a quasi-mystical quest both forward and back "home to the present." Halting lines and parenthetical asides trace her mythical descent:

> I go stumbling
> > (head turned)
> > > back to my origins:
> (if that's where I'm going)
> > to joy, my Jerusalem.
> Weeping, gesturing,
> I'm a small figure in mind's eye,
> diminishing in the sweep of rain or gray tears
> that cloud the far shore as jealous rage
> clouds love and changes it, changes vision.

(RA, 112–13)

The journey towards "caritas, claritas" is always threatened by a paralyzing return to "limbo" and by the distorting gaps between language and reality. The speaker herself falters, but the procession of the alphabet structures her journey and restores her to active "utterance," "continuance," and "vision." She returns from the underworld to the world she has known all along, now dismantled and reconstructed, the alphabet relearned. The poem ends with a familiar "ah! of praise," but this affirmation has now been matured and tested through a descent to an underworld of split psyche, nightmare, and thwarted language—an underworld whose more social and political realities surface in "From a Notebook."

The mystical wonder and celebration recovered in "Relearning the Alphabet" prove to be provisional and perhaps insufficient responses to political reality, for they are replaced with a renewed sense of darkness and paradox in *To Stay Alive,* published a year later (1971)—her only volume devoted entirely to political poetry. She republishes poems already in print and interpolates "From a Notebook" and "Interim" into a longer, more coherent sequence, "Staying Alive." Levertov struggles in this volume with the daily complexities of radical political action, death—both close to home and global—and language that is increasingly recalcitrant to her needs. She does, however, manage to break the paralyzing stasis of earlier poems, and *To Stay Alive* marks a turning point in Levertov's movement toward an "osmosis of the personal and the public, of assertion and of song."[12]

In addition to finding a way to reconcile her various polarities of consciousness, Levertov must discover a form that will include history and envision the future as well as "dig down / to re-examine" ("Staying Alive," "Part II," *TSA*, 40) the present. The long sequence form of "Staying Alive" allows a meditative breadth and temporal inclusiveness not possible in her shorter lyrics. Like its main precursor, *Paterson,* the sequence mixes lyric passages with prose, conversations, letters, public documents, and diary entries in a kinetic montage of Levertov's "inner/outer experience" during the sixties. Recurring themes and words reverberate like Poundian subject rhymes to give the poem structure and coherence. The formal alternations of prose and poetry allow a large rhythm of expansion and contraction, mirroring the manic-depressive, painful split which is both personal and national. Like *Leaves of Grass, Paterson,* and the *Cantos,* Levertov's is "a poem including history" as well as a poem included and inscribed in history: Levertov's personal case history is inseparable from and representative of the public events in which she is immersed.

The opening "Interim," which tells of a trip to the sea while awaiting her husband Mitchell Goodman's trial for war resistance, is now retitled "Prologue: An Interim." Past experience gains new significance in retrospect and in the new context of her ongoing political struggle. The "Prologue" also invokes Levertov's personal muse on behalf of the fallen culture and sets forth a major theme of the poem:

> O language, mother of thought,
> are you rejecting us as we reject you?
>
> Language, coral island
> accrued from human comprehensions,
> human dreams,
>
> you are eroded as war erodes us.
>
> (*TSA,* 22)

A primary mission in this poem is to rebuild a strong and healthy language to counter the polemical jargon and officialese assaulting the poet from both Left and Right. But this undertaking, fundamentally moral and political, must first be personal for Levertov. To all her other polarizations she now must add the most basic gap between words and action. She clings to the locus discovered in "Relearning the Alphabet": "Without a terrain in which, to which, I belong, / language itself is my one home, my Jerusalem"; yet throughout the poem she gropes for adequate expression: "I choose / revolution but my words / often already don't reach forward / into it— / (perhaps)" (*TSA,* 34); "*revolution,*" itself, she laments, is "the wrong word. . . . But it's the only / word we have . . ." (*TSA,* 41; second ellipsis in original). Such skeptical explorations reach toward dialogue to replace what Thomas Merton, in an essay written during the same period, calls "definitive utterance, to which there can be no rejoinder."[13] Levertov strains to maintain dialogue with her own conflicting extremes as well as to promote dialogue as a means toward progressive political change.

"Part I" opens with the refrain that pulses through the poem and structures its progression: "Revolution or death." For Levertov, this choice is highly personal, not just rhetorical, and though she must in good conscience answer "Revolution, of course," the long questioning poem explores the implications and complexities of this choice, deconstructing what first seems to be another absolute dichotomy. (There could, she realizes, be revolution *and* death—a possibility she must come to terms with.) Every choice reveals its alternative; all is provisional, qualified, irreconcilable: "And yet, yes, there's the death." The revolution she chooses "is the first that laughter and pleasure aren't shot down in," but it is also peopled by self-immolating and self-starving martyrs and violent demonstrators.

Her meditations on death first seduce Levertov back to Whitman, Swinburne, and Keats, where dissolution and forgetfulness offer tempting relief and intimations of mystical transcendence to the agonized poet: "Death lovely, / whispering, / *a drowsy numbness . . . / 'tis not / from envy of thy happy lot . . . / . . . river / winds somewhere to the sea*" (*TSA,* 30; second ellipsis added). In later sections, she elegiacally explores the suicides of two friends—one "trivial," one tragic. Only by contemplating the feel of death can Levertov begin to come to grips with its global significance. Like "revolution," it must be stripped of abstractness before it can be restored as a vital and meaningful term.

The opening of "Part II" plunges into the complexities of the present moment: "Can't go further. / If there's to be a / second part, it's not / a going beyond, I'm / still here. // To dig down, / to re-examine" (*TSA,* 40). Echoing the opening of Book II of *Paterson*—"Blocked. / (Make a song out of that: concretely)"— Levertov takes Williams's earlier American quest as a map for her own, in spirit as well as form. The climax of the poem—the "Diary" ended here in the previous volume—this section recounts her participation in the 1969 People's Park movement in Berkeley, an event that seems to have galvanized Levertov's radical consciousness. As "The War / come home to us" (*TSA*, 45) and her eyes are seared by tear gas, Levertov proclaims her radicalization and rebirth. Collective activism releases the static polarization brought on by her earlier traumas. Her choice of revolution is affirmative, harking back to her earlier celebratory mode and echoing the very early "Overland to the Islands," where "every step" is "an arrival":

> Revolution: a crown of tree
> > raises itself out of the heavy
> > flood . . .
>
> . . . .
> Maybe what seems
> evanescent is solid.
>
> Islands
> step out of the waves on rock feet.

(*TSA*, 47)

"I" becomes incorporated with "we" in Levertov's new identity in solidarity and action. The personal does not dissolve in the collective but gains force, definition, and liberation. Revolutionary transformation involves trial by fire and violence, but these are seen as temporary, cathartic stages of progressive political action, and Levertov welcomes them as active counterforces to numb immobility. If the recovery of joy and hope in this section is a bit facile in its Whitmanesque optimism ("O happiness / in the sun! Is it / that simple, then, / to live?" [*TSA*, 44]) the poem's continuing immersion in complicated events and emotions tells us that, in fact, it is not "that simple." Later she admits, "I keep / enduring such pangs of giving // birth or being / born" (*TSA*, 52) and "I forget anguish / as I forget joy" (*TSA*, 65).

With her newly won "tragic, fearful / knowledge of *present history*" (*TSA*, 66), Levertov transforms the choice between "revolution or death" to the conjunction of two life-giving forces: "revolution" and "poetry." Though this fusion does not relieve her pain or solve her dilemmas, it provides a new source of strength: "But when their rhythms / mesh / then though the pain of living / never lets up // the singing begins" (*TSA*, 74).

Levertov uses this affirmation to dig back into the "tunnel of daily life," now able to celebrate daily joys again, in solitude as well as solidarity. The movement back "home" reenacts the climax of "Relearning the Alphabet," which proves, in retrospect, merely to have been a preparation for this real transformation. Thus the core discovery of this long poem is a new politicized identity in the "Here and Now," which incorporates the past (history) and opens up the future (revolution). Levertov rediscovers happiness, love, heroes, song, and dance in a series of brief epiphanies, but her voice is urgent and these consolations are clearly provisional. Her lines step confidently forward until they are pulled back to the margin:

> only conjunctions
> > of song's
> > > raging magic
> > > with patient courage
> > > > will make   a new life:
> we can't wait: time is
> > > not on our side. . . .
>
> > > > > (*TSA*, 82)

She comes to understand that struggle—political as well as poetic—must be renewed daily. A new battle looms at the end— "news of invasion of Laos started to be 'official' "—and her poetic diary hangs in elliptical suspension: "O holy innocents! I have / no virtue but to praise / you who believe / life is possible . . ." (*TSA*, 84; ellipsis in original). Pragmatism and prayer mingle to form a provisional response to the complexities of good and evil. Her recovery of the luminous present moment, now irrevocably shadowed by the knowledge of evil, forms the foundation of Levertov's integration of personal and political, lyric and didactic in her later poems.

Images and themes of unreconciled duality reappear with renewed force in *The Freeing of the Dust* (1975), written after her trip to North Vietnam with fellow poet Muriel Rukeyser. The war now appears through the eyes of a witness, for Levertov regains the confidence that her refined vision can accurately convey what she observes: amputees, children in hospitals, nervous bomber pilots, the green landscape and business-as-usual ironically bestowing moments of "Peace within the / long war" (*FD*, 35). Rather than being paralyzed and benumbed, as before, Levertov has attained a more realistic vision which can include fluctuation and polarity without a nostalgic yearning for complete synthesis. *The Freeing of the Dust* balances divorce ("Divorcing") with reconciliation ("Libation"). It offers a model of dialogue in place of polarized monologue, recreating a contrapuntal conversation between a Russian poet and an American poet mediated by a translator, all of whom smile "in common knowledge" ("Conversation in Moscow"). As in Wallace Stevens's "Sunday Morning," where paradoxical pigeons fly "downward to darkness, on extended wings," Levertov's experienced vision embraces both "grief and delight entwined in the dark down there."

"Modes of Being" extends Levertov's familiar pattern of extreme opposites by exploring more fully the gaps between simultaneous good and evil (*FD*, 98–99). Four lyrical passages about private experience—"Indoors, reading, talking . . . What more / can love be than epiphany!"—alternate with three italicized passages of flat reportage describing men and women being tortured "*Near Saigon, / in a tiger-cage.*" These two "modes of being" are linked by the universal human gesture of stretching and reaching. The speaker and her companion "reach and enter / a new landscape of knowledge," "January's fist / unclenches," and "shadows yawn and / stretch to the east" at the same time an imprisoned man "*tries to stretch out his hand / and cannot*" and a woman "*tries to straighten her / cramped spine / and cannot.*" Rather than synthesizing these two simultaneous realities, the imagery and discrete formal divisions provide a chilling contrast between "that which is and / that which is." The poem moves beyond absolute polarization, however, as the speaker's imagination reaches toward both extremes:

> Joy
> is real, torture
> is real, we strain to hold
> a bridge between them open,
> and fail,
> or all but fail
>
> (*FD*, 99)

The emblematic gulf that dominates so many of her earlier political poems is now replaced by a more hopeful "bridge" constructed through imagination, moral vision, and language:

> What wings, what mighty arch
> of feathered hollow bones, beyond

span of albatross or eagle,
mind and heart must grow
to touch, trembling,
with outermost pinion tips,
not in alternation but both at once,
in one
violent eternal instant
that which is and
that which is . . .

(*FD*, 99)

Paradoxically, Levertov can both imagine this balance and admit its impossibility. Ending as an unanswered question, the poem stops short of transcendence and projects its conditional, almost sleight-of-hand reconciliation only through a supreme effort of language itself. The ending ellipses leave the reader, implicitly included in the speaker's "we," straining "to hold / a bridge . . . open."

Levertov remains haunted by her own question, however. "Unresolved" (*CB*, 103) is structured by the same paradox in "Modes of Being" and extends the attempt to make torture—here in El Salvador—real and comprehensible. Again, the poem juxtaposes grisly newsreel close-up with lyric responses to this other reality. Jostling the same knowledge of simultaneous good and evil, she finds a tone weary and resigned rather than painfully torn. The poem's image of a strangled bird descends from the "mighty arch" of wings imagined in "Modes of Being," frankly representing failure where before there was fragile desire:

We know so much of daily bread,
of every thread of lovingly knit compassion;

garments of love clothe us, we rest
our heads upon darkness; when we wake

sapphire transparency calls forth our song.
And this is the very world, the same, the world

of vicious power, of massacre.
Our song is a bird that wants
to sing as it flies, to be
the wings of praise, but doubt

binds tight its wire to hold down
flightbones, choke back breath.
We know no synthesis.

(CB, 104–5)

With this flat denial, Levertov reaches the limits of polarity, whose extremes she has explored obsessively and whose poetic possibilities she has exhausted. Her most recent political poems assume "no synthesis" and move beyond this impasse toward a more complex paradigm of dialogue—both spiritual and social— to bridge her knowledge of evil and her yearning for peace.

In her two most recent volumes, *Candles in Babylon* (1982) and *Oblique Prayers* (1984), Levertov extends the qualified optimism recovered in *The Freeing of the Dust* and relies more strongly than ever on the mysticism underlying all of her work. She has refined both her lyricism and her didacticism and integrates them in her current work with polished, pared-down language. She no longer leaps to the exclamatory epiphanies of her early lyrics or the blunt invective of some previous political poems; transcendence is now muted and provisional, political outrage now tempered by wisdom and experience. Above all, she tells us, poetic vision can no longer pretend to be neutral; yet the poet's gifts of heightened perception and expression offer hope in this "Age of Terror." Though moments of visionary affirmation are never purely innocent in Levertov's fallen world, her knowledge of evil is mitigated by a deep reverence for earthly life.

The set piece of *Candles in Babylon* is the sequence "Mass for the Day of St. Thomas Didymus"—a contrapuntal exploration of faith and doubt in the nuclear age. The solemn procession of liturgical sections works emotionally as an actual mass does to save the poem from ponderousness. Invocation, confession, praise, blessing, creed, song, and plea are modulated in a whole that, like "Relearning the Alphabet," is at once freely organic and highly structured. As in a mass, private emotions find release in communal ritual and, as in so many of Levertov's later political poems, the lyric voice is a collective "we" rather than a singular "I." Like Christian faith itself, Levertov's poetic mass assimilates a knowledge of evil and counters it with hope and praise, however qualified and diminished. The poem succumbs neither to transcendent ecstasy nor to absolute despair, but rests with an acceptance of fluctuating and irreconcilable extremes: "I believe and / interrupt my belief with / doubt. I doubt and / interrupt my doubt with belief" (*CB*, 110). Language is both divinely incarnate ("very word of / very word, / flesh and / vision" [*CB*, 111–12]) and threatened with extinction ("What of the emptiness, / the destructive vortex that whirls / no word with it?"). At the center of these circular dilemmas lies a "spark / of remote light" (*CB*, 115) salvaged from Levertov's original immanentist poetics. She prays not to an orthodox deity but to the spirit infusing "the ordinary glow / of common dust in ancient sunlight" (*CB*, 110). The mass inverts Christian hope at the end by placing tentative faith in mankind, who now has the almost overwhelming responsibility to shelter "a shivering God"—the Agnus Dei shorn of symbolism, "reduced" to a "defenseless . . . wisp of damp wool" (*CB*, 114).

In *Oblique Prayers,* the political concerns of the poems in the section "Prisoners" merge with the spiritual concerns in the final section, "Of God and of the Gods." The volume is infused with a renewed celebration of nature which, unlike mankind, knows "no clash / of opposites" ("The God of Flowers," *OP*, 77) and a rediscovery of immanence in fleeting moments and essential things of the world: "a sorrel grass, / a crust, / water, / salt" ("This Day," *OP*, 81). These celebrations, bridging Levertov's early and late poetry, are now more valuable for being less innocent, tinged by the knowledge that it is also "part of human-ness // to enter / no man's land" ("Oblique Prayers," *OP*, 82) and tempered by the dark forces compelling human history in a time when "we've approached / the last / the last choice" ("The Cry," *OP*, 44). Though she is able to envision transcendent unity in nature, Levertov continues to maintain dialogue with all-too-human oppositions in herself. In "Thinking about El Salvador," she finds silence the only logical and humane response to brutality; yet she overcomes the temptation to be mute in the desperately titled "Perhaps No Poem But All I Can Say And I Cannot Be Silent" and later in "The Antiphon," where "once more / all is eloquent" (*OP*, 84). In "Vocation," she praises "martyrs dying / passionately," through whom "we keep our title, *human,* // word like an archway, a bridge, an altar" and shows mature confidence in her own vocation as a "poet in the world" building "an archway, a bridge, an altar" through poetic language and moral vision (*OP*, 31).

Levertov's recent poems move beyond polarity to embrace both "anguish" and "affirmation." These terms, the emotional corollaries of good and evil in Levertov's lexicon, are no longer polarized but are yoked together to form the core of Levertov's later political aesthetic: "In our time, a political poetry untinged with anguish, even when it evokes and salutes moments of hope, is unimaginable. Yet—because it creates autonomous structures that are imbued with life and which stir the life of those who experience them—poetry is, in process and in being, intrinsically affirmative."[14] Increasingly, Levertov's affirmations are accepted reverently and offered generously as gifts of grace from a God "in the dust, / not sifted // out from confusion" ("This Day," *OP*, 80). The poet's task is to allow for both "anguish" and "affirmation" and to flesh out their relations. "Of Being" achieves, in form and thought, a rhythmic interlocking of these impulses, then moves beyond duality to a new realm of the sublime:

> I know this happiness
> is provisional:
>
>> the looming presences—
>> great suffering, great fear— . . .
>
> but ineluctable this shimmering
> of wind in the blue leaves:
>
> this flood of stillness
> widening the lake of sky:
>
> this need to dance,
> this need to kneel:
>> this mystery:
>>> ("Of Being," *OP*, 86)

The indented stanza makes room for the simultaneous reality of both "happiness" and "great suffering, great fear." The hope of salvation in "unmerited" and fortuitous "grace perhaps" is bolstered by Levertov's reworking of her original immanentist beliefs: "this mystery:" moves ahead of the other lines, and the ending colon points to a future the poet hardly dares to imagine or articulate.

Levertov has recently described the movement from agnosticism to faith evident in her latest poems:

I have been engaging, then, during the last few years, in my own version of the Pascalian wager, and finding that an avowal of Christian faith is not incompatible with my aesthetic nor with my political stance, since as an artist I was already in the service of the transcendent, and since Christian ethics (however betrayed in past and present history) uphold the same values I seek in a politics of racial and economic justice and nonviolence.[15]

This turn is clearly a natural outgrowth of Levertov's whole poetic endeavor for, as she goes on to say, the "acknowledgement, and celebration, of mystery probably constitutes the most consistent theme of my poetry from its beginnings."[16] We might recall, as Levertov no doubt expects us to, the Latin root of "religion"— "to tie back." To recover and forge connections, to bridge gaps, has been Levertov's fundamental impulse since her fall into the world of political experience. At once lyrical and ritualistic, poetic prayer bridges personal emotions and larger collective concerns. It seeks communion both horizontally, between humans, and vertically, between the human and the divine—both central modes of dialogue in Levertov's later political vision. Closely related to song and poetry, prayer reaffirms the poet's effort to restore language as a vehicle for political struggle: "Keep writing in the dark . . . / words that may have the power / to make the sun rise again" ("Writing in the Dark," *CB,* 101). Levertov's lyric prayers, read in the context of her political engagement, become a form of activism imploring the reader's own active engagement and response. John Berger finds inherent connections between poetry and prayer and makes explicit their relevance to political action. His statement aptly describes Levertov's efforts to mediate between the spiritual and the political:

> To break the silence of events, to speak of experience, however bitter or lacerating, to put into words, is to discover the hope that these words may be heard, and that when heard, the events will be judged. This hope is of course at the origin of prayer, and prayer . . . was probably at the origin of speech itself. Of all uses of language, it is poetry that preserves most purely the memory of this origin.[17]

Levertov's knowledge of the world and of the word have been deepened and enriched by political activism. She has lost irretrievably the innocent and easy epiphany of her early poems, for "Reason has brought us / more dread than ignorance did" (*CB,* 77). She has no illusions about the power of poetry to change political structures or to eradicate evil, and she offers no systematic program for social regeneration. Rather, her strength as a political poet lies in her appeal to celebrate what is valuable and to protest what is unconscionable. Her poems force us to see that both joy and terror are real in our world and challenge us to reconcile them for ourselves. Moreover, she is exemplary in her courage to speak from a clear moral and ideological position when much American poetry remains hermetic and socially disengaged. Levertov counters the unspeakable in our "Age of Terror" with dialogue, song, and prayer.

NOTES

1. My discussion focuses on the political poems in seven of Levertov's volumes, all published by New Directions in New York. The following abbreviations will be used in the text: *JL: The Jacob's Ladder* (1961); *SD: The Sorrow Dance* (1967); *RA: Relearning the Alphabet* (1970); *TSA: To Stay Alive* (1971); *FD: The Freeing of the Dust* (1975); *CB: Candles in Babylon* (1982); *OP: Oblique Prayers* (1984). "The World Outside" and "Life at War" appear in *Poems 1960–1967*. Copyright ©1961, 1966 by Denise Levertov Goodman. "Life at War" was first published in *Poetry*. "A Cloak" and "Relearning the Alphabet" appear in *Relearning the Alphabet*. Copyright ©1968 by Denise Levertov Goodman. "Modes of Being" appears in *The Freeing of the Dust*. Copyright ©1974, 1975 by Denise Levertov. "Unresolved" appears in *Candles in Babylon*. Copyright ©1982 by Denise Levertov. All poems are reprinted here by permission of New Directions Publishing Corporation.

2. Denise Levertov, "The Poet in the World," *The Poet in the World* (New York: New Directions, 1973), 115.

3. Levertov, "Great Possessions," *Poet in the World,* 106.

4. Charles Altieri, "Denise Levertov and the Limits of the Aesthetics of Presence," *Enlarging the Temple: New Directions in American Poetry During the 1960's* (Lewisburg, Pa: Bucknell University Press, 1979).

5. Levertov, "The Nature of Poetry," *Light Up the Cave* (New York: New Directions, 1981), 60.

6. For fuller discussions of Levertov's early poetry, see: Thomas A. Duddy, "To Celebrate: A Reading of Denise Levertov," *Criticism* 10, no. 2 (1968): 138–52; Ralph J. Mills, "Poetry of the Immediate," in his *Contemporary American Poetry* (New York: Random House, 1965), 179–96; Diana Surman, "Inside and Outside in the Poetry of Denise Levertov," *Critical Quarterly* 22 (1980): 57–70; and Linda Welshimer Wagner, *Denise Levertov* (New York: Twayne Publishers, 1967).

7. Robert Pack, "To Each Man His Own Muse," *Saturday Review,* 8 December 1962, 28–29, rpt. in *Denise Levertov: In Her Own Province,* ed. Linda Welshimer Wagner (New York: New Directions, 1979), 119–21.

8. For Levertov's own formulation of evil as "good in abeyance," see "Origins of a Poem," *Poet in the World,* 53.

9. Levertov, "On the Edge of Darkness: What is Political Poetry?" *Light Up the Cave,* 128.

10. James F. Mersmann, *Out of the Vietnam Vortex* (Lawrence: University of Kansas Press, 1979), 102.

11. "Relearning the Alphabet" is dated June 1968 to April 1969 and is almost contemporaneous with "From a Notebook: October '68–May '69," which I will examine in the context of its reworking in the subsequent volume, *To Stay Alive.* These two poems may be viewed as alternative responses to the events of this period, though the expansion and republication of "From a Notebook" as "Staying Alive" demands that they be read sequentially.

12. For a discussion of how Levertov works out the terms of lyric and didactic in *To Stay Alive,* see Paul Lacey, "The Poetry of Political Anguish," *Sagetrieb* 4, no. 1 (Spring 1985): 61–71.

13. See Thomas Merton, "War and the Crisis of Language," in *The Critique of War,* ed. Robert Ginsberg (Chicago: Henry Regnery, 1969), 99–119. Merton writes, "The language of the war-maker is *self-enclosed in finality.* It does not invite reasonable dialogue, it uses language to silence dialogue, to block communication, so that instead of words the two sides may trade divisions, positions, villages, air bases, cities—and of course the lives of the people in them" (113). Levertov refers to dialogue repeatedly in poems and essays, and this paradigm of communication underlies her political as well as aesthetic intents: "The poet develops the basic human need for dialogue in concretions that are audible to others; in listening, others are stimulated into awareness of their own needs and capacities, stirred into taking up their own dialogues, which are so often neglected" ("Origins of a Poem," 49); "A poet driven to . . . maintain a dialogue with himself, concerning politics, can expect to write as well upon that theme as upon any other" ("The Poet in the World," 115).

14. Levertov, "The Nature of Poetry," 60.

15. "A Poet's View," *Religion and Intellectual Life,* MS, 4.

16. "A Poet's View," 6.

17. John Berger, rev. of *Missing,* by Ariel Dorfman, *The Village Voice Literary Supplement,* September 1982, 11.

PART FOUR   *Gender*

SANDRA M. GILBERT

Revolutionary Love
Denise Levertov and the Poetics of Politics

In an age of psychic anxiety and metaphysical angst, Denise
Levertov's most revolutionary gesture is probably her persistent
articulation of joy—joy in self, delight in life, sheer pleasure in
pure *being*. In different poems, her frequently mystical self-
definitions achieve varying degrees of intensity: in "Stepping
Westward," for instance, she is "realistic," scrupulously celebrat-
ing "what, woman, // and who, myself, / I am," while in "Song
to Ishtar" she is more "fantastic," exulting that "the moon is a
sow . . . and I a pig and a poet." Yet at her best Levertov has
always expressed an exuberant self-knowledge, the mysterious
self-contact of what in "The Son" she called "the rapt, imperi-
ous, sea-going river," along with an appreciation of otherness
that continually leads her to seek new ways of affirming "Joy,
the, 'well . . . *joyfulness* of / joy.' "

Especially in her early collections, from *Overland to the Islands*
through *Relearning the Alphabet,* Levertov produces a succinct yet
detailed record of experience in which the perceiving mind, con-
fronting the apparent ordinariness of the world, is continually
surprised by joy. A section of "Matins," from *The Jacob's Ladder*
(1961), reveals the paradoxically insouciant reverence with which
this poet of the particular can celebrate the visionary pleasures of
daily reality:

> The authentic! I said
> rising from the toilet seat.
> The radiator in rhythmic knockings
> spoke of the rising steam.
> The authentic, I said
> breaking the handle of my hairbrush as I
> brushed my hair in
> rhythmic strokes: That's it,

Reprinted from *Parnassus* 12, no. 2/13, no. 1 (1985): 335–51.

that's joy, it's always
a recognition, the known
appearing fully itself, and
more itself than one knew.

Later in this suite of ceremonial praise "the real, the new-laid /
egg" and "the holy grains" of a child's breakfast are added to the
poet's hairbrush, her "steaming bathroom" and kitchen "full of /
things to be done" as loci of "Marvelous Truth," of the "terrible
joy"—the awesome, eternal delight—which is always, in some
sense, waiting to illuminate and transfigure the facade of the
ordinary.

That the *lares* and *penates* of the household seem to Levertov
to contain such symbolic potential is surely significant. Though
she is not an aggressively feminist poet, she is very much a
woman poet, or perhaps, more accurately, a poet conscious that
the materiality of her life as a woman is not matter to be tran-
scended; it is material in which poetry is immanent. Like "the
worm artist" in *The Sorrow Dance* who "is homage to / earth
[and] aerates / the ground of his living" (*Poems,* 176), this writer
consciously inhabits a domestic world whose grounds her words
record, revere, transform. Indeed, throughout Levertov's career,
the house itself becomes an emblem of not only physical but
spiritual shelter, its mysteries the secrets not just of habit but of
in-habitation.

The comparatively early "Overheard," from *O Taste and See*
(1964) suggests the literal resonance Levertov attributes to her
dwelling place:

A deep wooden note
when the wind blows,
the west wind.
The rock maple is it,
close to the house?
Or a beam, voice
of the house itself?
A groan, but not
gloomy, rather
an escaped note of
almost unbearable
satisfaction, a great
bough or beam

> unaware it had
> spoken.

(*Poems*, 106)

Suavely cadenced, with pauses whose careful timing emphasizes this artist's consistent attention to "where the silence is" as well as to the flow of her verse's "inner song" (*The Poet in the World,* 22, 24), this piece clearly represents Levertov's commitment to the skillful deployment of "organic form," an aesthetic strategy for which she has often been praised. But the very technique of "organic form," as Levertov defines it, cannot be separated from attention to, and celebration of, indwelling mysteries. "For me," she has written, "back of the idea of organic form is the concept that there is a form in all things (and in our experience) which the poet can discover and reveal" (*The Poet,* 7). Thus, with comparable fluency, a number of her other poems also explore both the personal and the poetic meanings of inhabitation.

"From the Roof," for instance (*Poems,* 51), begins with the poet in a wild wind, "gathering the washing as if it were flowers," meditating on a move "to our new living-place" and asking "who can say / the crippled broom-vendor yesterday, who passed / just as we needed a new broom, was not / one of the Hidden Ones?" The piece's final answer—"by design / we are to live now in a new place"—suggests the significance of place, of house, of "indwelling" to this artist. Similarly, "Invocation," which concludes *Relearning the Alphabet* (1972), dramatizes a family's preparation for moving with a prayer:

> O Lares,
>> don't leave.
>> The house yawns like a bear.
>> Guards its profound dreams for us,
>> that it returns to us when we return.

More playfully, "What My House Would Be Like If It Were a Person," in *Life in the Forest* (1978), incarnates the house itself as a mysterious, even mystical, creature:

> Its intelligence
>> would be of a high order,
>> neither human nor animal, elvish.
>> And it would purr, though of course,

it being a house, you would sit in *its* lap,
not it in yours.

At the same time, though, such a Levertovian vision of the house-as-personality is luminously complemented by a vision of the person-as-house. The beautiful "Psalm Concerning the Castle" (*Poems,* 217) almost seems to follow Gaston Bachelard's *Poetics of Space* in its scrupulously elaborated analysis of "the place of the castle . . . within me":

> Let the young queen sit above, in the cool air, her child in
> her arms; let her look with joy at the great circle, the
> pilgrim shadows, the work of the sun and the play of
> the wind. Let her walk to and fro. Let the columns,
> uphold the roof, let the storeys uphold the columns,
> let there be dark space below the lowest floor, let the
> castle rise foursquare out of the moat, let the moat be a
> ring and the water deep, let the guardians guard it, let
> there be wide lands around it, let that country where it
> stands be within me, let me be where it is.

But if the figure of the house itself is cherished by this woman poet, the activities associated with it are equally important to her. For Levertov, the ancient female tasks of keeping and cleaning, sewing and baking, loving and rearing, often become jobs as sacred as the apparently humdrum task of spinning the prayer wheel in the archaic temple—which is not to say that she is the "Dear Heloise" of poetry but rather that she is a sort of Rilke of domesticity, turning her talent for what the German poet called *einsehen* ("inseeing") toward those supposedly mundane but really central occupations which bring order out of the chaos of dailiness. Whether gathering rebellious laundry or stirring holy grains, she means to invest her housework (and her spouse's) with meaning, and she is often awestruck by its implications. As early as *Here and Now* (1957) she celebrates the dull job of "Laying the Dust"—"What a sweet smell rises / when you lay the dust" (*Collected,* 48)—and a year later, in *Overland to the Islands* (1958), she develops a metaphor of sewing to which she returns in her most recent collection, *Oblique Prayers* (1984). "I would like," she says in the earlier verse, "to make . . . poems . . . mysterious as the silence when the tailor / would pause with his needle in the air," (*Collected,* 78), and in the later she notes that "a day of spring" is "a needle's eye / space and time are passing through like a swathe of silk" (*Oblique*, 87). With the same intensity, moreover, "The Acolyte," in *Candles in Babylon* (1982), enters a large, dark, enigmatic kitchen to explore a woman's sense of the magical ambitions inspired by bread baking:

> She wants to put
> a silver rose or a bell of diamonds
> into each loaf;
> she wants
>
> to bake a curse into one loaf,
> into another, the words that break
> evil spells and release
> transformed heroes into their selves;
> she wants to make
> bread that is more than bread.
>
> (*Candles*, 69)

But of course, as the proverb would have it, the loaf that rises in the oven is often really (that is to say, symbolically) the child, and it is the child—her son Nikolai—for whom Levertov most often finds herself stirring the holy grains. From "The Son," in *The Sorrow Dance* (1967), to "He-Who-Came-Forth," in *Relearning the Alphabet,* a poem whose title works off the first line of "The Son," she exults in the miraculous separateness of the life to which she has given birth: "He-who-came-forth was / it turned out / a man," exclaims the first text, while the second marvels that his "subtle mind and quick heart. . . . now stand beyond me, out in the world / beyond my skin / beautiful and strange as if / I had given birth to a tree."

Perhaps even more than in her poems about and to her son, however, Levertov elaborates her sense of the strangeness, as well as the joy, of *relationship* in a number of erotic poems about married love. Though her work has often been discussed in terms of stylistic innovations associated with the Black Mountain School, though she is generally classified as a "neo-Romantic," and though she is frequently seen as a determinedly political poet, Levertov is not often defined as what used to be called a "love poet." Yet, especially in *The Jacob's Ladder* (1961), *O Taste and See* (1964) and *The Sorrow Dance* (1967), she has produced a set of remarkable verses, poems which, like Christina Rossetti's sonnet sequence *Monna Innominata,* dramatize the female side of the story of desire. These poems are sometimes lushly sensuous, as in "Song for a Dark Voice"—

> Your skin
> tastes of the salt of Marmora,
> the hair of your body casts
> its net over me.
>
> *(Poems, 25)*

—or "Our Bodies"—

> Your long back,
> the sand color and
> how the bones show, say
>
> what sky after sunset
> almost white
> over a deep woods to which
>
> rooks are homing, says.
>
> *(Poems, 145)*

Thus, mythologizing male beauty the way male poets have traditionally celebrated and sanctified female beauty, they suggest the Song of Songs in which an Eve, untaught silence and submissiveness, might have given voice to her erotic love for Adam. More, melodiously articulated and passionately phrased, they imply the essential connection between "the authentic" miracles of the physical house and the inescapable authenticity of the body, whose "terrible joy" the house holds and reveals. "A Psalm Praising the Hair of Man's Body," for instance, hints at the theology of Eros which Levertov more openly expresses in "Eros at Temple Stream" or "Hymn to Eros":

> Husband, thy fleece of silk is black,
>   a black adornment;
> lies so close to the turns of the flesh,
> burns my palm-stroke.
> . . . .
> Hair of man, man-hair, hair of
> breast and groin, marking contour as
>   silverpoint marks in cross-
>   hatching, as river-

                    grass on the woven current
                    indicates ripple,
        praise.

(*Poems*, 154)

In other love poems, however, Levertov explores the tension
between the desire for merging with the beloved that is mani-
fested in her erotic verses and the inexorable separateness of
lovers. "Bedtime" begins with near fusion—"We are a meadow
where the bees hum, / mind and body are almost one"—but
moves to an acknowledgment of what Whitman called the "soli-
tary self": "by day we are singular and often lonely" (*Poems*,
167). Similarly, "The Ache of Marriage," which deserves to be
quoted in its entirety, dramatizes the paradoxes of separateness-
in-togetherness, unity and duality:

            The ache of marriage:

            thigh and tongue, beloved,
            are heavy with it,
            it throbs in the teeth

            We look for communion
            and are turned away, beloved,
            each and each

            It is leviathan and we
            in its belly
            looking for joy, some joy
            not to be known outside it

            two by two in the ark of
            the ache of it.

(*Poems*, 77)

"*It is leviathan*": though, as I have already noted, Levertov is
not an aggressively feminist writer, her rigorous attentiveness to
the realities of her own life as a woman has inevitably forced her to
confront the contradictions implicit in that condition. Desire en-
traps lovers in an ark—a covenant as well as a Noah's ark steering
toward survival—that is also an ache, an institution in which the
married pair are buried as in the belly of the whale. "Don't lock
me in wedlock, I want / marriage, an / encounter—" (*Poems*, 140)

the poet exclaims in "About Marriage," yet, despite her reverence for those details of desire and domesticity which manifest "the authentic," she often implies that the wife-mother who is an artist, a woman who *sees* and says what she sees, can never be wholly one with her life, for to see is to be set apart by the imperatives of perception and expression. Where the clean and comely homemaker wears "a utopian smock or shift" (*Poems,* 143) and, "smelling of / apples or grass," merges with the nature of her life and the life of nature, the artist-wife, "dressed in opals and rags," separates herself from the kindly routines of the household.

In a number of poems, therefore, Levertov characterizes herself as *two* women—the one who lives, loves, nurtures, and the one who observes, sings, casts spells. Such a strategy of doubling is of course a traditional one for women artists: as Susan Gubar and I have argued elsewhere, nineteenth-century writers from Charlotte Brontë to Emily Dickinson frequently imagined themselves as split between a decorous lady and a fiercely rebellious madwoman. Interestingly, however, where her precursors experienced such splits as painful if liberating, Levertov usually describes them as purely liberating, further sources of "the, 'well . . . *joyfulness* of / joy.' " The early "The Earthwoman and the Waterwoman," from *Here and Now* (1957), dramatizes polarities of female experience that appear throughout most of the poet's subsequent volumes. The wholesome, nurturing "earthwoman" has children "full of blood and milk," while her opposite, the prophetic "waterwoman / sings gay songs in a sad voice / with her moonshine children" (*Collected,* 31); at night, while the earthwoman drowses in "a dark fruitcake sleep," her waterwoman self "goes dancing in the misty lit-up town / in dragonfly dresses and blue shoes." Yet despite the opposition between these two, both are exuberant, both celebrate "the authentic" in its different manifestations.

The speaker of the later "In Mind," from *O Taste and See* (1964), is more frankly confessional about her relationship to these antithetical selves, and franker, too, about the pain that at least one of them, the mystically self-absorbed waterwoman, may cause to others. "There's in my mind a woman / of innocence," the poet explains, a woman who "is kind and very clean . . . but she has / no imagination" (*Poems,* 143). But the double of this woman, she adds, is a "turbulent moon-ridden girl // or old woman . . . who knows strange songs"—and *she* "is not kind." Unkind though she may be, however, the visionary singer inexorably exists, and significantly Levertov does not apologize for her existence. On the contrary, even while in "The Woman" (*The Freeing of the Dust,* 1975) she concedes the problems that the female split self poses for a "bridegroom"—

> It is the one in homespun
> you hunger for
> when you are lonesome;
>
> the one in crazy feathers
> dragging opal chains in dust
> wearies you. . . .

—she is adamant about this complex psychic reality: "Alas, / they are not two but one," she declares, and her groom must "endure / life with two brides" (*Freeing,* 53).

In fact, it is particularly when she undertakes to analyze and justify female complexity that Levertov makes her most overtly "feminist" political statements. "Hypocrite Women," from *O Taste and See,* simultaneously expresses contempt for "a white sweating bull of a poet" who declared that "cunts are ugly" and rebukes women for refusing to admit their own strangeness, their own capacity for prophetic dreaming. Cunts "are dark and wrinkled and hairy, / caves of the Moon," yet

> when a
> dark humming fills us, a
>
> coldness towards life,
> we are too much women to
> own to such unwomanliness.
>
> Whorishly with the psychopomp
> we play and plead. . . .

(Poems, 142)

Similarly, "Abel's Bride," in *The Sorrow Dance* (1967), urges acquiescence in the female mystery that is associated with the confrontation of earthwoman and waterwoman, a confrontation enacted in the interior household where vision and domesticity coexist. Though "Woman fears for man [because] he goes / out alone to his labors" (and by implication, his death), she must recognize her own complex fate: "her being / is a cave, there are bones at the hearth" (*Poems,* 163). In fact, those—both male and female—who do not acknowledge the "dark humming" of the spirit that imbues the flesh with meaning are like "The Mutes" (also in *The Sorrow Dance*), inarticulate men whose "groans . . . passing a woman on the street" are meant to tell her "she is a female / and their flesh knows it" but say, instead,

> "Life after life after life goes by
>
> without poetry,
> without seemliness,
> without love."
>
> *(Poems,* 197)

Finally, indeed, Levertov declares that it is precisely in her womanhood—in its tangible flesh of earthwoman as well as in its fluent spirit of waterwoman—that her artistic power lies:

> When I am a woman—O, when I am
> a woman,
> my wells of salt brim and brim,
> poems force the lock of my throat.
>
> *(Freeing,* 49)

Given such a visionary and mystically (if not polemically) feminist commitment to female power, it is not surprising that some of Levertov's strongest and best-known poems offer homage to the muse-goddess whom she sees as patroness of her poetry. Among her earlier verses, the piece called "Girlhood of Jane Harrison," in *With Eyes at the Back of Our Heads* (1960), suggests one of the forces that shaped her thought on this matter, for in her monumental *Prolegomena to the Study of Greek Religion* (1903) the British feminist-classicist had sought to document the dominance of the Great Mother in ancient Greek culture. Levertov's famous poem "The Goddess," also in *With Eyes at the Back of Our Heads,* plainly devlops Harrison's theories as its praises the deity "without whom nothing / flowers, fruits, sleeps in season, / without whom nothing / speaks in its own tongue, but returns / lie for lie!"—the goddess who empowers not only the flowering grounds on which the earthwoman lives but also the strange songs of the waterwoman. Similarly, "The Well," in *The Jacob's Ladder,* as well as "Song for Ishtar" and "To the Muse," in *O Taste and See,* celebrate "The Muse / in her dark habit" and with her multiple manifestations. Finally, that this divinity inspires and presides over the essential solitude in which the woman poet inscribes her tales of earth and water is made clear in "She and the Muse," from the recent *Candles in Babylon,* a poem which shows how, after "the hour's delightful hero" has said "*arrivederci,*" the "heroine . . . eagerly" returns to the secret room of art, where "She picks a quill, / dips it, begins to write. But not of him" (*Candles,* 67). In the last analysis, the joyfulness of this woman's life and love is *made* authentic through the joy of language, the pleasure of musing words in which "the known" appears "more itself than one knew."

Although Levertov's joy is sometimes playful ("The authentic! I said / rising from the toilet seat"), it is rarely ironic or skeptical. Neither the relieved exstasis of the sufferer momentarily released from pain (the kind of exhilaration sometimes enacted by, say, Sylvia Plath) nor the brief tentative reconciliation to things-as-they-are of what we might call the *eiron maudit* (the kind of affirmation sometimes dramatized by Robert Lowell), Levertov's delight in existence depends, rather, on the steady celebratory patience of the believer who trusts that if you wait long enough, if you abide despite forebodings, the confirming moment of epiphany will arrive. Thus she assimilates those metaphysical anxieties which Wordsworth in a very different context defined as "fallings from us, vanishings" into a larger pattern based on faith in the inevitability of joy renewed.

Even some of her verses about absence—the actual or imminent absence of self, body, spirit—suggest confidence in the restoration of presence. "Gone Away," in *O Taste and See,* confesses that "When my body leaves me / I'm lonesome for it," but depends on a knowledge that the physical self will return, while two mirror poems, "Looking-Glass" (also in *O Taste and See*) and "Keeping Track" (in *Relearning the Alphabet*), trace the "shadow-me" in the glass "to see if I'm there" and, by implication, to verify an expected sense of authenticity. Even more dramatically—and more characteristically—"To the Muse," in *O Taste and See,* maintains that though the poet, the "host" of the house of art, fears that his aesthetic patroness is hiding,

all the while

> you are indwelling,
> a gold ring lost in the house.
> *A gold ring lost in the house.*
> You are in the house!

And the mystery of creativity is precisely that the muse's "presence / will be restored" (*Poems*, 99).

Inevitably, perhaps, for a poet of Levertov's bent, a poet who trusts that a thread of potential joy is woven into every inch of the fabric that constitutes daily reality, any ripping or clipping of that secret, sacred thread threatens cataclysm. Thus, like such other poets of affirmation as Blake, Shelley, Whitman, or in our own age Bly, she is a deeply political writer—and I am using the word "politics" in its most ordinary sense, to mean public matters having to do with "the policies, goals, or affairs of a government" (*American Heritage Dictionary*). For in the "real" world, it is political action—the burning of villages, the decapitation of villagers, the building of bombs—that most threatens the authority of daily joy. Yet, paradoxically enough, despite their often revolutionary intensity, Levertov's most artistically problematic poems are precisely those no doubt overdetermined verses in which she explicitly articulates her political principles.

Comparatively early in her career, Levertov began to try to find a way of confronting and analyzing the horrors of a history—especially a twentieth-century history—which denies the luminous integrity of flesh-and-spirit. But even one of her better poems in this mode, "Crystal Night" (in *The Jacob's Ladder*), now seems rhetorically hollow, with its generalized description of "The scream! / The awaited scream" which "rises," and "the shattering / of glass and the cracking / of bone" (*Poems*, 68). The better-known "Life at War," in *The Sorrow Dance*, is more hectic still, in its insistence that

> We have breathed the grits of it [war] in, all our lives,
> our lungs are pocked with it,
> the mucous membrane of our dreams
> coated with it, the imagination
> filmed over with the gray filth of it

and in its editorial revulsion from the complicity of "delicate Man, whose flesh / responds to a caress, whose eyes / are flowers that perceive the stars" (*Poems*, 229).

In a splendid essay on verse in this mode ("On the Edge of Darkness: What is Political Poetry?" in *Light Up the Cave*, 1981), Levertov herself observes, about the "assumption by partisan poets and their constituencies that the subject matter carries so strong an emotive charge in itself that it is unnecessary to remember poetry's roots in song, magic, and . . . high craft," that such a belief is "dangerous to poetry" (*Light,* 126). Yet in most of her political verse she seems herself to have disregarded her own astute warning. Because she has little taste or talent for irony, her comments on social catastrophe lack, on the one hand, the sardonic ferocity that animates, say, Bly's "The Teeth Mother Naked at Last" (e.g., "It's because we have new packaging for smoked oysters that bomb holes appear in the rice paddies"), and, on the other hand, the details of disillusionment that give plausibility to, say, Lowell's "For the Union Dead" (e.g., "When I crouch to my television set, / the drained faces of negro schoolchildren rise like balloons"). At the same time, despite the impressive sincerity of her political commitment, her exhortations fail to attain (as perhaps postmodernist exhortations inevitably must) the exaltation of, for instance, Shelley's "Men of England, wherefore plough / For the lords who lay ye low?"

Still, as Levertov's personal commitment to the antinuclear movement and to support for revolutionary regimes in Central America has intensified, the proportion of politicized work included in her published collections has risen drastically. *Oblique Prayers* (1984) contains a section of ten manifestos, most of which, sadly, dissolve into mere cries of rage and defiance. The tellingly titled "Perhaps No Poem But All I Can Say And I Cannot Be Silent," for instance, protests against "those foul / dollops of History / each day thrusts at us, pushing them / into our gullets" (*Oblique,* 35) while "Rocky Flats" depicts "rank buds of death" in "nuclear mushroom sheds," and "Watching *Dark Circle*" describes the experimental "roasting of live pigs" in "a simulation of certain conditions" as leading to "a foul miasma irremovable from the nostrils" (*Oblique,* 38, 39). Though I (along with, I suspect, the majority of her readers and admirers) share most of Levertov's political convictions, I must confess that besides being less moved by these poems than I have been by the more artful verses of Bly, Lowell, and Shelley, I am rather less moved than I would be by eloquent journalism, and considerably less affected than I would be by a circumstantially detailed documentary account of the events that are the subjects of Levertov's verses, for certainly there is little song, magic, or high craft in some of their phrases. The muse is still, I trust, "indwelling" in this poet's house, but she has not presided over some of the writer's recent work.

To be sure, the muse *has* inspired several of Levertov's political verses. "Thinking about El Salvador," in *Oblique Prayers* opens with the poet's confession that "Because every day they chop heads off / I'm silent / . . . for each tongue they silence / a word in my mouth / unsays itself," and concludes with a poignant vision

> of all whose heads every day
> float down the river
> and rot
> and sink,
> not Orpheus heads
> still singing, bound for the sea,
> but mute.
>
> (*Oblique*, 34)

And the much earlier "A Note to Olga (1966)" dramatizes the poet's sudden vision of her dead sister at a political rally:

> It seems
> you that is lifted
>
> limp and ardent
> off the dark snow
> and shoved in, and driven away.
>
> (*Poems*, 239)

But what moves these poems, as opposed to Levertov's less successful polemics, seems to be not ferocious revulsion but revolutionary love—not the hate that is blind to all detail except its own rhetoric ("foul dollops") but the love that sees and says with scrupulous exactitude the terror of the severed heads that are "not Orpheus heads" and the passion of the ghostly Olga, "limp and ardent." And as these works show, such rebellious *caritas*, perhaps as surely as Bly's ironic inventiveness, Lowell's meticulous weariness, or (even) Shelley's hortatory energy, can impel the poetics of politics.

In fact, the phrase "revolutionary love" itself is from Levertov's fine essay on Pablo Neruda: "Poetry and Revolution: Neruda is Dead—Neruda Lives" (in *Light Up the Cave*), a piece that beautifully complements and supplements her meditation on political poetry. "Neruda's revolutionary politics," she declares here, "is founded in revolutionary love—the same love Che Guevara spoke of. Revolutionary love subsumes a bitter anger against oppression and oppressors. . . . But revolutionary love is not merely anthropocentric; it reaches out to the rest of creation."

For, she adds, Neruda's celebrations of animals and vegetables, of the earth and sky and sea, "are not irrelevant, dispensable, coincidental to his revolutionary convictions, but an integral part of them" (*Light,* 133–34).

About Levertov's own revolutionary love, with its often brilliantly precise elaborations of the joyfulness of joy, the same statement could be made. Yet it is instructive to compare her expressions of "bitter anger" with those of her Chilean precursor. Neruda's classic "The United Fruit Co.," for instance, begins with scathingly sardonic, surrealistic detail:

> When the trumpet sounded, it was
>
> all prepared on the earth,
> and Jehovah parceled out the earth
> to Coca-Cola, Inc., Anaconda,
> Ford Motors, and other entities:
> The Fruit Company, Inc.
> reserved for itself the most succulent,
> the central coast of my own land,
> the delicate waist of America.
>
> (trans. Robert Bly,
> Neruda, and Vallejo, *Selected Poems,* 85)

And even more strikingly than Levertov's "Thinking about El Salvador," Neruda's poem ends with a terrifying image:

> Indians are falling
> into the sugared chasms
> of the harbors, wrapped
> for burial in the mist of the dawn:
> a body rolls, a thing
> that has no name, a fallen cipher,
> a cluster of dead fruit
> thrown down on the dump.

Though of course it is intellectually coherent with the poem's theme ("sugared chasms," "a cluster of dead fruit"), this brilliant detail, in which we recognize "the known / appearing fully itself," is an image shaped by revolutionary love, by the love that yields itself not so much to editorial convictions as to the muse's telling, the goddess's indwelling.

When Levertov is at her best, such love underlies both her

celebrations and her cerebrations; indeed, precisely because she is not an artist of irony or disillusionment but a poet of revolutionary love, she succeeds at recountings of the authentic in daily experience and fails at what Swift called *saeva indignatio*. Clearly, moreover, she knows this in some part of herself. One of the best poems in *Candles in Babylon* is "The Dragonfly-Mother," a piece in which Levertov reexamines the split between earthwoman and waterwoman specifically in terms of her own split commitment to, on the one hand, political activism, and, on the other hand, poetry.

> I was setting out from my house
> to keep my promise
>
> but the Dragonfly-Mother stopped me.
>
> I was to speak to a multitude
> for a good cause, but at home
>
> the Dragonfly-Mother was listening
> not to a speech but to the creak of
> > stretching tissue,
> tense hum of leaves unfurling.

"Who is the Dragonfly-Mother?" the poem asks, then goes on to answer that she is the muse, "the one who hovers / on stairways of air," the one—by implication—who sees and says the authentic in the ordinary, the revolutionary love continually surprised, and inspired, by joy. Her imperatives are inescapable: "When she tells / her stories she listens; when she listens / she tells you the story you utter."

It is to such imperatives that, one hopes, this poet will continue to be loyal, for what the Dragonfly-Mother declares, over and over again, is that the political is—or must be made—the poetical: the fabric of joy should not be ripped or clipped, yet the activist artist must struggle to praise and preserve every unique thread of that fabric, against the onslaughts of those who would reduce all reality to "foul dollops." Toward the end of this poem, Levertov seems to me to express the central truth of her own aesthetic, the truth of the joy *and* the pain born from revolutionary love:

Dragonfly-Mother's
a messenger,
if I don't trust her
I can't keep faith.

(Candles, 13–15)

RACHEL BLAU DUPLESSIS

The Critique of Consciousness
and Myth in Levertov, Rich,
and Rukeyser

I want to be able to separate in myself what is old and cyclic, the recurring history, the myth, from what is new, what I feel or think that might be new.
—Doris Lessing, *The Golden Notebook* (1962)

In the decade and a half that saw the anticolonial, black, Vietnamese, and women's movements flourish, three women poets, Adrienne Rich, Muriel Rukeyser, and Denise Levertov, invented self-exploratory and culturally reevaluative quest plots, so that the act of cultural criticism became their central lyric act, from the critique of language and consciousness to its necessary extension, the discussion of the individual in history.

The poets saw themselves contributing to the undermining of cultural structures repressive of women first by reevaluating canons of proper language and proper subject. With their deliberate use of taboo words, and with the thematic purpose these words symbolize, the poets provided support for an argument made in "Professions for Women."[1] Virginia Woolf traces the process by which a woman creates from her life and the contradictions of her consciousness the new context in which she has permission to speak and act in autonomous, fearless ways. First, she must "kill the angel in the house," that self-sacrificing, charming, flirtatious phantom who always pleases others, never herself. The death of the angel of self-repression, that is, the critique of old consciousness, hypothetically insures that there will be no sex-linked taboos on women's self-exploration.

In "Hypocrite Women," Denise Levertov asks what specific female constraints can prevent or inhibit one's choosing to make life a pilgrimage.[2] The answer: women repress whatever they feel—even their own self-doubt—to preserve a generous, unruffled surface, while they "mother man in his doubt," encouraging the nuances and moods necessary for his self-expression. The

Reprinted from Rachel Blau DuPlessis, *Writing Beyond the Ending* (Bloomington: Indiana University Press, 1985), 123–41 and 229–33.

women really feel cold, moonstruck, self-absorbed: in a word, "unwomanly." To hide the paradox of "unwomanliness," they assume the mask their culture has long made available: flirtation used as self-repression. In doing so, they also hide the intensity of the conflict from themselves. The judgment "Whorishly with the psychopomp / we play and plead—" alerts us to what is at stake. This traditional guide of souls from Greek mythology, crucial to spiritual development, is assailed by a teasing display of charm, which the women use as a deliberate strategy of refusal, rejecting their capacity for growth and denying their inmost selves. Key terms such as "to mother" and "whorishly," and the image of cutting dreams "like ends of split hair," are linguistic allegories criticizing women who, concerned simply with pleasing men, tailor their responses to ignore messages of myth and dream, always so vital in Levertov. By self-censorship, women deny themselves the challenge of soul making.

The women have agreed with the man that they—that their "cunts"—are ugly. But in this poem, the word *cunt* has been used openly and carefully as a counterstrategy of affirmation. The explicit naming of sexual organs and bodily functions in this and contemporaneous poems by women uncensors taboo words, and by so doing, constructs a critique of the cultural values of propriety and complicity that have kept these words—and females themselves—unspeakable.

Muriel Rukeyser's "Despisals"[3] likewise poses forbidden words like "asshole," "shit," and "clitoris" to explore the social implications of self-hatred. Rukeyser argues that the ghettoization of parts of the body precedes and in some way has caused the ghettos of the city. Through the creation of individual consciousness, reproduced in the upbringing of every child, an intolerant, destructive society is also formed. The poem studies the continuity of repression from the individual psyche to the collective city.

Through the flat, bold words of "Despisals," Rukeyser has also dramatized the power of the reader's assumptions. For a person is likely to be startled at the forbidden words, shocked that the poet did not censor herself. Since the poem concerns the rejection of shame and contempt, readers find that their internalized expectations for the poem's tone or diction are a version of the "despisals" criticized therein. The poem causes the reader to examine the repressive function of canons of right language by its delegitimation of linguistic taboos.

In order for a woman to accomplish Woolf's second task,

aggressive truth telling from female experiences, she must rejoin the internal struggle between censorship—respect for dominant ideology—and expression of muted insights. The expression of a woman's feelings can be achieved only by delegitimating narrative patterns embodying the social practices and mental structures that repress women. The writer must "break the sentence" of beliefs and the sequence of plot structures that express them.

Adrienne Rich's "Snapshots of a Daughter-in-Law" (1958–60) is an outstanding example of this critique of consciousness. As Rukeyser and Levertov confront canons of respectable language, so Rich has to pit herself against acceptable canons of subject: "I had been taught that poetry should be 'universal,' which meant, of course, non-female."[4] As an act of self-defense, she excludes the pronoun "I" from the work (although she ends with "we"), uses allusions to expert opinion, and chooses a title with ironic reference to "feminine" sources of authority: her marital status and family relationships.

Indeed, like a feminist *Waste Land* in its "loaded gun" allusiveness, the poem answers, sometimes in a relentlessly dismissive way, some of the problems posed by male culture. Rich even uses *The Second Sex* of Simone de Beauvoir the way T. S. Eliot used Jesse Weston. There is a tissue of reference to such classic modernist texts as Yeats's "Leda and the Swan." When Yeats asks, "Did she put on his knowledge with his power / before the indifferent beak could let her drop?" Rich responds, "A thinking woman sleeps with monsters. / The beak that grips her, she becomes," turning the question back, and showing an ambivalent judgment about the possession of phallic power and knowledge. Anger, rupture, and a wounding self-initiation define this text.

The three poems of the first section discuss the intricate but limited patterns of behavior of women in Rich's own family. They have few options. The mother lives through memories of past elegance; yet because she does not think, but only feels, all her experience is "useless."[5] The daughter-in-law hears and, with a deep self-denying perversity, represses unseen voices that call on her to rebel or to be selfish, demands she cannot begin to fulfill. The third poem exposes sisters without sisterhood, who express the monstrous dimensions of their self-hatred through hostility toward each other. At one and the same time, the poet is isolated from other women and implicated in their paralysis, anger, and disintegration. She is torn between her sense of being exceptional and her protofeminist identification with women as a structurally separate group. Such a bleak sketch of the options available to women—frustration taking shape as vagueness, madness, bitchiness—demands some causal explanation, which the poet discovers in the next section by referring to and analyzing classic literary texts that evoke the history of women's condition and the fate of their gifts.

When a woman as gifted as Emily Dickinson appears—an image of Rich herself—she is compelled to pursue her ideas and images in the interstices of domestic life, a life that exists in diffuse, interruptible contrast to explosive power.[6] Alternately, endless domestic tasks will give shape to a woman's life. She will put all her energy into upkeep, not into living, "dusting everything on the whatnot every day of life."

If domesticity is one social expectation that shapes a woman's personality and to which her gifts must conform, the demands of beauty are another. The woman is idol, objectified by the necessity of preserving a sleek and beautiful surface, and powerless because of artifice.

The section that follows, with its oblique citation from Campion, argues that courtship also immobilizes women.[7] The accomplished woman bending over a lute is not immersed in art for its sake or for hers; song is one of the ornaments of her beauty; art enhances her as an icon. Love, along with domesticity and beauty, is the third term creating the traditional boundaries that mold and define women. Woman is a social construct, not, as in much lyric, an idealized vision. Each of these three terms of women's condition creates typical traits: the combination of repressed power and actual powerlessness; the bitterness of a person prevented from full fruition; a "keenness" about nature and human relationships that comes from dependence on love.

Having summed up the classic expectations, Rich turns to modern touchstones of cultural attitudes toward women, identifying in each case, with concision and subtlety, the complex psychological paralysis and kinds of failure that have been the lot of women who internalize or are controlled by male opinion. She recalls how Mary Wollstonecraft was reviled by men for her analyses of the status of women. But Diderot's praise of their lush flowering arouses women to self-pity and infinite regrets for their past potential; they are tacitly forgiven for a lack of accomplishments.

Rich caustically challenges both majority opinion about women and women's complicity with it.

Our blight has been our sinecure:
mere talent was enough for us—
glitter in fragments and rough drafts.

Sigh no more, ladies.
                    Time is male
and in his cups drinks to the fair.
Bemused by gallantry, we hear
our mediocrities over-praised,
indolence read as abnegation,
slattern thought styled intuition,
every lapse forgiven, our crime
only to cast too bold a shadow
or smash the mold straight off.

For that, solitary confinement,
tear gas, attrition shelling.
Few applicants for that honor.

                                        (*PSN,* 50)

Women are praised precisely because their work has not called
male "superiority" and male analysis into question. Safe and
childlike, mental invalids, women may be patronized generously
because of their failure to grow and to preserve. Rich exposes the
double face of the prevailing culture: its paternal protection of
female mediocrity and its destructive attack on female boldness.

Given what she says, any woman must reinvent herself; hence
at the end of the poem, she is compared to the helicopter, half bird,
half knife. To construct her new consciousness, the woman must
at one and the same time sever her allegiance to the destructive
views of the past and transcend the presence of destructive ideolo-
gies in herself, producing that critique distinctive of twentieth-
century women writers, "not to pass on a tradition, but to break
its hold over us."[8]

Levertov, Rich, and Rukeyser share a concern for individual
mental structures and their cultural roots. They see that the con-
tents of consciousness curtail the work of the imagination. There-
fore, they mount a critical attack on dominant patterns of percep-
tion and practice.

Both for historical reasons and to extend their analysis of con-
sciousness further, all three poets write about political situa-
tions—the Vietnam War, and, in Rukeyser's case, the two World
Wars. The same concern to investigate, to criticize, to protest

against the commonplaces of perception and behavior that ani-
mates their poems about women leads the poets to examine politi-
cal forces and power relations that inform individual conscious-
ness. The Vietnam War becomes a focal issue, since, in a historical
sense, it is the concrete political reality in which they feel impli-
cated, and, in a symbolic sense, it epitomizes the destructive val-
ues and acts that the old consciousness can produce. The Vietnam
War also demystified the colonial-imperial relation. This swift
delegitimation of a national mission made the process of critique
especially sharp, a development that had, in turn, two intellectual
effects on the generations to which these poets belonged: contin-
ual attention to the critical analysis of ideology on one hand, and,
on the other hand, the spiritual hope for an ungridded area of
human activity without ideology—giving access to an epiphanal
or purely experiential truth. These two effects are, of course,
contradictory.

As a group, the poems that comment on the war and talk
about political protests ask how the individual psyche is related
to history. To phrase the question somewhat differently, they ask
how to apply the model of personal changes of consciousness to
produce social change. In "Breaking Open," Rukeyser docu-
ments a series of linked conversions and communions that ex-
tend personal change outward to small groups.[9] In her terms,
"breaking open," will result from a knowledge of our historical
and our personal moments and must lead to a transformation of
both—history through psyche and psyche through history. An-
other meditative political poem of recent years, Levertov's "Stay-
ing Alive," longs for the revolutionary "life that / wants to live,"
as opposed to the deadly "unlived life."[10] Social change begins—
as in Rukeyser—with individual witnesses to the new life, who
try to demonstrate in the present the values and relationships the
changed society would bring. Levertov and Rukeyser share one
response to the question of changing society.[11] They go deeper
into themselves, not as an act of rejection or a declaration of
autonomy, but from a belief that inwardness is one necessary
path to social transformation. Their documentary poems about
politics and the war return dramatically to a concern for con-
sciousness and changes in the self.

In poems contemporaneous with the Vietnam War, Adrienne
Rich linked male sexuality and personal life to war. In "The
Phenomenology of Anger" Rich is a combatant, and the battle-
field is her consciousness. War parallels the patriarchal oppres-
sion of women. Domination, depersonalization, and dehuman-

ization are the vectors of the patriarchal psyche; multiplied and extended on a national scale, these male traits are, in Rich's view, an Ur-political explanation for the Vietnam War and its atrocities.[12] Social dislocation and war stem from an estrangement, at some original moment, between "female" and "male" components of the human psyche. Rich pursues this split, conducting an examination of psychic life to trace the colonial relation to its origins.

On one level Rukeyser's "Breaking Open," Levertov's "Staying Alive," and Rich's "The Phenomenology of Anger" record an impasse: the near impossibility of creating social change only through changing consciousness. However, the poets write as if continuing to know more and feel more—rage in Rich, communion in Rukeyser, participation in Levertov—could create social change by the explosive needs of consciousness itself. But in another sense, these poems about the interaction of history and consciousness reveal that nothing—not the most hidden aspects of the psychic life of the individual—exists apart from the pressures of a historical era.

The gendered, historically sculpted person, realizing the dimensions of her opposition to dominant ideologies, breaks the repeating sentences and sequences of that dominance in myths of critique. These myths entail critical perceptions about the nature of women. They recast long-sanctified plots, especially quest patterns, and reenvision such familiar figures as the hero, the lady, and the reborn god. The poems are so strongly reevaluative that they may even appear antimythological ("No more masks! No more mythologies!"), precisely because they record the realization that certain prime myths are invalid and crippling for women: "a book of myths / in which / our names do not appear." Indeed, the poems are often self-evaluative, recasting the poet's prior work.

One of the most curious is Rukeyser's "The Poem as Mask."[13] Explicitly antimythological, the poem is also an act of self-criticism, written in direct opposition to an earlier "Orpheus."[14] The older poem, constructed like a court masque of English tradition, uses the power of music as organizing symbol, centers on a static drama of transformation, and ends with a song of unity. The figure of Orpheus—the poet reborn as a god, the fragments of the human reunited as the divine, a transcendent experience that gives power to the self—is a motif of great resonance for Rukeyser.[15] Yet in "The Poem as Mask," she brings her earlier poem into question by deliberate acts of self-examination and self-criticism, showing that the myth she had so lovingly chosen and carefully shaped is an impediment to her quest. "The Poem as Mask" states that she had censored her feelings, writing *him, god, myth,* when she meant *me, human, my life.* As a woman, she had been unable to affirm her "torn life"—the loss of love, a dangerous birth, the rescue of self and newborn child. Her former use of the myth blunted her sense of personal reality; it was a "mask" of covering, not a "masque" of unity and joy. So she makes a vow at the end of the poem: "No more masks! No more mythologies!" But while this vow is understandably anti-mythological, a cry against alien patterns imposed on women's lives, the poem's final lines present a renewed myth based on concrete feelings of peace, blessing, and wholeness. The new myth comes from within the self, as the orphic experiences in the historical life of the poet that offer inspiration and rebirth.

Another matching set of mythopoetic works by Rukeyser concerns Oedipus and the sphinx: "Private Life of the Sphinx" from *The Green Wave* (1948) and "Myth" from *Breaking Open* (1973).[16] Both poems work with revisionary strategies. The first makes a serious, pulsing lyrical displacement to the sphinx's side of things; she redefines herself away from male power in order to become a perpetual questioner. However, this early version of the myth accepts that the answer to her riddle must still be *man*. This is exactly the answer delegitimated by Rukeyser's later, jokey, joyous "Myth," in which the universal is abruptly particularized and the answer that "everyone knows" is called into question (*CP*, 278, 498). Rukeyser plays on the generic "mankind" by having her sphinx pointedly note that, despite Oedipus's assumption, the abstract noun in question does not, from her perspective, include womankind. The sphinx's deflating reduction of universal assumption to untenable opinion makes the poem a critique of consciousness through critical allusions not only to the classical story but to an earlier poem.

Denise Levertov's major mythopoetic work, "Relearning the Alphabet," chronicles a journey of the self and a rediscovery of the roots of vision.[17] The loss of contact with sources is solved by a pilgrimage in which each letter of the alphabet marks the route. The form is thus a primer of meaning, teaching the reader to attend to concrete experience that bears a special resonance or pitch. To the loss of both self and love, Levertov first proposes a false solution: the will, imagistically related to the cold moon.

But inner avatars, who take the form of men, compel her to stop. Only by retracing the steps of her journey, that is, by a self-critical reassessment, can the true path be found.

The "U" section states:

> Relearn the alphabet,
> relearn the world, the world
> understood anew only in doing, under-
> stood only as
> looked-up-into out of earth
>
> (*RA,* 119)

The focus on *under-stood* is a call for a return to basic detail, to the event rooted in concrete, daily life. For this understanding, the poet forges the syntactically entangled set of prepositions ("up-into out of"), situating herself in the real at that moment, always decisive in Levertov, when its inner energy is known.

In "Relearning the Alphabet," the hero is a woman, and it appears that she is also her own prize or treasure, for she rediscovers that authentic self.

> In childhood dream-play I was always
> the knight or squire, not
> the lady:
> quester, petitioner, win or lose, not
> she who was sought.
> The initial of quest or question
> branded itself long since on the flank
> of my Pegasus.
>
> (*RA,* 116)

Yet although the poem can be read as a myth of the woman-hero finding the woman-captive and freeing her, Levertov is not comfortable with this. She states that she is only the knight or quester and rejects the implicit role of the captive self or muted lady.

The formal use of the alphabet is also a measure of how far Levertov allows herself to go into critique. As the poem's significant action is the "relearning" of the most ordinary things, what is more basic than the alphabet, what more ubiquitous, or more taken for granted? So the alphabet form focuses subtle attention on building blocks of consciousness: here the form works critically. However, the alphabet is a self-limited area for critique, since the letters must finally be put back into the accustomed order. The material of reality is "relearned," not revised; the alphabet is the sign of that familiar order, reinvested with wonder, but not called into question. As a corollary, Levertov remains engaged with cyclic and archetypal patterns, unlike the other two poets.

Adrienne Rich's work during this period also centers on a critique of the stories and meanings that have patterned a dominant perspective. "Diving into the Wreck," specifically antimythological, perturbed by the existing cultural "book of myths," creates a new myth, similar to Rukeyser's in its focus on the act of criticism and in its centering on reality.[18]

In "Diving into the Wreck," descent, detection, and exploration are metaphors for the acts of criticism. The poet, as an undersea diver, takes a journey down to an individual and collective past, where some mysterious, challenging "wreck" occurred that no prior research or instruction can clarify. We discover that the wreck is the personal and cultural foundering of the relations between the sexes. Her exploration moves to the unembellished and apparently unmediated perception of

> the thing I came for:
> the wreck and not the story of the wreck
> the thing itself and not the myth.
>
> *(PSN,* 197)

Like Rukeyser, but in a darker tone, Rich places her emphasis beyond the culturally validated frames of story and myth, on the absolute and concrete perception of the seeker. The diver spends much of the poem in descent to arrive at dissent, moving deeper than the surface of meanings and atmospheres in which it is "natural" to be the way we are. Further, the diver goes beyond the "ending" of the implied story of a wreck to examine clues to alternative stories that—first unnoticed—would otherwise be doomed to be permanently muted. The "book of myths" contains sentences and sequences that do not name properly, keeping things invisible or unspoken. But if explored from this muted experiential perspective without the scripts of narrative, the wreck will yield alternative meaning.

In the act of detection, the analysis of the wreck, the poet discovers that she has herself become the object of the search: "I am she: I am he // whose drowned face sleeps with open eyes" *(PSN,* 198). This discovery of multiple, androgynous, unifying identities is part of the truth of the wreck. The holistic "one" who is revealed underwater is constructed of opposites before their split: I and we, she and he, dead and living, speaker and spoken, individual and collective, cargo and instruments, seeker and sought.

In this poem of journey and transformation, Rich is tapping the plots of myth while reenvisioning the content. While there is a hero, a quest, and a buried treasure, the hero is a woman; the quest is a critique of old myths; the treasure is the whole buried knowledge of the relations between the sexes that cannot yet be brought to the surface, and a self-definition won only through the act of criticism.[19]

In a traditional "transformation myth," according to Erich Neumann, a male hero (like Perseus) engages in a struggle or quest to liberate a captive woman, and possibly a treasure, from a female monster. At the successful end of the struggle, the hero marries the captive, having extricated her from the coils of the "terrible mother," a snake or dragon, who represents the captive's own dangerous and despised matriarchal past. The captive woman is the necessary contributor to the hero's development, representing a fruitfulness and creativity that he appropriates and that transforms him. The hero severs (or rescues) the creative, supportive, enriching aspects of the female from the baleful, destructive, devouring aspects, becoming the custodian of the "good" and the repressor of the "wicked" aspects of female power. "With the freeing of the captive and the founding of a new kingdom, the patriarchal age comes into force."[20] This kind of tale offers marriage to its female character, quest and control to its male, and, in addition, makes the female relatively impotent.

The ultimate intention of "Diving into the Wreck" is to call this patriarchal myth into question. Rich does so by constructing her oppositional version of the origin and history of consciousness. If we were to take Rich's myth as a simple reversal of Neumann's model, it would be easy to say that in the underwater journey of the self, she too finds her opposite. But displacement is not her aim. Unlike the fecund captive-treasure of the patriarchal myth, this character is dead, arrested in the strained posture of unfulfilled searching. Far from being the answer, s/he is one complex part of the question the wreck poses. The new "fruitful center" in Rich's myth has become the creative antagonism of the woman-hero to traditional consciousness and old patterns of myth—an antagonism aroused by the fact that the book of stories and explanations excludes her. In the course of her journey, a new woman has been invented, one appropriating her own fruitfulness and power. She is both hero and treasure, a unity not achieved by heterosexual bonding but by anticolonial quest.[21]

Besides being critiques, the myths of Rich and Rukeyser in this period of work are nonstatic and nonarchetypal. Rejecting the unchanging, unhistorical types—hero, captive, treasure, reborn god—the poets make these new myths historically specific inventions. They are lyric documents entailing perceptions of a changing self in a historical context, reinterpreting elements of the quest or motifs of rebirth by a reevaluation of who the poets are, the time and place they have entered, and the cultural stances their lives were expected to embody. In both poets, the rupture of sequences, the "splitting open" and delegitimation of constituted stories, occurs oppositionally outside "the guidelines of orthodoxy," as Rich said of Dickinson.[22] This is why the critiques of consciousness are a necessary first step to the poems that reevaluate myth.

Further, these myths replace archetypes with prototypes. They do not investigate moments of eternal recurrence, but rather break with the idea of an essentially unchanging reality. Prototypes are original, model forms on which to base the self and its action—forms open to transformation, and forms, unlike archetypes, that offer similar patterns of experience *to* others, rather than imposing these patterns *on* others. A dictionary definition reveals the significant distinction between the words.[23] While both archetype and prototype "denote original models," an archetype "is usually construed as an ideal form that establishes an unchanging pattern for all things of its kind." However, "what develops from a prototype may represent significant modification from the original." A prototype is not a binding, timeless pattern, but one critically open to the possibility, even the necessity, of its transformation. Thinking in terms of prototypes historicizes myth.

Criticizing the nature of myth is one of the reevaluations that women writers consciously undertake, for their own lives allow them to see the culturally repressive functions of archetypes, and their own experiences of personal and social change, recorded in poems about consciousness and politics, belie the illusion of a timeless, unhistorical pattern that controls reality.

Reassessment by an intense examination of conscience is characteristic of these mythic poems as a group. At the same time, it marks the intense self-questioning and internal debate of Rich's coming out as a lesbian.[24] Since about 1974, Rich has adopted a lesbian feminist perspective to situate this critical examination of culture, trying thereby to create an irrevocable distance between dominant and alternative/oppositional social practices. So, in part, Rich uses the term "lesbian feminist" as we have been using the terms "feminist" or "critical" throughout this study, to describe a person who has made an analytic severing from certain patriarchal cultural practices, whose acts of oppositional deliberation have brought her to "the other-side of everything"—to the questioning of primary institutions of social, sexual, and cultural organization.[25] Rich's lesbian stance is consistent with the perspective of all the writers who are the subject of this study.

Rich's most theoretical statement on sexuality criticizes heterosexuality, showing how it is one institution of the sex–gender system, psychosexually and socially produced. Although heterosexuality has seemed like a part of nature, it can be called into question by a critical approach that deuniversalizes it, taking it from the realm of biology and setting it into the realm of politics.[26] The rhetorical purpose of the essay is to shift the relative weights of dominant and alternative sexualities, so that, by the end, the "lesbian continuum" seems dominant as well as attractive, while heterosexuality seems not only a minor position for species survival, but an unpalatable one. Rich redefines the category of lesbian to include not only women who are sexually and erotically bound (what she calls "lesbian existence") but also women who are in any way affiliated with other women or not connected to men—single women, independent women, women who aid other women—as well as any activity of nurturance and support in which women are mutually engaged. Thus the term "lesbian continuum" broadens the meaning from a sexual minority to an oppositional and women-identified behavior whose scope is much greater than had been suspected. The poles of dominant and alternative are shifted; more than a delegitimation of main culture by an oppositional stance, this is a capture of centrality by a perspective once falsely or ignorantly considered of only secondary importance.

Shifting the term *lesbian* from the purely sexual to a widely social and cultural arena still preserves the depth charge of shock inherent in what had been a deeply taboo sexual affiliation. Rich has, in fact, always been concerned to find a stance that cannot possibly be appropriated by main culture because it embodies such a definitive critical negation of the status quo. Rich's use of the term lesbian, and choice of lesbianism, satisfied her as a way

of publicly establishing the most radical outsider status in rela-
tion to such institutions of gendering as the oedipal crisis and
heterosexuality.[27]

Self-revisionary poems followed Rich's declaration of lesbian
existence. "Natural Resources," one of the important poems in
The Dream of a Common Language, reassesses earlier stages of
Rich's work, represented by "Snapshots of a Daughter-in-Law"
and "Diving into the Wreck" respectively.[28] "Natural Resources"
begins with the image of a descent to a treasure, with evident
parallels to the earlier poem. There is a palpable difference, how-
ever, between the well-equipped, technologically supported but
brilliantly isolated scuba diver, and the miner in this poem, who
more clearly suffers the consequences of her labor: body bent,
lungs filled with dust. The miner is an ordinary woman; the
diver had been exceptional. Rich insists, rejecting the allegorical
nature of her diver, that this miner is "no metaphor" (*DCL,* 60).

The treasure in "Diving into the Wreck" was found with the
recognition of the essential human identity of the two sexes,
which, once present, had been severed in a primeval event whose
meanings reverberate through history and psyche. Hence the
treasure is a buried but pulsing presence of wholeness in the
androgynous unity of the sexes. In contrast, the treasures of
"Natural Resources" are the constant and perpetual acts of fe-
male labor, which preserve and remake "a universe of humble
things" (*DCL,* 66).

These acts are depicted, with a lacerating vision, as the acts of
women uniquely, in distinction to men.

> I am tired of faintheartedness,
> their having to be *exceptional*
>
> to do what an ordinary woman
> does in the course of things.
>
> (*DCL,* 64)

Domestic tasks, once seen by Rich as debilitating and grating
taxes on female talent, are here pensively celebrated as virtually
the only stay against male aggression and destructiveness.

In addition, "Natural Resources" shows an entirely different
definition of "culture" than did "Snapshots"—more anthropo-
logical and social than specifically literary and artistic, the culture
of workers, not literati. This argues that women produce civiliza-
tion, in ordinary and communal acts. It is not surprising that the

only literary allusion in "Natural Resources" (one remembers that "Snapshots" was filled with citations) occurs when the poet speaks of men, as if the strategy of citation helps identify the tedium of these repeated notions from high culture. The turn from a "botched civilization"—it is Ezra Pound's "Hugh Selwyn Mauberley" that is cited—seems to complete a movement that began with the modernist response to World War II, and that has various manifestations in the Woolf of *Three Guineas,* the H.D. of *The Gift,* and the Lessing of *Four-Gated City.*

Rich's anger, explored for several of the poem's sections, emerges in the stern declaration exactly opposed to "Diving into the Wreck": "there are words I cannot choose again; / *humanism androgyny.*"[29] In "Natural Resources," then, the poet no longer seeks a term in which the positive elements of male and female can be reconciled, or, indeed, any term in which "man" is taken as the center, or part of the center, of the universe.[30] But more than that, debate about the permanent validity of humanism is current among radical thinkers, both socialist and feminist. It is not that this antihumanism implies nonhumanitarian behaviors, but rather that the universalizing assumptions of humanism about the needs and aspirations of all "(hu)mankind" are found to be bereft of meaning because they do not acknowledge people's formation as specific, historically rooted subjects. In her exposition of Louis Althusser's antihumanist position, Janet Wolff provides a gloss that can apply to Rich as well: that humanism wrongly posits people "who somehow pre-exist the contingencies of their material and social lives."[31]

But Rich's antihumanism has also coexisted with an unmediated appeal to myth. The debate between archetype and prototype—mythic and social dimensions of narrative—may recur in oscillation because these terms sum up two fundamental positions. Myth can be seen as a sacred or primal verity touched within the poem, a statement that by its very nature offers an unmediated gist beyond social grids and ideological expectations; indeed, it is construed as a way to transcend these. Mediation of any sort, including the social practices of language and literary convention, tends then to be overlooked or minimized. Language is seen as a function of nature or the body, both of which are treated as entities whose essential part is hardly touched by culture. Alternatively, myth can be viewed as narrative that is at root historically occasioned, related to questions of power and ideology, performing certain functions: "language generat[ing] reality in the inescapable context of power," in Donna Haraway's phrase.[32] The two positions are separated by their views of the possibility for historical change in narrative. These positions both come into Rich's work in the books of poetry (to date) that she has published since the appearance of *Poems Selected and New* in 1974, and are the subject of intense debate.[33]

These works also make specific reference to romance, among other plots and images by which women are culturally produced. *The Dream of a Common Language* draws on a new love relationship in the poet's life. And indeed, early poems in both *The Dream of a Common Language* and *A Wild Patience* present the two-woman couple in ways ranging from pure sensuality to wary marginality. Despite the power of this bond, the poems do not so much celebrate passion and yearning (for "*Tristan und Isolde* is scarcely the story," DCL, 33) as stand as a warning, even in the midst of personal bliss, not to make of that lesbian bond a *solitude à deux,* a thralldom, a privileged world. For, Rich says, even about passion and growing trust, "I can't call it life until we start to move / beyond this secret circle of fire" (*DCL,* 9). The 1981 and 1983 volumes use the lesbian couple as an ethical and intellectual situation in which probing questions can be asked by women together in a "laboratory," like Woolf's Chloe and Olivia. Typically, the poet establishes a bond not of coupledom but of "twainship" with other women, intellectually passionate and demanding of both herself and this sister a commitment to understanding and to struggle. So the lesbian couple is not a new form of romance, and the sexual tie is not its sole justification. "Women are made taboo to women—not just sexually, but as comrades, cocreators, coinspirators."[34] The passion in these poems is, then, not primarily for sensual fulfillment, but rather for creating the kind of social and community fulfillment among women that responds critically to that nineteenth-century narrative paradigm evoked in the allusion to the *Liebestod* of Tristan and Isolde.

Yet there is a subtle debate between two of the books as well, which rejoins the themes that have concerned us here. Some of the most ecstatic moments of *The Dream of a Common Language* and *A Wild Patience* are also their most ecstatic temptation: to be free of speech altogether, for it is a tainting script.[35] This setting aside of language comes at the contact of a daughter with a mythic mother: the Minoan snake goddess in "The Image"; the Eleusinian sprouting wheat in "Cartographies of Silence"; the "homesick" contact with the mother in "Transcendental Etude."

Speechlessness, the intuitive grasp of the body's codes and of nurturing, beautiful objects, all associated with the mother-daughter bond, are such a temptation because they seem safer and truer than a speech that has been culturally contaminated. To be free of speech is, of course, impossible, yet the yearning is still affirmed through the mythic imagination and the maternal body.

Rich's ideas about language express and are related to the search for a bond that is pre-gridded, natural, and therefore authentic. She hopes to know and speak from a voice of pure gesture and sensation:

> *If you can read and understand this poem*
> *send something back: a burning strand of hair*
> *a still-warm, still-liquid drop of blood.*

> *(WP, 7)*

As one part of this enterprise, Rich has outlined in "Sibling Mysteries" an alternative path out of the oedipal crisis, an account that does not equalize the maternal with the paternal in a bisexual oscillation. Rich postulates that the maternal is and can remain the parent of authority. The argument hopes to affirm a purely natural bond that exists between female bodies before culture has severed it, and to which one could return, if the veneer of oedipalization were stripped.

> The daughters never were
> true brides of the father
>
> the daughters were to begin with
> brides of the mother
>
> then brides of each other
> under a different law

> *(DCL, 52)*

The sense that better learning and knowing will occur in natural language inspires the end of *The Dream of a Common Language,* in which a woman walks away from "argument and jargon" and begins to piece together a quiltlike amalgam of natural materials, a witch's brew contrived for the white magic of female transformation.

Yet even a work of art that claims this natural discourse of silks, whiskers, and shells, insofar as it is made or constructed, insofar as acts of intention draw it together, is in contradiction to the poetics on which it claims to be based. The call for "no masks" and "no mythologies" is, after all, made up of acts of displacement to another story or the delegitimating of a dominant narrative in favor of the fictions of the muted. As Margaret Homans shrewdly notes, even "Diving into the Wreck," with its pointed rejection of the "book of myths," still shows the speaker's life dependent on her mediating face mask.[36] One may equally well note that Rukeyser's comments rejecting myths lead simply to a more pluralistic music and choreography, rejecting the modernist use of myth as scaffolding and the separation of mythopoesis and history in favor of an equally potent myth of immanence.[37]

Homans's criticism of certain contemporary women writers, Rich among them, is based on an argument about the inherent fictiveness of language. Language in its innermost structure (the relation of signifier to signified) draws on dualism and division; there is never any direct or natural correlation between word and thing, but only a set of conventional attachments, learned behaviors subtly deployed. Homans argues that there develop certain constructs based on this law of twos: opposition, which may valorize one side, not the other; hierarchy, setting one side above the other; appropriation, assimilating one side to the other. Faced with these formulations and struck by the fact that, as women, they are always the other side in dualistic systems, some women poets may try to exorcise these dualisms by fiat, declaring that they have done with their position in otherness, and therefore with fictiveness. They henceforth propose to live happily ever after in a unitary world where word does equal thing, and where women "tell the truth" about their lives as if a "truth" that exists beyond the fictions and languages in which it is told could be reached by special folk (in this case, females).[38] Homans's statement of the problem is elegantly accomplished.

With the search for a natural language being so thwarted by the nature of language itself, one may well ask why poets are thus tempted when they will inevitably be so deceived in the search for a pure discourse of things. Rich's activity in defining a female poetics offers some suggestion. Such a search seems to signal a rupture with the conventionalized correlations of word and thing, because the poet becomes aware of muted words that cannot be said, like "lesbian," aware of invisible things that are unaccounted for, like feelings in motherhood, or bonding between women. Such a poetics is, therefore, a signal of frustration with convention and a sign of ideological dissent, a desire to rewrite culture by the critical examination of the "natural"; that is, by uncovering that which our current social and linguistic practices currently exclude. The postulating of monistic discourse is, then, a poetics that signals ideological critique, the valorizing of oppositional in contrast to dominant.

The debate between gesture and language in Rich quickens in *A Wild Patience* and culminates in "Turning the Wheel," its final poem, where the debate is affiliated with archetypal mythic quest on one hand and prototypical historical research on the other, the spiritual truth tested by historical skepticism. The very title of this self-reflective poem indicates a change of direction. The poem is set in the Southwest, and, despite the Indians and the landscape, it conscientiously avoids primitivism and nostalgia, rejecting "an archetypal blur" of history turned into myth, the "false history" of a woman who does not have the courage to ask of texts and artifacts her particularist questions (*AWP*, 54, 53). Rather than making one-dimensional pictures of the Indian women who survive, colonized, half powerful and half self-hating, Rich instructs herself to "forget the archetypes . . . do not pursue / the ready-made abstraction, do not peer for symbols" (*AWP*, 56). Instead she evokes a flawed and self-contradictory reality.

This rejection of universals rejoins the theme of the book as a whole, continuing the twinning ties to women, yet examining difference, anger, pain, resistance, in order not to romanticize any kind of tie between women. Indeed, there are a number of overtly self-critical remarks in which Rich draws herself back from romanticizing women (as in the poem about Ethel Rosenberg), and there are as well poems that notably contain rifts or misunderstandings, or are critical of female heroes.

It is therefore consistent that at the end of "Turning the Wheel," Rich turns away and refuses to visit the majestic and intransigent Grand Canyon, "the female core of a continent." A visit to the Grand Canyon had seemed obligatory, because of the force that site had in Rich's imagination.

> Seeing those rocks   that road   in dreams   I know
> it is happening again   as twice while waking
> I am travelling to the edge   to meet the face
> of annihilating and impersonal time
> stained in the colors of a woman's genitals

> (*AWP*, 59)

While she begins by driving eagerly to this mythic place, willing to be transfixed by its massive symbol of time, sexuality, and gender, still on this one day, the journey is rejected: "Today I turned the wheel refused that journey" (*AWP*, 59). The reasons for the refusal are particular, intimate, immersed in a specific life's history, the discovery that the "world beyond time" would be too taxing to confront. When Rich makes the refusal of this iconic meeting, the debate between the prototypical and the archetypal seems (perhaps temporarily) to have resolved in favor of the historically and personally specific, not the symbolic.

The same concern to reassert continual journeys and the provisional in a meditative context of self-reflection and in the context of chosen communities occurs in *Sources;* even though it would be easy and gratifying to "rest among the beautiful and common weeds I can name," the task of such naming and journeying is ceaseless. "There is no finite knowing, no such rest" (*S*, 35). Rich is concerned here to reestablish the primacy for her work of the New England tradition of self-scrutiny, joined with an acknowledgment of the Jewish community, to which she had silently belonged. Self-scrutiny is one part of Rich's generally existentialist project: the lived ethics of "transcendence"—de Beauvoir's challenge in *The Second Sex* that women should claim choice, liberty, and enterprise and thereby transform the static polarization of (male) Self and (female) Other that has structured Western ideology. This claim of choice has been recast by Rich to end *Sources:*

> I mean knowing the world, and my place in it, not in
> order to stare with bitterness or detachment, but as a
> powerful and womanly series of choices: and here I
> write the words, in their fullness:
> powerful;   womanly.

(*S*, 35)

At the same time, by writing the word *womanly* with all that it implies of immanence and rootedness in matter, Rich disaffiliates from the pure transcendence that de Beauvoir idealized.[39]

As becomes especially clear from Rich's self-critical poems and from her lyrical discussions of history and myth, the debate between the true and the fictive, between a spiritual and historical stance, between "experience" and mediation, and between archetype and prototype has long structured Rich's work and may continue to express her versions of the project of twentieth-century women's writing.

NOTES

1. Virginia Woolf, "Professions for Women," *Collected Essays*, vol. 2 (New York: Harcourt, Brace and World, 1967), 44.

2. Denise Levertov, *O Taste and See* (New York: New Directions, 1964), 70.

3. Muriel Rukeyser, *The Collected Poems of Muriel Rukeyser* (New York: McGraw-Hill, 1978), 492. Abbreviated as *CP*.

4. The poem appears in Rich, *Poems Selected and New, 1950–1974* (New York: W. W. Norton, 1975), 47–51. Abbreviated as *PSN*. The citation is from Rich, "When We Dead Awaken: Writing As Re-Vision," *On Lies, Secrets, and Silence, Selected Prose, 1966–1978* (New York: W. W. Norton, 1979), 44. Abbreviated as *LSS*.

5. Rich's recounting of her own mother's history offers not only background and context for the portrait in the first section of "Snapshots," but confirmation, as well, of the pattern that was discussed in chapter 6: the role played by observation of the thwarted career of a maternal artist in the forming of the daughter's artistic ambition. "Once married, she gave up the possibility of a concert career, though for some years she went on composing, and she is still a skilled and dedicated pianist." *Of Woman Born: Motherhood as Experience and Institution* (New York: W. W. Norton, 1976), 221.

6. Two versions of the poem exist, each with different lines from Dickinson. "This is the gnat that mangles men" emphasizes the sapping of energy by diffusion; "My life had stood—a loaded gun" suggests explosive, possibly disciplined power. In "Vesuvius at Home: The Power of Emily Dickinson," Rich examines in 1975, years later than the poem, the canny strategies by which Dickinson accomplished her work. Domesticity and withdrawal to her family's house are viewed differently in "Snapshots" and in the essay.

7. As Rich stated in a 1972 interview with *The Saturday Review*, "The whole convention of lyric poetry is written in a sense as a misleading script for women" (22 April 1972, 56–59).

8. "When We Dead Awaken," *LSS*, 35.

9. *CP*, 527–35.

10. Denise Levertov, *To Stay Alive* (New York: New Directions, 1971), 29.

11. They shared more than that as well. During this period, as Levertov later recalled, Rukeyser was an exemplary personal figure. The poets went to Hanoi together in 1972 as activists in the antiwar movement, and several of Levertov's poems are dedicated to Rukeyser—"The Unknown" and "Joy" in *The Sorrow Dance* and "In Thai Binh (Peace) Province" in *The Freeing of the Dust*. Their relationship—"as

colleagues who became friends—fellow votaries of Poetry who were also mothers and political allies"—had a further dimension. "After my mother died in 1977, when I told Muriel forlornly that I felt myself to be a middle-aged orphan, she said, 'Oh, I'll adopt you. You'll be my Adopted Something.' She meant that and I felt it, felt warmed and strengthened." "On Muriel Rukeyser," *Light Up the Cave* (New York: New Directions, 1981), 194.

12. The poem is in *PSN,* 198–202. In 1973, Rich wrote: "The bombings, for example, if they have anything to teach us, must be understood in the light of something closer to home, both more private and painful, and more general and endemic, than the institutions, class, racial oppression, the hubris of the Pentagon, or the ruthlessness of a right-wing administration: the bombings are so wholly sadistic, gratuitous and demonic that they can finally be seen, if we care to see them, for what they are: acts of concrete sexual violence, an expression of the congruence of violence and sex in the masculine psyche." *LSS,* 109.

13. From *The Speed of Darkness, CP,* 435. Elly Bulkin reads this and other opening poems in this book as coming-out poems; Rukeyser participated in the 1978 lesbian poetry reading at the Modern Language Association. " 'A Whole New Poetry Beginning Here': Teaching Lesbian Poetry," *College English* 40, no. 8 (April 1979): 884–85.

14. "Orpheus," *CP,* 291–300.

15. Muriel Rukeyser, *The Life of Poetry* (New York: Current Books, 1949), discusses the composition of "Orpheus."

16. *CP,* 278–80, 498.

17. Denise Levertov, *Relearning the Alphabet* (New York: New Directions, 1970), 110–21. Abbreviated as *RA.* The poem is dated 1968–69.

18. From *Diving into the Wreck, Poems 1971–72,* reprinted in *PSN,* 196–98.

19. There are some uncanny resemblances between the imagery of Margaret Atwood's *Surfacing* and that of Rich's "Diving into the Wreck," which suggest either that Rich assimilated the novel within her poem (which was written in 1971, the year that Atwood was published in Canada), or, more likely, that the act of critique in which both writers were engaged led them to similar patterns of visualization. These include, in Atwood: the drowned brother's face; the father's camera; the album of pictographs and drawings that become instruction; the "forgetting the reason" for coming to the woods; and the drowned father/fetus/self who is confronted. In Rich: the "drowned face with open eyes"; the camera as part of the equipment; the "book of myths," which, read differently, become "maps"; the forgetting "what one is here for"; the dead body inside the wreck that must be investigated.

20. Erich Neumann, *The Origins and History of Consciousness,* Bollingen Series 42 (Princeton: Princeton University Press, 1954), 199.

21. This moment of fusion ("I am she: I am he") is, in a later poem, transposed and rearticulated, without heterosexuality. "*I am the lover and*

the loved, / home and wanderer, she who splits / firewood and she who knocks, a stranger / in the storm." "Transcendental Etude," in *The Dream of a Common Language, Poems 1974–77* (New York: W. W. Norton, 1978), 76. Abbreviated as *DCL.*

22. *LSS,* 183.

23. *The American Heritage Dictionary,* s.v. "ideal."

24. This process was publicly completed by 1975, when Rich published poems in the anthology *Amazon Poetry,* ed. Joan Larkin and Elly Bulkin (New York: Out and Out Books, 1975). This point is made by Judith McDaniel in *Reconstituting the World: The Poetry and Vision of Adrienne Rich* (New York: Spinsters, Ink, 1978).

25. See, for example, Charlotte Bunch: "*Lesbian-feminist theory,* as a critique of male supremacy and heterosexism, is a perspective, analysis and commitment that can be embraced by anyone, gay or straight, female or male—just as socialism or Pan-Africanism are theories that can be adopted by anyone regardless of race, sex or class." "Lesbian-Feminist Theory" (c. 1978), in *Women and the Politics of Culture,* ed. Michele Wender Zak and Patricia A. Moots (New York: Longman, 1983), 417–18.

26. Rich, "Compulsory Heterosexuality and Lesbian Existence," *Signs* 5, no. 4 (Summer 1980): 631–60. Rich's position is consistent with that held by Blanche Weisen Cook, " 'Women Alone Stir My Imagination': Lesbianism and the Cultural Tradition," *Signs* 4, no. 4 (Summer 1979): 718–39. See especially Cook's definition of lesbian: "Women who love women, who choose women to nurture and support and to create a living environment in which to work creatively and independently," 738. In the debate occasioned by Rich's essay, in *Signs* 7, no. 1, Ann Ferguson, criticizing as romanticized the overarching cross-cultural, cross-historical approach positing a "lesbian continuum," points out that if this perspective were applied too literally, women who had any nurturing or mutually interested connections with men—women like Virginia Woolf or H.D.—would be definitionally excluded from the category lesbian, which, given everything, would not see them whole. "Patriarchy, Sexual Identity, and the Sexual Revolution," *Signs* 7, no. 1 (Autumn 1981): 158–72.

27. In "One Is not Born but Made a 'Woman,' " (Paper delivered at the Simone de Beauvoir Conference, The Second Sex—Thirty Years After: A Commemorative Conference on Feminist Theory. New York, September 1979), Monique Wittig similarly insisted that "woman" is the name given to a female being who has been socially constructed and historically sculpted by patriarchal relations. What does one call the new woman who has formulated herself in a critical resistance to patriarchy? Wittig too answers *lesbian.* The point is similarly polemical and lexical, offering a new name with old connotations, and using the force of the taboo to declare one's rupture from the dominant. The implication that lesbianism is the highest stage of critique occurs in passing.

28. *DCL*, 60–67. Other moments of reassessment, which I do not have the space to discuss here, can be traced in Rich's writing on Emily Dickinson throughout her career. When she writes the poem "I Am in Danger—Sir—" (1964), she characterizes Dickinson as "you, a woman, masculine in single-mindedness"; when she writes "The Spirit of Place," with its section on Dickinson, she corrects the attribution of singlemindedness to a "masculine" sensibility by giving firm attention to the poet's maternal lineage and her defining love for Sue Gilbert. *PSN*, 84, and *A Wild Patience Has Taken Me This Far* (New York: W. W. Norton, 1981), 40–45 (abbreviated as *AWP*). Furthermore, she vows to reject any future discussion of Dickinson, condemning these exercises as self-centered acts of appropriation, insensitive to Dickinson's desire for privacy.

29. The word *androgyne* also occurs in "The Stranger," written in 1972, the same year as "Diving into the Wreck"; the line "I am the androgyne" refers to a new fused person. This poem does not appear in Rich's *Poems Selected and New*, because, as Rich has commented, androgyny now seems to be a "liberal" solution to the woman question, one that cares more about liberating men than women. See Elly Bulkin, "An Interview with Adrienne Rich (October 1976)," *Conditions One* (1977): 61–62. Susan Friedman has discovered a parallel kind of self-critical change undertaken to deemphasize interest in male transformation or situation. The version of "When We Dead Awaken: Writing as Re-Vision" in *LSS* removes a section that had once evinced a welcoming interest in male change. "H.D. and Adrienne Rich: An Intertextual Study," *Signs* 9 no. 2 (Winter 1983): 228–45.

30. The degree to which this represents a shift can be measured by Rich's comment (1972) about mythic narrative (e.g., in *Wuthering Heights*), which offers an "archetypal bond between the split fragments of the psyche, the masculine and feminine elements ripped apart and longing for reunion," *On Lies, Secrets, and Silence*, 90. This remark provides a context for "Diving into the Wreck"; at that point, Rich considered that the hierogamic version of a heterosexual love plot could extend into the romantic quest for soul making. Marriage could be a "continuation of her self-creation," in *Jane Eyre*. At the same time, this essay ("Jane Eyre: The Temptations of a Motherless Woman") was the first to discuss maternal-sororal ties as a major source of soul making in that novel.

31. Janet Wolff, *The Social Production of Art* (London: Macmillan, 1981), 130.

32. Donna J. Haraway, "In the Beginning was the Word: The Genesis of Biological Theory," *Signs* 6, no. 3 (Spring 1981): 479.

33. Already referred to, these are *DCL*, *AWP*, and *Sources* (Woodside, Calif.: The Heyeck Press, 1983), a poem in twenty-three parts, dated August 1981–August 1982 (abbreviated as *S*). This may be a good time to remark that with Rich, as with several other authors discussed in

this book (Lessing, Walker, Brooks, Atwood, Piercy, Russ, and Morrison among them), we are, at this date in 1983, talking about living writers, whose capacity for change, modulation, reiteration, externally directed debate, and internally produced self-criticism should not be underestimated.

34. Rich, *Of Woman Born,* 255.

35. Joanne Feit Diehl discusses this desire and Rich's distrust of language in " 'Cartographies of Silence': Rich's *Common Language* and the Woman Poet," *Feminist Studies* 6, no. 3 (Fall 1980): 539–44.

36. Margaret Homans, *Women Writers and Poetic Identity: Dorothy Wordsworth, Emily Brontë, and Emily Dickinson* (Princeton: Princeton University Press, 1980), 223.

37. I have argued this in an early version of this chapter, in *Shakespeare's Sisters,* ed. Sandra M. Gilbert and Susan Gubar (Bloomington: Indiana University Press, 1979), 280–300.

38. Indeed, Homans's book suggests an essential project for feminist poetics: "Hierarchy in language must be undone in other ways than by denying otherness," 40.

39. These critical questions about de Beauvoir were elegantly posed by Mary Lowenthal Felstiner, in "Seeing *The Second Sex* through the Second Wave," *Feminist Studies* 6, no. 2 (Summer 1980): 267–71.

GEORGE BOWERING

Denise Levertov

In the two hundred years prior to the writings of Emily Dickinson there were no women poets of prominence in North America. Between the times of Dickinson and Denise Levertov there have been a few, though most of the great women Modernists wrote fiction. H.D. is the best female poet in the short history of the United States, but vital work came from Marianne Moore and Gertrude Stein. The highly overrated poems of Edna St. Vincent Millay and Amy Lowell have long faded from sight except in the rose-tinted glasses of academe. Lorine Niedecker and Marya Zaturenska and Mina Loy helped to make the way for the many fine women poets working in the last part of the twentieth century.

But in the middle of the century, and into the sixties and seventies and eighties, Denise Levertov, who came to America in 1948, commands the grove. In what was to become known as the New American Poetry, she was only one among the leaders and champions, but her poetry, like Robert Creeley's, persuaded the new and common reader that it was accessible, while being at the same time in the post-Williams modern stream.

In addition, her work through the end of the sixties was all centered on the religious view, as I have described it in reference to Emily Dickinson's poetry. She extended the idea of poetry *as* religion, writing: "I believe poets are instruments on which the power of poetry plays" (*The Poet in the World,* 3). But she says that poets are not thus passive; they are also makers, so that poetry comes from shared activities, human with hobgoblin, mind with mystery.

Denise Levertov's poetry shows a mind's activity far different from that of Anne Bradstreet. Mrs. Bradstreet was surrounded by family and community thoroughly Puritan and powerful in the Puritan isolation of New England. Denise Levertov traces her descent on her mother's side from a Welsh tailor and mystic,

---

Excerpted from George Bowering, "Three Ladies of Spirit in New England," *Imaginary Hands: Essays* (Edmonton, Alberta: NeWest Press, 1988), 73–94.

243

Angell Jones of Mold, and on her father's side from Russian Hasids, the last of which, her father, experienced a conversion to Christianity and a desire to join Judaism with Christianity. That varied background or confusion may be taken as a representative determinant for the nature of American poetry in the last half-century, in which the names of the poets themselves indicate that spiritual considerations will be liberated from any mainline English Protestant domination: Levertov, Zukofsky, Ginsberg, Corso, Kerouac, Reznikoff, Rexroth, Oppenheimer, etc. There is something here that may be analogous to the situation in American music, where some of the names may be English, but the colours reflect truths that were not self-evident in eighteenth-century Massachusetts.

Denise Levertov is also confronted by the nature of spiritual unconsciousness among the whole community of people in the twentieth century—or rather, *we* are. *With Eyes at the Back of Our Heads* (1960) is the name of her first widely distributed American book. The title poem is modernly elusive about the aims, chances, prospects, of mortal folk, but adds that elusiveness to Emily Dickinson's espousal of nature. In the poem we hear an interesting modern development of an image of clothing. Whereas Dickinson had imaged her faith as raiment torn and resewn to fit comfortably, Levertov writes of hers this way:

> The doors before us in a facade
> that perhaps has no house in back of it
> are too narrow, and one is set high
> with no doorsill. The architect sees
>
> the imperfect proposition and
> turns eagerly to the knitter.
> Set it to rights!
> The knitter begins to knit.
>
> For we want
> to enter the house, if there is a house,
> to pass through the doors at least
> into whatever lies beyond them,
>
> we want to enter the arms
> of the knitted garment. As one
> is re-formed, so the other,
> in proportion.
>
> (*With Eyes at the Back of Our Heads*, 9)

The eyes at the back of our head see that while we are walking toward the narrow, maybe deceiving doors of some indefinite palace before us, we are walking away from clear beauty and loveliness behind us on this earth.

A good portion of Denise Levertov's poetry is given to celebrating colors and flavors, the sustenance of the senses. One of her early books is called *O Taste and See.* She feels no guilt for these appetites, as Anne Bradstreet would, and she feels no need to be defiant about them, as Emily Dickinson would. The celebration of the senses is not done under the reproachful eyes of a paternal God. The modern poet does not often call God by that name except in irony or other rhetoric. Levertov seeks unstated spiritual significance in emotional honesty, precise attention to the natural, exercise of pity, mercy, peace and love. Not that God is dead, unless by that is meant that he no longer wears Talmudic and Mosaic disguises and fright-beards. Levertov uses images of nature's things to speak of more abstract feelings, but not with such consciously stated intentions as are to be found in Thoreau and Dickinson:

> I like to find
> what's not found
> at once, but lies
>
> within something of another nature,
> in repose, distinct.
>
> ("Pleasures,"
> *With Eyes at the Back of Our Heads,* 17)

For Dickinson that would include the pearl, the just and our thought. Something like those might be the twentieth-century self:

> "Are we
> what we think we are or are we
> what befalls us?"
> ("Seems Like We Must Be Somewhere Else,"
> *With Eyes at the Back of Our Heads,* 19)

That is going at least a step beyond Emily Dickinson's feeling that God is knowable.

Many of Levertov's poems express and name the loneliness of the human individual, so often a realization of modern writers that it may be taken as true for us, at least to the extent that the Puritan world-picture seemed true in Massachusetts in 1650. But it is that loneliness that forces the imaginative act—the individual will fall down inside herself or she will try to find some possible communion. In Levertov's poem called "The Communion," the act is not made between a petitioning servant and a superior god, but as "an accord" among things living: the poet, a frog, a bowl of plums. In the act of communion the poems tend to open moments outward, as do those of Emily Dickinson, with the difference that here there is no talk of Eternity. Rather the moment may teach the observation of the world as it is, even surprising, even irrational, even if the old values and meanings are violated:

> The cat is eating the roses:
> that's the way he is.
> Don't stop him, don't stop
> the world going round,
> that's the way things are.
> The third of May
> was misty; fourth of May
> who knows. Sweep
> the rose-meat up, throw the bits
> out in the rain.
> He never eats
> every crumb, says
> the hearts are bitter.
> That's the way he is, he knows
> the world and the weather.

> ("The Sage,"
> *With Eyes at the Back of Our Heads*, 29)

One of Levertov's poems is called "Everything That Acts Is Actual" (*Selected Poems*, 13). Her greatest debt as a poet is to William Carlos Williams, the champion of what he called plain language and ordinary concrete things as the materials of poetic reference. People have flapped down on the kind of poem that results, saying that mundane materials do not permit any flight of the imagination in the poem. But the eyes and the other senses may be as close to the divine as any speculative brain, if not closer. The shaman's sticks and bones are as much signs of human spiritual imagination as abstracted theology may be. The actual is in the act, and in the soul's music that emerges, as

Wallace Stevens knew, plunking on his blue guitar. Denise Levertov may have had Blake's "Everything that is, is Holy" in mind when she made her above title, and the muse is watching not only at the inkwell:

> The authentic! I said
> rising from the toilet seat.
> The radiator in rhythmic knockings
> spoke of the rising steam.
> The authentic, I said
> breaking the handle of my hairbrush as I
> brushed my hair in
> rhythmic strokes: That's it,
> that's joy, it's always
> a recognition, the known
> appearing fully itself, and
> more itself than one knew.
>
> ("Matins," *Poems 1960–1967*, 59)

With no expressed thoughts of afterlife, and hence no impulse to call this life either a vanity or a dream, the poet keeps eyes open and walks "deeper into Imagination's / holy forest." She uses the biblical image of Jacob's ladder as a title of a book (*The Jacob's Ladder*, 1961) and an image to show the nature of the imagination's ascent. Even the angels ascending and descending the steps depend on the mind that has reinvented that spiritual conveyance. The ladder is not "a radiant evanescence." Rather:

> a man climbing
> must scrape his knees, and bring
> the grip of his hands into play. The cut stone
> consoles his groping feet. Wings brush past him.
> The poem ascends.
>
> ("The Jacob's Ladder," *Poems 1960–1967*, 39)

Continuing the movement of Emily Dickinson and Walt Whitman, Levertov denies all separation between the material and the divine.

Thus too the concept of death is here much different from the Puritan one. Death is not an alternative to humble life, nor is it a pathway to Eternal life. Life and death are inadequate and partial names for the process perceived in mercy and love:

The pastor
of grief and dreams

guides his flock towards
the next field

with all his care.
He has heard

the bell tolling
but the sheep

are hungry and need
the grass, today and

every day. Beautiful
his patience, his long

shadow, the rippling
sound of the flock moving

along the valley.
("A Cure of Souls," *O Taste and See,* 20)

Paradise is the endless movie of the world, perceived within the individual, perceived with a mystical metaphor in which the individual apprehends that there is no final cosmic separation between the interior history and the exterior forever.

In the seventies Levertov's poems tended more and more to express popular protest against political targets, and to use the language of the "movement," but in the midsixties they tended toward mystic-romantic subjects, influenced as they were by the work of Robert Duncan (who was himself to turn to the Vietnam War and other political issues); they may be said to be based on the early Hasidic sense of mystery, and the devotion to "the actual." There is less direct talk to the soul's experience than in the poems of the fifties, more making of ritual, more arranging of the magic materials by one who functions as a spellbinder or alchemist. Undescribed spirit-figures seem to be moving about the daily house and forest. In "The Prayer" the poet tells how in Greece she prayed to Apollo, and was probably heard instead by the goat-god.

The mysteries are never merely anterior to people. They are part of them. In "Earth Psalm" the poet worships the mortal after saying that she "could replace / God for awhile" (*O Taste and See,* 80). (The fact that she puts the word "replace" at the end of a very short line suggests the literal, as re-place.) The mysteries are not something to be nervous of as they were to the Puritan poet, just as reason is not now man's highest attribute or gift on earth. Writing about H.D., Levertov mentioned an imaginative act that would have repelled Anne Bradstreet: "not to flood darkness with light so that darkness is destroyed, but to *enter into* darkness, mystery, so that it is experienced" (*The Poet in the World,* 246). (Levertov's critical language is always simple.) Mrs. Bradstreet would have called that a pagan step, over-asserting as always, but touching some truth. (I know that I sound unkind to Mrs. Bradstreet, but think about the way her community would treat us.)

For Denise Levertov's views on reason and poetry, see her article, "An Approach to Public Poetry Listenings" (*Light Up the Cave*), in which she appeals against overrationalizing of an approach to or from poetry, and the damage done by the New Criticism and textbook poets. The poems in *The Jacob's Ladder* attend to diffuse divinity, seen in action between a human being (his body and all) and all things, none perfect, none theoretical. "Come into Animal Presence" is the title of one poem. The moon is not perfect and cold. It is flawed. The flawed human sight picks out intensities and unusual lights in the common world.

Emily Dickinson's image of a humanized God is remembered in Levertov's "absurd angel of happiness." In "The Novices" (from *O Taste and See*) the speaker watches communicants enter the woods to find a mystery which they neither fear nor try to explain. In this world the child and the primitive see eidetically, as Whitman would have it, without systems of abstract enquiry, and that is the way to encounter moments of illumination. While she is hosing dirt off an old brick wall (one with a history, presumably), Denise Levertov the poet sees an

> archetype
> of the world always a step
> beyond the world, that can't
> be looked for, only
> as the eye wanders,
> found.
>
> ("The Garden Wall," *O Taste and See,* 60)

Serendipity instead of doctrine. Or the doctrine of Duncan's wandering eye.

I think that what may have been coming clear is that Denise Levertov represents a twentieth-century American cosmos (poetical) quite different from those represented by the two earlier women. This is true not only because of her exotic origin. The American artist in the seventeenth century tended to draw from two places outside America—England and the Classical Mediterranean. The Transcendentalists added German romanticism, and flirted with their own peculiar notions of Brahmanism. After the middle of the twentieth century, through mass print and superelectronics and jet stream, the New England poet draws on eclectic nodes. Levertov's poems are made in Maine, but also in Russia, Mexico, Greece, and Egypt. She, like Bradstreet and Dickinson, has her important New England influences or associations—Charles Olson, Robert Creeley, John Weiners. But literary United States is no longer lodged in Boston, or Massachusetts, or New England. Those are unrealistic geographical and theological determinants. There is little doubt that Levertov's quasi-pantheism has some of its sources in New England thought (and she did use Emersonian language in calling her poetry organic), but it is part of an interior cosmos that also houses mysteries from further East. (See "A Ring of Changes" in *With Eyes at the Back of Our Heads*.) When Levertov says

> let the oranges
> ripen, ripen above you,
> you are living too, one
> among the dark multitude—
>
> ("Under the Tree,"
> *With Eyes at the Back of Our Heads*, 46)

we hear of a process quite different from Anne Bradstreet's "Meditations," those rigid allegories. We see a development of poetic sensibilities, from simile to metaphor. Emily Dickinson made many poems in which she rides in angel-directed vehicles of the sky, and Levertov says:

> I in my balloon
> light where the wind
> permits a landing,
> in my own province.
>
> ("An Ignorant Person,"
> *With Eyes at the Back of Our Heads*, 50)

—which is not necessarily Manhattan or a county of Maine.

Religiously, if we are now using that term, Levertov seems to move especially to gods of fertility, of the natural cycle, of death as part and motive of life—the Mexican god of Spring, Xochipilli, for instance. One of the most frequently seen images in the Levertov poem is a seed. In the sixties the poems concentrated on the sexual nature of a woman in conjunction with the rest of the universe:

> The moon is a sow
> and grunts in my throat
> ("Song for Ishtar," *O Taste and See,* 3)

Levertov could take advantage of the twentieth-century consciousness of archetypes that speak from mortals' feelings about mysteries; not being constricted by Christian allegory, she could draw on mankind's whole world of magic and ritual. Modernism made it possible for the poet to choose her tradition. Levertov sees a snake, for instance, as good and beautiful, and not only with Emily Dickinson's paganlike perversity. She hardly ever speaks of God, except as he appears in a painting, or folklore, as part of someone else's spiritual scene.

In her earliest poems she often spoke of poetry as religion in a Dickinsonian sense. "I long for poems of an inner harmony in utter contrast to the chaos in which they exist" (*The Poet in the World,* 3), she once said. Her position there was similar to that of Yeats, whose eclectic spookiness always seemed to have a Christian base. In the poem "Art," she said that she wanted artists to work with "hard, strong materials," to strive for longevity in a flowing and malleable world (*The Poet in the World,* 129)—art as alternative to the faults in the mortal world. Very Yeatsian.

But later, while not disposing of the concrete and homely materials, she came to a position in her "Three Meditations," a poem on the purpose of a poet, at which she agrees with the emblem she takes from a poem by Charles Olson:

> the only object is
> a man, carved
> out of himself, so wrought he
> fills his given space, makes
> traceries sufficient to
> others' needs
> (here is

```
            social action, for the poet,
            anyway, his
            politics, his
            news)
               ("Three Meditations," Poems 1960–1967, 31)
```

That may correspond in her ethic to the Puritan idea of fulfilling God's purpose. Here we see something else about the poet's spiritual position in America. Anne Bradstreet was spokeswoman for the religious norms of her community. Emily Dickinson chose to worship God at home. In "The Grace-Note," Denise Levertov shows a Sabbath scene in which an underground artist stands in the shape of the Crucified while a cop frisks him, looking for a sacramental herb the community's lawmakers do not condone. "Nothing / is new to him and he is not afraid" (*Poem 1960–1967*, 56).

There is a curious poem near the end of *O Taste and See* that seems to suggest the other two women I have been referring to. It is called "In Mind":

```
            There's in my mind a woman
            of innocence, unadorned but

            fair-featured, and smelling of
            apples or grass. She wears

            a utopian smock or shift, her hair
            is light brown and smooth, and she

            is kind and very clean without
            ostentation—
                        but she has
            no imagination.
                              And there's a
            turbulent moon-ridden girl

            or old woman, or both,
            dressed in opals and rags, feathers

            and torn taffeta,
            who knows strange songs—

            but she is not kind.
                                 (O Taste and See, 71)
```

In retaining the homely materials, and walking deep into the sacred forest of the imagination, Denise Levertov is looking for a way to be the complete woman and poet, spiritually whole in a world that looks fragmented in any intellectual or philosophical scan.

What seems to be required is an admission that there are no final certainties that remove the merest responsibility from the individual:

> It could be what I'm waiting for is
> not here at all.
>
> ("Notes of a Scale,"
> *Collected Earlier Poems 1940–1960,* 103)

—as well as complete self-reliance such as the Transcendentalists never dreamed was needed in a century nowhere as terrifying as this one. Twentieth-century man is irremediably alone in a world he cannot hope to justify, and his spiritual resources are called upon to make him brave with no theoretical rewards for bravery. Denise Levertov's model for that brave man or artist is the blind man of her poem, "A Solitude," which ends with these words:

> and now he says he can find his way. He knows
> where he is going, it is nowhere, it is filled
> with presences. He says, *I am.*
>
> (*Poems 1960–1967,* 72)

Levertov would go on to give more and more of her attention to the politics of the peacemakers, but she would never give up the forest, and she would never give up the spirit that lives in it. Her 1984 volume was called *Oblique Prayers.* Its last section was called "Of God and of the Gods." The poet's sense of life's lightness and the endurance of the mystery are the frames and substance of a poem called "Of Being":

> I know this happiness
> is provisional:
>
>> the looming presences—
>> great suffering, great fear—
>
>> withdraw only
>> into peripheral vision:

but ineluctable this shimmering
of wind in the blue leaves:

this flood of stillness
widening the lake of sky:

this need to dance,
this need to kneel:
                    this mystery:
                        (*Oblique Prayers*, 86)

PART FIVE *Religion*

ROBERT DUNCAN

Denise Levertov and the Truth of Myth

"The sentimentality destroys some of the poems," a recent mentor of poetic proprieties writes of Denise Levertov's work:

> It is not sentimentality about the poor, her troubles, dying rabbits or sunsets, but rather sentimentality about words like "seraphic" and "demonic." Subway entrances become "steps to the underworld." In *From the Roof* she says: "who can say / the crippled broom-vendor yesterday, who passed / just as we needed a new broom, was not / one of the Hidden Ones?"

"Who indeed?" then the contemptuous critic sneers. Does he suppose he is dismissing out of hand the silly personal fancy of the poetess? He seems ignorant of the world of Jewish mysticism, the generations of a living community to which Denise Levertov's imagination here belongs, and into which, through her father, rabbi and then Christian priest, translator of the Zohar, she was born. But he is not ignorant, for referring to another poem, "Illustrious Ancestors," he grows scornful here of her pretension as he sees it to some spiritual claim. Actually, in the poem, remembering her paternal ancestor the Rav of Northern White Russia and her maternal ancestor Angell Jones of Mold, she lays no claim but "Well, I would like to make, / thinking some line still taut between me and them, / poems direct as what the birds said,

> hard as a floor, sound as a bench,
> mysterious as the silence when the tailor
> would pause with his needle in the air.

But for the modern demythologizing mind, our sense of a life shared with the beings of a household, our sense of belonging to generations of spirit, our ancestral pieties, must be put aside. And then, back of the critic's outrage at this poem, was the fact that he was confronted again by such as the broom vendor: for meditations of Angell Jones, Denise Levertov tells us, "were sewn into coats and britches."

"In the rather prosaic life of these poems," the critic protests: "the truth is that a broom vendor is a broom vendor." He does not seem aware that it is in his own eyes that the life of these poems becomes "rather prosaic" nor that he shows forth in his contempt for the thought at all that a mere broom vendor might be "one of the Hidden Ones" a hubris that is fearful.

In the belief in the Hidden Zaddik, the divine wisdom that the least of men may be illumined by, the Chassidic masters speak not only to the Jewish community but to our common humanity. In the fairytales of every people there are stories of those who will not recognize in the wretched and contemptible even, the presence of a divine life. A little Clod of Clay, "trodden with the cattle's feet," sings in Blake's poem:

> Love seeketh not Itself to please,
> Nor for itself hath any care,
> But for another gives its ease,
> And builds a Heaven in Hell's despair.

"That is only a fairytale! The truth is . . ." Our modern-minded critic here is that very proud, ugly and ungracious stepsister, eager to see through the pretentiousness of things, who, directed to the source of treasure, finds Mother Hulda to be only a tiresome old housewife and the work that Mother Hulda asks of her to be no more than dreary tasks. Our whole American Way of Life is designed to save the householder from his household myths, from the lifestory of working in which he has his communion with the house; as in the factory, the worker, no longer a maker, is removed from his work. Works become commodities, and the ends of labor, not in the grains of the field or the goods produced, but in the wages, benefits and social approval earned. Tables and chairs, "the house, the fruit, the grape," that the poet Rilke saw, "into which the hope and meditation of our forefathers had entered," become props. "Now there come crowding over from America empty, indifferent things, pseudo-things, dummy-life," Rilke writes: "The animated, experienced things that share our lives are coming to an end and cannot be replaced."

It is the very idea that there is a miraculous grace ever about us, a mystery of person, that our modern critic refuses to allow. Personality takes the place of the individual living soul. The broom vendor or the Vietnamese Communist has not earned or has forfeited his reality as a person. "A holy man becomes a holy man only by incredible physical sacrifice," Denise Levertov's critic admonishes. This is the very voice of the Protestant ethic as Weber defined it in his *Capitalism and the Protestant Ethic*. The presumption can only increase:

> Denise Levertov wants to have a prosaic housewiferly life, and find her kitchen step-ladder in Jacob's Ladder. It won't work. Her reading of the lives of saints is sentimental.

Everywhere there is the ready suspicion and accusation that the poet has not really *earned* or *deserved* to have wonder manifest in the poem, as if wonder came from some power of the writer's and was not a grace recognized by the writer in the reality of things. The world then is filled with "prosaic" things, broom vendors, housewiferly life, and kitchen stepladders, that do not deserve our poetic attentions, or that need to be seen as deep images of the psyche before they become poetic. As things in themselves, they won't work.

For career poets, both the Jacob's Ladder, the stairway of rosy stone "that takes / a glowing tone of softness," that Denise Levertov sees in her poem, where angels' feet "only glance in their tread, and need not / touch the stone," but where a man "climbing / must scrape his knees, and bring / the grip of his hands into play," and the household kitchen ladder, are high-minded or trivial sentimentalities in light of the very real ladder of status. Where, looking upward, the ambitious professional sees spirits elevated above their just deserts and, looking downward, sees spirits who had better not put on airs.

JOAN F. HALLISEY

Denise Levertov's "Illustrious Ancestors"

The Hassidic Influence

Denise Levertov's work is ordinarily seen in the mainstream of American literature. She has been placed, on occasion, in the Emersonian visionary tradition.[1] In recent years, she has been clearly recognized as a poet who refuses to be silent in times of political and social crises.[2] The multicultural aspect of her work, however, has been, for the most part, unexplored.

Levertov speaks, with pride, of her multicultural background in her essay, "The Sense of Pilgrimage," in *The Poet in the World* and in her memoir about her mother, "Beatrice Levertoff," in her recently published collection of prose works, *Light Up the Cave*. In the earlier reflection, the poet makes reference to an early poem, "Illustrious Ancestors" (*Overland to the Islands*), which she believes reveals the "definite and peculiar destiny" that she and her sister shared by their having among their ancestors two men who were living during the same period (late 1700s and early 1800s) but in very different cultures, who had "preoccupations which gave them a basic kinship (had they known of one another and had [they] been able to cross the barriers of language and religious prejudice)."[3] Denise and Olga felt that this "kinship" must be recognized in heaven or that somehow on earth it would be "unified and redeemed" through them.

One of her paternal ancestors, Schneour Zalman, "The Rav of Northern White Russia,"[4] was the founder of the Habad branch of Hasidim, and the other, in her mother's ancestral line, was Angell Jones of Mold, a tailor, teacher, and preacher to whom Daniel Owen, "the Welsh Dickens," was apprenticed. The shop of Angell Jones's son (the poet's great uncle) served as a kind of literary and intellectual salon in the 1870s.[5] Levertov believes that the presence of figures like these in a person's imagination

Reprinted from *MELUS*, 9, no. 4 (Winter 1982): 5–11.

can help to create a kind of "personal mythology" and function as a source of confidence and inspiration for the artist.[6]

Denise Levertov's most immediate "Illustrious Ancestors," her parents, Paul and Beatrice Levertoff, were themselves story-tellers, writers, and her mother an artist, who encouraged their daughters to develop this "kind of personal mythology" by listening, reading, and writing. The elder Levertoffs' lives were also an obvious source of inspiration to their daughters. In "Beatrice Levertoff," Levertov tells us that in 1910, Beatrice Spooner-Jones left Wales to go to Constantinople as a teacher. Before long she met Paul Levertoff, a young Russian Jew who had "converted to Christianity and had begun his lifelong task of attempting to reconcile Christians and Jews."[7] They were soon engaged, returned to Wales to meet Beatrice's relations, were then married in London, and went to live in Warsaw, which was then part of the Russian Empire. From Warsaw they went to Germany, where they eventually became prisoners of war, under house arrest, in Leipzig. After the Armistice, they were "displaced persons" in Denmark before they were able to cross the mined North Sea to England and, eventually, settle for many years in the London area. In the two decades that followed, Mrs. Levertoff educated her daughters at home; wrote a novella and an unpublished children's novel; and worked long and selflessly rescuing refugees from Hitler and finding homes and work for them in Britain.[8] (A paper remains to be written about Denise Levertov's dearest and most influential "Illustrious Ancestor," her mother.) The Levertoffs' consciousness of their own "roots" and their commitment to justice and reconciliation in their lifelong "search for community" deeply touched the poet. Her own life and work are a credible testimony to this influence.

Levertov remembers the many hours that her parents spent reading aloud to each other, as well as to the children, during those London years. Among the books and tales that most early affected her imagination were Bunyan's *The Pilgrim's Progress* and Anderson's *The Snow Queen and The Bell*. She was also listening to the stories and novels of Andrew Lang, Beatrix Potter, Willa Cather, Dickens, Jane Austen, and the Brontës, and reading, with her sister, the poetry of Auden. And it was at this time, too, that Paul Levertoff was telling his family the Hasidic tales,[9] whose influence this study will examine.

As we learn from her 1965 interview with Walter Sutton and from my own unpublished 1977 interview with the poet, Denise

Levertov was obviously moved by Martin Buber's *Tales of the Hasidim:*

> Hasidism has given me since childhood a sense of marvels, of wonder. . . . The Hasidim were a lot like the Franciscans, although in both movements there was a recognition and joy in the physical world. And a sense of wonder at creation, and I think I've always felt something like that. . . . I think that's what poems are all about.[10]

In his Preface to the Tales, Buber speaks of the belief of the Hasidim as a "joy in the world as it is, in every hour of life in that world, as that hour is." Levertov's response indicates that she is at ease with the "belief"—and, indeed, her own poetry often *does* portray a sense of wonder along with "a recognition and joy in the physical world."

One feels this "sense of wonder," particularly, in Levertov's later poetry in which she considers the myth "numinous"—"spiritually elevated."[11] In this poetry in which the myth is "numinous" and in her response to the Hasidic tales there is a sense of the sacred glimpsed in and through the particular instance of the momentary, the secular, and the worldly. In her poem "Notes of a Scale," the persona tries to interpret the "physical world" / "the painting within itself" through "open windows looking down"—"at noon with twilight overtones."[12] The boy/the fisherman in the distance "maintains dialog with his heart," while balancing his fishing rod—joyful in his being, his "doing":

> A glass brimming, not spilling,
> the green trees
> practising their art.
> 　　　　　"A wonder
> 　　　from the true world,"
> he who accomplished it
> 　　　"overwhelmed with the wonder
> which rises out of his doing."

Levertov's note for the poem refers the reader to "The True Wonder," an anecdote of Rabbi Elimélekh of Lijensk in Buber's *Tales: The Early Masters.* Part of this anecdote is relevant to Levertov's appreciation of the legacy of "joy in the physical world . . . and wonder at creation" that she received from the Hasidim:

> But those who work something because God gives them power to do it know of no whence and no how, and the wonder which arises out of their doing, overwhelms them themselves. And this is what Pharaoh meant "Do not pretend to me. Get you a wonder from the true world so that it may testify for you."[13]

One *does* get a "sense of the sacred" in the "testimonies" of this anecdote and poem—glimpsed through a particular instance of the momentary, the secular, the worldly.

For many of the Hasidic teachers and Levertov, "Man is [in Emerson's words] a center for nature running out threads of relation through everything."[14] Note the words from the *Tales of the Hasidim: Later Masters* that Levertov used as the epigraph for *The Jacob's Ladder,* "The Ladder":

> Rabbi Moshe (of Kobryn) taught: It is written: "And he dreamed and behold a ladder set up on earth." The "he" is every man. Every man must know: I am clay, I am one of the countless shards of clay, but "the top of it reached to heaven"— my soul reaches to heaven; "and behold the angels of God ascending and descending on it"—even the ascent and descent of the angels depend on my deeds.[15]

Levertov's poem, "The Jacob's Ladder," speaks to her understanding that, in fact, much *does* "depend on [her] deeds." Jacob's "ladder"/"stairway" is not just

> a thing of gleaming strands
> a radiant evanescence
> for angels' feet that only glance in their tread,
>   and need not
> touch the stone.
>
> It is of stone.
> . . . .
> A stairway of sharp
> angles, solidly built.
> One sees that the angels must spring
> down from one step to the next, giving a little
> lift of wings:

and a man climbing
must scrape his knees, and bring
the grip of his hands into play. The cut stone
consoles his groping feet. Wings brush past him.
The poem ascends.[16]

In my own interview with Levertov and in subsequent corre-
spondence and conversation, it was clear that she does, in fact,
see the poet as "a center for nature running out threads of rela-
tion through everything"—and that she considers this task a
responsibility that is both precarious and awe-filled. The "scrap-
[ing]" and "groping" are crucial for the "birth process" ("ascen-
[sion]") of the poem.

Levertov's poet/"man climbing" would become the dreamer/
visionary of "The Broken Sandal"—a poem that echoes the
above-mentioned anecdote of Rabbi Moshe and the sentiment of
"The Jacob's Ladder":

Dreamed the thong of my sandal broke.
Nothing to hold it to my foot.
How shall I walk?
                    Barefoot?
The sharp stones, the dirt. I would
hobble.
And—
Where was I going?
Where was I going I can't
go to now, unless hurting?
Where am I standing, if I'm
to stand still now?[17]

In "Sparks," the poet speaks of receiving a poem from a poet
who is feeling the "sharp stones" and "hurting"—but *not* "stand-
[ing] still":

A letter with it
discloses, in words and between them,
a life opening, fearful, fearless,
thousand-eyed, a field
of sparks that move swiftly
in darkness, to and from
a center. He is beginning
to live.[18]

During a 1963 reading Levertov said that this poem relates to "being where we are and still doing all we can."[19] In the Hasidic tale, "Most Important," we are told that soon after the death of Rabbi Moshe, Rabbi Mendel of Kotzk asked one of his disciples: "What was most important to your teacher?" The disciple thought and then replied: "Whatever he happened to be doing at the moment."[20]

"Sparks" recalls the Hasidic belief that "in the primeval creation preceding the creation of our world, the divine light-substance burst and 'sparks' fell into the lower depths, filling the 'shells' of the things and creatures of our world."[21] In her poem, "The Necessity," which Levertov considers "a kind of testament,"[22] she speaks of "each part / of speech a spark / awaiting redemption."[23] This recalls her earlier words about the "kinship" between her "Illustrious Ancestors" that must be recognized in heaven or that somehow on earth must be "unified and redeemed" through her "sparks." Given the Hasidic belief concerning "sparks" and her understanding of the consciousness that the poet must bring to his/her work, it appears that Levertov is telling us here that it is the duty and privilege of the poet to discover or uncover and to "translate" the sacred that is found in the secular. Her use of the title "Sparks," with the implications of its meaning and her speaking of "a life opening, fearful, fearless / thousand-eyed, a field / of sparks that move swiftly / in darkness," portrays a poet who is "beginning to live" (in Jungian terms, becoming "conscious"), and Levertov is concerned, as the Hasidim were, with relating consciousness to the Divine. Once again, there is a strong indication that the poet believes with Rabbi Moshe that "even the ascent and descent of the angels depend on [her] deeds."

The Hasidic influence is also evident in the elegy "In Obedience" that Levertov wrote for her father. She speaks about it in *The Poet in the World:* the poem

> tells of doing a wild, solitary dance among the fireflies in a New England garden one night while my father lay dying in London; a joyful dance of love and mourning. It was only later that I learned that my father rose from his bed shortly before his death to dance the Hasidic dance of praise.[24]

The elegy itself records a type of "spiritual" journey on the poet's part. Her final lines speak of a feeling that any of us might have:

I dance

for joy, only for joy
while you lie dying, into whose eyes
I looked seldom enough, all the years,
seldom enough with candid love. Let my dance
be mourning then,
now that I love you too late.[25]

In his Preface to *The Tales: The Early Masters,* Buber tells about a Rabbi who said that "a story must be told in such a way that it constitutes help in itself." And he told:

> My grandfather was lame. Once they asked him to tell a story about his teacher. And he related how the holy Baal Shem used to hop and dance while he prayed. My grandfather rose as he spoke, and he was so swept away by the story that he himself began to hop and dance to show how the Master had done. From that hour on he was cured of his lameness. That's the way to tell a story![26]

This tale surely appealed to the daughter of a consummate story-teller. Likewise, the "telling" of her story "constitute[d]" a help in itself for the poet. She sees in this experience the seeds of a legend that take on the dimension of myth: "Might not some descendant of his or mine say some day to a son or daughter, 'We are of a line that dances in mourning and dances a joyful dance in the hour of death?' "[27] Olga Levertoff also mentioned this "Hassidic dance" in her poem, "The Ballad of My Father," writ- ten in 1963. Denise and Olga were again recognizing a "kinship" with their "Illustrious Ancestors" and attempting to "unif[y] and redeem it" through their poetry.

NOTES

1. Hyatt H. Waggoner, *American Poets: From the Puritans to the Pres- ent* (New York: Dell, 1968), 619–22.

2. The author is preparing an article, "The Poet Responds to Disillu- sion in the American Dream," that addresses, in part, critical appraisals of this most recent work.

3. Denise Levertov, *The Poet in the World* (New York: New Direc- tions, 1973), 70.

4. Denise Levertov, "Illustrious Ancestors," reprinted from *Over-*

land to the Islands (1958) in *The Jacob's Ladder* (New York: New Directions, 1961), 87.

5. Denise Levertov, *Light Up the Cave* (New York: New Directions, 1981), 238.

6. Levertov, *The Poet,* 70.

7. Levertov, *Light Up,* 241.

8. Levertov, *Light Up,* 242.

9. See Levertov, "The Sense of Pilgrimage" in *The Poet in the World,* 62–86.

10. Original transcript of Walter Sutton's "A Conversation with Denise Levertov," *Minnesota Review* 3–4 (December 1965).

11. *The American Heritage Dictionary* defines *numen* (pl. *numina*) as 1. The presiding divinity or spirit of a place. 2. The spirit believed by animists to inhabit certain natural objects. 3. Creative energy regarded as a genius or demon dwelling within one; and *numinous* as 1. Of or pertaining to a *numen,* 2. Spiritually elevated.

12. Denise Levertov, *With Eyes at the Back of Our Heads* (New York: New Directions, 1960), 34–35.

13. Martin Buber, *Tales of the Hasidim: The Early Masters* (New York: Schocken Books, 1948), 262.

14. Ralph Waldo Emerson, "The Uses of Great Men," *Representative Men: And Miscellanies* (Boston: Houghton Mifflin, 1929), 10.

15. Martin Buber, *Tales of the Hasidim: The Later Masters* (New York: Schocken Books, 1948), 56.

16. Denise Levertov, *The Jacob's Ladder* 37.

17. Denise Levertov, *Relearning the Alphabet* (New York: New Directions, 1970), 3.

18. Denise Levertov, *O Taste and See* (New York: New Directions, 1964), 15.

19. Linda Wagner, *Denise Levertov* (New York: Twayne Publishers, 1967), 41.

20. Buber, *Tales: Later,* 173.

21. Buber, *Tales: Early,* 333.

22. Levertov, *The Poet,* 43.

23. Levertov, *The Jacob's Ladder,* 56.

24. Levertov, *The Poet,* 70.

25. Denise Levertov, *Overland to the Islands* (Highlands, N.C.: Jonathan Williams, 1958), 15.

26. Buber, *Tales: Early,* iv–v.

27. Levertov, *The Poet,* 70.

JOYCE LORRAINE BECK

Denise Levertov's Poetics and
Oblique Prayers

In Denise Levertov's poem, "The Instant," from *Overland to the Islands,* a moment of illumination occurs when mist and clouds roll away to show forth the distant peak of Mt. Snowdon shining in the gleam of early morning. Suddenly, "Light / graces the mountainhead / for a lifetime's look, before the mist / draws in again" (65–66). Levertov has spoken of this poem and of the title poem of her collection *With Eyes at the Back of Our Heads* as one of those stages in her life's journey that are "moments of vision presaging the secret that will bring the seeker to his goal, but which are quickly forgotten again, or hidden again from the imagination, just as the head of Snowdon, Eryri, is hidden again as the mists return" (*PW,* 72). As a representative combination of the sublime and the mundane, Ralph J. Mills finds "The Instant" characteristic of Levertov's poetics. It is both "an abbreviated narrative, dramatic in character," and "a spiritual adventure of a nearly ineffable sort" (113). There is indeed a religious meditative element in Denise Levertov. It has at least three sources—the Christian inheritance of her immediate background, her upbringing as a child of a Church of England clergyman; her ancestral roots in Judaism and her affinity for Hasidism; and finally the "natural supernaturalism" of her romantic poetics.

If "The Instant" is a good example of what Mills terms her "visionary disposition," it still retains its status as a "poem of fact," one "emerging from ordinary circumstances and immediate life, and returning there" (Mills 114).[1] Levertov often associates the imagination with exquisitely realistic detail. The work of the imagination is "its far-reaching and faithful permeation of those details that in a work of art, illuminate the whole" (*PW,* 203). In "A Note on the Work of the Imagination," she attributes the graphic intensity of a recent dream to the power of imagination to introduce "exquisite realistic detail" into dream as into

Reprinted from *Religion and Literature* 18, no. 1 (Spring 1986): 45–61.

art. In the dream a radiant glimmer had led her to approach nearer her own image in a mirror where she saw "a network of little dew or mist diamonds" sprinkled in her dark hair. She finds this realistic detail, provided by the creative unconscious—the imagination—surprisingly appropriate to a dream in which she had "been walking in the misty fields in the dew-fall hour," and concludes. "I awoke in delight, reminded forcibly of just what it is we love in the greatest writers—what quality, above all others surely makes us open ourselves freely to Homer, Shakespeare, Tolstoy, Hardy—that following through, that *permeation* of detail—relevant, illuminating detail—which marks the total imagination at work. . . . It was Imagination put seed pearls of summer fog in Tess Durbeyfield's hair . . . and it was the same holy, independent faculty that sprinkled my hair with winter-evening diamonds" (*PW,* 204).

But if Levertov associates the imagination with detailed literary realism, such literary detail is not synonymous with what she calls elsewhere "the authentic," which she repeatedly praises in her well-known poem "Matins":

> The authentic, I said
> breaking the handle of my hairbrush as I
> brushed my hair in
> rhythmic strokes: That's it,
> that's joy, it's always
> a recognition, the known
> appearing fully itself, and
> more itself than one knew.
>
> (*JL,* 57)

Levertov's attention to authenticity is often rigorous. She subjects objects to intense scrutiny, affirming her knowledge of what she sees by looking and naming, seeking to know both the inner and outer compositions of things. Such knowledge comes from what she calls "disinterested intensity":

"Disinterested intensity," of which Rilke wrote, then is truly exemplary and affective intensity. What Charles Olson has called a man's "filling of his given space," what John Donne said of the presence of God in a straw—"God is a straw in a straw"—point toward that disinterest. The strawness of straw, the humanness of the human, is their divinity; in that intensity is the "divine spark" Hasidic lore tells us dwells in all created things. . . . Only by the light and heat of these divine sparks can we see, can we feel, the extent of the human range. They bear witness to the possibility of "disinterest, freedom, and intensity." (PW, 51–52)

Levertov stresses again and again in her prose writings her definition of poetry as a revelation of the meanings or patterns of experience. As the poet contemplates or "muses" in the temple of life, meaning is revealed to her: "To contemplate comes from 'templum, temple, a space for observation, marked out by augur.' It means, not simply to observe, to regard, but to do these things in the presence of a god. And to meditate is 'to keep the mind in a state of contemplation'; its synonym is 'to muse,' and to muse comes from a word meaning 'to stand with open mouth'—not so comical if we think of 'inspiration'—'to breathe in.' " The organic form of existential experience is revealed to the disinterested, musing, attentive poet as poetry: "So—as the poet stands open-mouthed in the temple of life, contemplating his experience, there come to him the first words of the poem, if there is to be a poem. The pressure of the demand and the meditation on its elements culminate in a moment of vision, of crystallization, in which some inkling of the correspondence between those elements occurs; and it occurs as words" (PW, 8). Levertov's poetics, like the art of the poet she refers to in "Origins of a Poem," combines musing or meditation—what Emerson in "Poetry" calls "the intellect being where and what it sees"—with articulation, "sharing the path or circuit of things through forms and so making them translucid to others" (PW, 50).

According to Albert Gelpi, Levertov deliberately maintains the tension of the meeting of mind and nature. It is in this sense that "hers is a sacramental notion of life; experience is a communion with objects which are in themselves signs of their own secret mystery" (123). Levertov has said herself, in "Some Notes on Organic Form," that organic poetry is based on "an intuition of an order, a form beyond forms in which forms partake, and of which man's creative works are analogies, resemblances, natural allegories" (PW, 7). Mills believes that Levertov's art teaches us what the French theologian Jacques Maritain affirms in Art and Scholasticism, that "our art does not derive from itself alone what it imparts to things; it spreads over them a secret which it first discovered in them, in their invisible substance or in their endless exchanges and correspondences."[2] Gelpi notices that while Levertov's All-Day Bird is "gripped by joy," it is "the pressure of his skill as singer," his ability to discriminate, which enables him to shape his song "closer to what he knows" (124). Levertov, in her prose writings, acknowledges two Muses or sources of poetic truth: rational discrimination, the Apollonian guide who directs her in craftsmanship or in deliberate imaginative creation; and meditation, the Beatific "breath" or Spirit who reveals to her the invisible substances of organic forms, or the Archetypes that arise from very deep associations.

Two such archetypes in Levertov's poetry, Knight and Muse, point toward the simultaneously descriptive and meditative poetic described by Mills and Gelpi and by her own prose. In her essay "A Sense of Pilgrimage," she has reflected on both of these symbols, drawing out some of their associations. The questing knight or pilgrim wandering through "imagination's holy forest" may be a successor of Chrétien de Troyes's Percival, Malory's Galahad, or Spenser's Red Crosse Knight. But there are more immediately personal linkings. Levertov remembers also the longing she had as a child to "step backward into time and become a page or knight errant." As a member of "The Church of England's Children's League: Knights of St. Richard," she saw herself as a knight on a journey through states or phases of being in life's pilgrimage, her feelings drawn both from Arthurian legends and from the "Prayer of St. Richard." In her use of the word "pilgrim," in one of her earliest poems, "Ballad," she recognizes the influence of the hymn which she loved best as a child, Bunyan's "He who would valiant be." *The Pilgrim's Progress* and Hans Andersen's *The Snow Queen* also presented a "definitely Christian sense of the nature of the life-pilgrimage." The figure of the questing pilgrim-knight attracted her to the Charles Kingsley version of the Argonauts and the many tales in the Andrew Lang collections. She singles out as typical the story called "The Water of Life" in which, "passing through many trials and dangers, the protagonist 'walked and walked' until she finally came to the top of a great mountain and found the well or pool of living water" (*PW,* 66). Years later, in "Relearning the Alphabet," the letters *P* and Q recall "petitioner" and the recurrent "quester":

> In childhood dream-play I was always
> the knight or squire, not
> the lady:
> quester, petitioner, win or lose, not
> she who was sought.
> The initial of quest or question

branded itself long since on the flank
of my Pegasus.
Yet he flies always
home to the present.

(RA, 116)

Much more mysterious than the questing knight-errant is the second recurring figure in Levertov's poetry, the Muse. The Muse, who sometimes accompanies and inspires the poet-pilgrim-knight on the quest, and sometimes appears as "she who is sought," as the spiritual home to which the Pegasus flies, seems to be a double figure, corresponding to Levertov's sense of the poet's twofold power for articulation and for contemplation. Her Muse is both seer and maker, prophet and craftsman. She said, in "A Sense of Pilgrimage," that her Muse is one who both sees deeply (often appearing mysteriously or unexpectedly) and sings skillfully. The act of verbalization, when skillful or masterful, leads the poet to the full perception of organic forms or transcendent prototypes. Poets are "instruments on which the power of poetry plays," she says, "but they are also *makers,* craftsmen: It is given to the seer to see, but it is then his responsibility to communicate what he sees, that they who cannot see may see, since we are 'members of one another' " (*PW*, 3).

The Muse may be a successor of Homer's Athena, Dante's Beatrice, or Spenser's Gloriana. Then again, she may be the type of Hagia Sophia, of Jerusalem the Golden, or of Lady Eloah. But—like the figure of the Knight—this Muse also has deeply personal associations for Levertov. In "The Well" and in "To the Muse" she notes the resemblance of her vision of the Muse to "the face of a certain actress," but the face resembles in turn the face of a figure who occurs and reoccurs in the tales of George MacDonald, such as "The Princess and the Goblin," "The Princess and Curdie," and such shorter stories as "The Golden Key" or "The Wise Woman." This personage is "the young/old grandmother," whose spinning room in a tower, where the gold ring waits to be found, "is hard to find at will, even though it is part of the house one inhabits" (*PW*, 74). In "To the Muse," she is one who chooses and abides:

I have heard it said,
and by a wise man,
that you are not one who comes and goes

but having chosen
you remain in your human house,
and walk

in its garden, for air and the delights
of weather and seasons.

Who builds
a good fire in his hearth
shall find you at it
with shining eyes and a ready tongue.

(TS, 25)

Still, the Muse must be cultivated by any poet who wants her
around: when the "host" fails her, she goes into hiding. She
cannot be forced or coerced, but only discovered through a kind
of "active reticence," or "wise passiveness"—as well as a "leap of
faith," a generous and courageous commitment, made in a spirit
of fear and trembling, to a loved and mysterious, "known/
Unknown" source.

Likewise, in "The Goddess," she is the figure of Truth who
tosses the protagonist out of Lie Castle:

She in whose lipservice
I passed my time,
whose name I knew, but not her face,
came upon me where I lay in Lie Castle!

Flung me across the room, and
room after room (hitting the walls, re-
bounding—to the last
sticky wall—wrenching away from it
pulled hair out!)
till I lay
outside the outer walls!

The Goddess of Truth is She

without whom nothing
flowers, fruits, sleeps in season,
without whom nothing
speaks in its own tongue, but returns
lie for lie!

(EBH, 53)

This poem, Levertov remarks, is not based on dream but on an actual waking vision. The poem's energy, she believes, "arises from an experience of awakening to the truth and to the necessity for truthfulness—an experience sufficiently profound to produce the image of truth as a Goddess, to produce that image spontaneously, and not by means of the conscious effort of allegory to find similes" (*PW,* 72).

In other places Levertov links the figure of the Muse with an "inexhaustible source," a "vast, irreducible spirit" summoned by the exercise of writing poetry. In her essay "Origins of a Poem" she relates the Muse to the divine in both poet and reader: "The poet—when he is writing—is a priest; the poem is a temple; epiphanies and communion take place within it. The communion is triple: between the maker and the needer within the poet; between the maker and the needers outside him—those who need but can't make their own poems (or who do make their own but need this one too); and between the human and the divine in both poet and reader. . . . When the poet converses with this god he has summoned into manifestation, he reveals to others the possibility of their own dialogue with the god in themselves" (*PW,* 47). Writing the poem, in this view, becomes the poet's means of "summoning the divine," or the Muse.

The relationship of the Muse to the poet-pilgrim-knight errant is central in Levertov's poetry. In "The Well" the poet stands on a bridge crossing a stream while the Muse, in her dark habit, wades into deep water to a spring where she fills her pitcher to the brim and then opens the doors of the world by spelling the word "water" in the poet's left palm. In this poem the Muse remains a mysterious figure whose connection with the poet is only obscurely suggested:

> In the baroque park,
>   transformed as I neared the water
>   to Valentines, a place of origin,
> I stand on a bridge of one span
> and see this calm act, this gathering up
>   of life, of spring water
>
> and the Muse gliding then
>   in her barge without sails, without
> oars or motor, across
>   the dark lake, and I know

no interpretation of these mysteries
    although I know she is the Muse
and that the humble
    tributary of Roding is
one with Alpheus, the god who as a river
    flowed through the salt sea to his love's well

so that my heart leaps
    in wonder.

                                                        (JL, 38–39)

"The Illustration," her sequel to "The Well," brings the traveling
soul and its Muse together at the Place of Origin by way of a
winding road:

Months after the Muse
had come and gone across the lake of vision,
arose out of childhood the long-familiar
briefly forgotten presaging of her image— . . .

a star come to earth burned before the
closed all-seeing eyes
of that figure later seen as the Muse.

By which I learn to affirm
Truth's light at strange turns of the mind's road,
wrong turns that lead
over the border into wonder,

mistaken directions, forgotten signs
all bringing the soul's travels to a place
of origin, a well
under the lake where the Muse moves.

                                                        (JL, 40)

When the Muse and the questing knight come together, the
spirit of here-and-now or of "the present" is united with the
romantic spirit of quest, of what she calls "longing to wander
toward other worlds." Levertov finds in the "Olga Poems" a
poem that brings the pilgrim to the end of his pilgrimage, as it
were. All her other poems based on the underlying conception of
life as "A Vale of Soulmaking" are "written, one might say, on

the road; this one looks back at a life that has ended, or come full circle." But, she concludes, "The purpose of pilgrimage that I hope emerges is not merely what is known as 'a good death'; the candle doesn't just get relit at the end of all the darkness, but is somehow to be miraculously kept alight all the way through" (*PW,* 80). The knight errant who wanders through imagination's holy forest in Levertov's poetry is accompanied and inspired by the Candlelight of Truth. In these paired figures, time and eternity, imaginative detail and a sense of divine presence are reconciled. The figures of the questing knight and the Muse together best constitute a symbol for Levertov's poetic of pragmatic, practical, or peripatetic Neoplatonism.[3]

If art is, as Levertov has said, "the act of realizing inner experience in material substance," the poet may realize or substantiate in her art, her being, and her actions the inspirations or inner dialogues of her Muse. She may, like Apollo, or the artist Levertov refers to in her "Origins of a Poem," "give body and future to 'the mysterious being hidden behind the eyes' " or the Muse. Levertov's own poetry, when inspired by her Muse, becomes what she calls, following Martin Heidegger, "a realization, quite literally 'realization,' making real, substantiation"; her acts, when inspired by her Muse, become symbolic acts or sacraments; and her visions become revelations. Such, we should expect, is also true of the poet-pilgrim-knight in the poems. The Muse is made apparent, or visible, through and in the figure of the knight errant or traveller and the continuing quest. In her poem "A Letter to William Kinter of Muhlenberg," Levertov finds "the profound Christian symbolism of the stations of the Cross dimly apprehended as the model for spiritual pilgrimage." This pilgrimage is in turn "imaged forth in a reference to the peripatetic discourse of personages in *The Zohar*":

> Zaddik, you showed me
> the Stations of the Cross
>
> and I saw
> not what the most abstract
>
> tiles held—world upon world—
> but at least
>
> a shadow of what
> might be seen there if mind and heart

gave themselves to meditation,
deeper

and deeper into Imagination's
holy forest, as travelers

followed the Zohar's dusty
shimmering roads, talking

with prophets and
hidden angels.

(JL, 44)

Levertov's Muse is both the end or goal of the quest and she who is present and inspires all along the way. The Muse is found or realized "when the travelling soul and its Muse are brought together at the Place of Origin by way of a winding road." Yet the Muse is also like a candle or star that is somehow "miraculously kept alight all the way through." Levertov's grail is found in the act of finding, when the seeker and the sought are one. The knight errant and the Muse together constitute the poet's whole Self, her becoming in her Being. In the poem "The Wings," the poet-pilgrim contemplates herself as a traveler sprouting "embryo wings" and going or continuing onward, "on one wing":

But what if,
like a camel, it's

pure energy I store
and carry humped and heavy? . . .

What if released in air
it became a white

source of light, a fountain
of light? Could all that weight

be the power of flight?
Look inward: see me

with embryo wings, one
feathered in soot, the other

blazing ciliations of ember, pale
flare-pinions. Well—

could I go
on one wing,

the white one?

(SD, 11–12)

Levertov's Muse is realized when one cannot tell the questing
knight from the Muse, the poet-pilgrim from the Light of Truth.
In poems such as "Voyage," from *The Freeing of the Dust,* the
reticent artist, the Muse or Goddess of Truth, the questing pil-
grim, the true inner self are drawn together in revelations of
absolute presence and freedom. In her early poem "Matins," she
shows that fear of the Divine can be the beginning of wisdom
even in the midst of the mundane. In the recent "Benedictus,"
from "Mass for the Day of St. Thomas Didymus," she moves
into the "known/unknown," de-centered center, drawing to-
gether writing with spirit, word with windripple, song with
silence, to articulate beatitude in a medieval/contemporary poly-
phonic sequence:

Blessèd is that which comes in the name of the spirit,
that which bears
the spirit within it.

The name of the spirit is written
in woodgrain, windripple, crystal,

in crystals of snow, in petal, leaf,
moss and moon, fossil and feather,

blood, bone, song, silence,
very word of
very word,
flesh and
vision.

(CB, 111–12)

Levertov's Apollonian or rational "guide," then, does not
dominate the Sacred Muse of beatitude so as to deny her activity
and nullify her wisdom; rather, he creates, interacts, and cor-

responds with her. Levertov's poetic is not defined through, or as, craft alone. Her Apollonian "guide" has not cast out Poly-hymnia and set himself up as tyrant or idol. Her knight or squire, the "quester, petitioner" of "Relearning the Alphabet," has come to understand what so many benighted pilgrims, left like Orestes to wander in Hades, have yet to learn, that "transmutation is not / under the will's rule":

> The door I flung my weight against
> was constructed to open   out
>   towards me.
>
> In-seeing
> to candleflame's
> blue ice-cavern, measureless,
>
> may not be forced by sharp
> desire.
>
>   (RA, 117)

Both her poet-persona and her Muse are (simultaneously or inter-mittently) active and passive, perceptive and receptive. As she reminds us in her conversation with Walter Sutton, her notion of organic form is really "based on the idea that there is form in all things—that the artist doesn't impose form upon chaos, but discovers hidden intrinsic form—and on the idea that poems can arrive at their form by means of the poet's attentive listening, not only his listening but also his experience and by means of his accurate transcriptions of that experience into words" ("Conversation" 22). While she recognizes the need for a well-developed ego, a strong conscious intellect, and a mastery of craft on the part of the Apollonian poet-persona, she also stresses the value of that reticence, or restraint, which leaves the door open to Spirit and allows the promptings of the Muse of grace.

Levertov's Muse of beatitude, the holy "breath" and "dim star" of her poetry, is an active faculty, a "source of mind's fire," whose presence she regards with reverence and joyfully celebrates:

> Joy—a beginning.   Anguish, ardor.
> To relearn the ah! of knowing in unthinking
> joy: the belovéd stranger lives.
> Sweep up anguish as with a wing-tip,
> brushing the ashes back to the fire's core.

Like Julia Kristeva's *"jouissance,"* Levertov's "joy" is born of "cosmic connection," of a realized link between the poet-persona and the Muse of meditation, the personal and the cosmic, a link leading the way to the eternal.[4] As she turns in the forest, relearning the alphabet, all utterance takes the poet step by hesitant step into "that life beyond the dead-end," to a place not evoked, but discovered upriver:

> *Sweep up*
> *anguish as with a wing-tip:*
>
> the blaze addresses
> a different darkness:
> absence has not become
> the transformed presence the will
> looked for,
> but other: the present,
>
> that which was poised already in the ah! of praise.
>
> *(RA,* 120)

The Goddess/poet-pilgrim-knight is one of the old yet new metaphors that Denise Levertov has contributed to English and American letters while on her "life's pilgrimage." By traveling through imagination's holy forest, she may, indeed, have approached, now and again, the shrine of the "well or pool of living water" and found there not only continuance, but Spirit's candleflame, holiness:

> The forest is holy
> The sacred paths are of stone.
> A clearing
> The altars are shifting deposits of pineneedles,
>   hidden waters,
>   streets of choirwood,
>   not what the will
>   thinks to construct for its testimonies.
>
> *(RA,* 119)

If the end, or purpose, of pilgrimage in Levertov's poetics is holiness—as it has been in most journeys to Jerusalem or traditional grail quests—then holiness, here, is synonymous with wholeness. Such integrity includes wholeness of vision, for Levertov is a poet who "subtly points the way to see with whole sight" (Mills 118). But it is also a matter of full humanity. If the poet shares the spirit of theologian Martin Buber in always saying "thou" to the persons, occasions, and objects she encounters, that is simply an expression of "her imagination's essential humanizing gesture toward every aspect of existence" (Mills 104). In her essay "Poems by Women," she has written that both women and men have to resist polarization and become more fully human, which is a question of "the humane comprehensions of the perceptive and receptive being in balance." Those poems which enrich the lives of readers and which demonstrate "that transcendence of gender which is characteristic of the creative mind" may, in this very act, have an effect beneficial to the body politic (100).

Holiness, as wholeness, of both person and place is hinted at in several of her poems. In "Kingdoms of Heaven," for example, the poet-pilgrim asks if "to believe it's there / within you / though the key's missing / makes it enough? As if / golden pollen were falling // onto your hair from dark trees" (TS, 12). In "The Goddess" she tells a similar story of a new heaven and new earth about to be more fully manifest: "I bit on a seed and it spoke on my tongue / of day that shone already among stars / in the water-mirror of low ground" (EBH, 43). The letter R in "Relearning the Alphabet" finds the poet suddenly released into "a soft day, western March;" where "a thrust of birdsong / parts the gold flowers thickbranching / that roof the path over" (RA, 116–17). A later poem, "The Many Mansions," presents an expanded view of a whole, or holy, universe—a place of universal harmony and abundance where each is unique yet all are holy, or whole. Here she speaks of "the world of the white herons," perfect yet undefiled, and of the knowledge her vision of that world gave:

> it was not a fragile, only, other world,
> there were, there are (I learned) a host,
>
> each unique, yet each having
> the grace of recapitulating
>
> a single radiance, multiform.
>
> (CB, 116)

We can surmise that the "Oblique Prayers" of Levertov's most recent volume have been answered when "no man's land," a gray place without clear outlines, a "mere not-darkness," gives way, in "The Antiphon," to a new land where "all is eloquent," a land very like a regained or rediscovered English garden Paradise, where all is blessed:

>   —rain,
>   raindrops on branches, pavement brick
>   humbly uneven, twigs of a storm-stripped hedge revealed
>   shining deep scarlet,
>   speckled whistler shabby and
>   unconcerned, anything—all
>   utters itself, blessedness
>   soaks the ground and its wintering seeds.
>
>   (*OP*, 84)

As an awe so quiet she doesn't know when it began fills the poet-pilgrim and a gratitude begins to sing in her, daybreak arrives and the wind begins to shimmer in blue leaves. Then we know, as we did and did not know before, that Denise Levertov's Muse is and has been the Spirit of Holiness, Lady Sophia-Gloriae, the living Light, Wordsworth's "Wisdom and Spirit of the universe." The pilgrim–poet has returned to the Vale, to Grasmere or Stanford Rivers, rediscovered the splendor in the grass, and regained "the glory and the dream," the visionary gleam of the celestial light.

Religious aspects have been implicit in Denise Levertov's poetry from the first. William Packard, in his 1971 interview for the *New York Quarterly,* notes in her poetry the use of religious words such as "hymn," "psalm," "communion wine," and "pilgrimage," and questions her, "What does the word 'religious' mean to you?" Her answer might be taken as a comment not only upon the religious aspects of her art but upon its sources: "The impulse to kneel in wonder. . . . The sense of awe. The felt presence of some mysterious force whether it be what one calls beauty, or perhaps just the sense of the unknown—I don't mean 'unknown' in the sense of we don't know what the future will bring. I mean the sense of numinous whether it's in a small stone or a large mountain" (18–19). Using similar "religious words" in her poem "Of Being," from "Of God and of the Gods," in *Oblique Prayers,* the poet speaks of

this flood of stillness
widening the lake of sky:

this need to dance,
this need to kneel:
                    this mystery.

(86)

Lorrie Smith, in a recent interview for the *Michigan Quarterly Review,* notes with interest that Levertov's "religious and spiritual concerns" have become more explicit in the latest volumes (601). This prompts the poet to mention a passage she has recently found in Ruskin which she might have used as a preface for "Of God and of the Gods" had she found it before *Oblique Prayers* went to press. She cites a long section from this essay, in which Ruskin refers to "the totality of spiritual powers delegated by the lord of the universe to do, in their several heights or offices, parts of his will respecting men or the world." Ruskin's passage could also be interpreted as an oblique commentary upon the sources of his own, and of Levertov's, artistic inspiration. After alluding to his innate acceptance of "the testimony and belief of all ages to the presence in heaven and earth of angels, principalities, powers, thrones and the like," he concludes that he knows for an indisputable fact "that no true happiness exists nor was any good work ever done by human creatures but in the sense or imagination of such presences" (602). Levertov in *Oblique Prayers,* like Ruskin in the essay she cites, seems concerned to show that no true happiness exists, nor is any good work done by human artists or pilgrim-poets, without the direct or indirect influence or inspiration of that God "busy at the loom. Among the berry bushes" (78).

Religious questions other than those explicitly about "God and the gods," however, are also raised in the *Michigan Quarterly Review* interview—questions, for example, about belief, incarnation, humanity, and orthodoxy. In her responses Levertov clarifies the human and personal emphases which have always been apparent in her poetry and are best symbolized, perhaps, in her figure of the pilgrim-poet or "travelling soul" wandering through "imagination's holy forest." In doing so she gives evidence, once again, of her abiding unwillingness to separate religious issues from human ones. Her initial idea for "Mass for the Day of St. Thomas Didymus," from *Candles in Babylon,* she says, "was just

283

to use those forms which had been so nourishing as a structure for composers through so many centuries and see what I could do with them in poetry. So it started off, paradoxically, as an agnostic mass. In the process of writing it, I moved somewhere" (603). In answer to the religious question which arises next of whether or not "Mass for the Day of St. Thomas Didymus" is "Christian, in an orthodox sense," the poet responds with a comment on the incarnation: "Well, it gets to the incarnation. I now define myself as a Christian but not a very orthodox one, and I think that there is a way of looking at Christian faith as involving the cooperation of man. I think that's part of the meaning of the incarnation" (603).

Perhaps because of her early encounters with the Goddess of Truth whose strong arm flings her from "Lie Castle," though, Levertov's poetry—however eclectic it may be—is not lacking in uprightness or integrity. As her poem "The Goddess" testifies, she has not been bereft of the judgments of that Goddess of righteousness "without whom nothing / flowers, fruits, sleeps in season, / without whom nothing / speaks in its own tongue, but returns / lie for lie!" (*EBH*, 153). Lady Eloah may indeed be an authentic and appropriate name for the mysterious yet provident Muse of glory the poet often associates with Wisdom and regards with awe and wonder—as might God of hosts, powers, or gods. But her sacred Muse may also have other sacred names. Jacques Maritain, in *Art and Scholasticism,* affirms that there exists a "real inspiration" which "comes from the living God" by which "the first Intelligence" gives the artist "a creative movement" superior to the yardstick of reason. Following Thomas Aquinas, he distinguishes this divine inspiration from "the essential supernatural inspiration proper to the gifts of the Holy Spirit" and concludes that in order for an art to arise that is truly liberated by grace, "both forms of inspiration must be joined at its most secret source" (66, 210). Levertov too in her latest volumes of poetry seems to recognize or acknowledge a joining or coming together of more than one kind of poetic inspiration or creative movement at a mysterious source.

In the last poem of "Of God and of the Gods," the poet celebrates the grace and liberating power of that Muse who has inspired her journey all along the way. She acknowledges the creative strength of Spirit—of "breath," of "*ruach*"—and of those "forms the spirit enters." We are led to understand from "Passage" that the "light that is witness and by which we witness" is present still, moving over the meadow of long grass, for, even now "green shines to silver where the spirit passes." Here the speaker addresses a different darkness, a darkness from out of which light has broken anew. We are invited, then, to see and to say, to hear and to sing, to dance and to kneel with the poet:

Wind from the compass points, sun at meridian,
these are forms the spirit enters,
breath, *ruach,* light that is witness and by which we witness.

The grasses numberless, bowing and rising, silently
cry hosanna as the spirit
moves them and moves burnishing

over and again upon mountain pastures
a day of spring, a needle's eye
space and time are passing through like a swathe of silk.

(*OP,* 87)

NOTES

I use the following abbreviations for works by Denise Levertov: *Candles in Babylon,* CB; *The Jacob's Ladder,* JL; *O Taste and See,* TS; *Oblique Prayers,* OP; *The Poet in the World,* PW; *Relearning the Alphabet,* RA; *The Sorrow Dance,* SD; *With Eyes at the Back of Our Heads,* EBH.

1. Hayden Carruth, in his review of *The Poet in the World* for *The Hudson Review* notes that Levertov's philosophical and tempermental base is in Neoplatonism. Nonetheless, unlike many writers who share this broad Neoplatonic provenance, she "never, or hardly ever, steps outside her role as a working poet aware of the practical and moral relationships between herself and her poetic materials: her experience, her life, her humanity." If she is a visionary poet, she "rarely veers into mystical utterance for its own sake." Rather, she "keeps her mind on the reality of imaginative process" (475). For further discussion of moral relationships and "social concern" in Levertov's poetics see Wagner, "Here and Now" 975–76; Levertov, "Everyman's Land" 231–36, and "Poetry and Political Engagement" 4–6; as well as Rexroth 44–45. On Levertov's "visionary disposition" or "spiritual consciousness" see Bowering 77–84, Younkins 40–48, and Gitzen 328–41.

2. Jacques Maritain, *Art and Scholasticism,* quoted in Mills, 105.

3. Levertov's "incorporative consciousness" is discussed by Harris 33–48. See also DuPlessis 280–300, Bowering 78–84, and Mottram 152–62. Levertov's paired figures may also be considered as reconciling movement and rest, motion and stillness. However, this does not mean that true "rest" is inactive; on the contrary, such "stillness" is the purest act. Levertov quotes Heidegger in "Hölderlin and the Essence of Po-

etry," who writes, "Poetry looks like a game and is not. A game does indeed bring men together, but in such a way that each forgets himself in the process. In poetry, on the other hand, man is reunited on the foundation of his existence. There he comes to rest; not indeed to the seeming rest of inactivity and emptiness of thought, but to that infinite state of rest in which all powers and relations are active" (*PW*, 50–51). For a more detailed study of Levertov and Heidegger see Rosenfield 195–213.

4. On "cosmic connection," "joy," "*jouissance,*" and "eternity" see also Cox 158.

WORKS CITED

Bowering, George. "Denise Levertov." *Antigonish Review* 7 (1971): 76–87.

Carruth, Hayden. "Levertov." *The Hudson Review* 27 (1974): 475–80.

Cox, Harvey. *Religion in the Secular City: Toward a Postmodern Theology.* New York: Simon, 1984.

DuPlessis, Rachel Blau. "The Critique of Consciousness and Myth in Levertov, Rich, and Rukeyser." *Feminist Studies* 3, nos. 1–2 (1975): 199–221. Rpt. in *Shakespeare's Sisters*. Ed. Sandra M. Gilbert and Susan Gubar. Bloomington: Indiana University Press, 1979. 195–213.

Gelpi, Albert. "*O Taste and See.*" *The Southern Review* 2 (1968): 1032–35. Rpt. in Wagner, *Province* 123–25.

Gitzen, Julian. "From Reverence to Attention: The Poetry of Denise Levertov," *Midwest Quarterly* 16 (1975): 328–41.

Harris, Victoria. "The Incorporative Consciousness: Levertov's Journey from Discretion to Unity." *Exploration* 4 (Dec. 1976): 33–48.

Kristeva, Julia. "Women's Time." Trans. Alice Jardine and Harry Blake. *Signs* 7, no. 1 (1981): 13–35.

Levertov, Denise. *Candles in Babylon.* New York: New Directions, 1982.

———. *Collected Earlier Poems: 1940–1960.* New York: New Directions, 1979.

———. "Conversation with Denise Levertov." With Walter Sutton. *The Minnesota Review* (1965). Rpt. in Wagner, *Province* 22–40.

———. " 'Everyman's Land': Ian Reid Interviews Denise Levertov." *Southern Review: An Australian Journal of Literary Studies* 5 (1972): 231–36.

———. *The Freeing of the Dust.* New York: New Directions, 1975.

———. "An Interview with Denise Levertov." With Lorrie Smith. *Michigan Quarterly Review* 24 (1985): 596–604.

———. *The Jacob's Ladder.* New York: New Directions, 1961.

———. *Oblique Prayers.* New York: New Directions, 1984.

———. *Overland to the Islands.* Highlands, N.C.: Jonathan Williams, 1958. Rpt. in *Collected Earlier Poems.*

———. "Poems by Women." Rpt. in Wagner, *Province* 98–100.

———. *The Poet in the World.* New York: New Directions, 1973.

———. "Poetry and Political Engagement: A Conversation with Denise Levertov." With Judith H. McDowell. *English in Texas* 11 (1979): 4–6.

———. *Relearning the Alphabet.* New York: New Directions, 1970.

———. *The Sorrow Dance.* New York: New Directions, 1967.

———. *O Taste and See.* New York: New Directions, 1964.

————. *With Eyes at the Back of Our Heads.* New York: New Directions, 1960.

Maritain, Jacques. *Art and Scholasticism.* 1962. Trans. Joseph W. Evans. Notre Dame: University of Notre Dame Press, 1974.

Mills, Ralph J. "Denise Levertov: Poetry of the Immediate." *Contemporary American Poetry.* New York: Random, 1965. Rpt. in Wagner, *Province* 103–18.

Mottram, Eric. "The Limits of Self Regard." Parnassus 1 (1972): 152–62.

Rexroth, Kenneth. "Bearded Barbarians or Real Bards?" *The New York Times Book Review,* 12 Feb. 1961, 44–45.

Rosenfield, Alvin H. "The Being of Language and the Language of Being: Heidegger and Modern Poetics." *Boundary* 4 (1976): 535–53. Rpt. in *Martin Heidegger and the Question of Literature: Toward a Postmodern Literary Hermeneutics.* 1976. Ed. William V. Spanos. Bloomington: Indiana University Press, 1979. 195–213.

Wagner, Linda Welshimer, ed. *Denise Levertov: In Her Own Province.* Insights II: Working Papers in Contemporary Criticism. New York: New Directions, 1979.

————. "Matters of the Here and Now." Rev. of *The Poet in the World. The Nation,* 22 June 1974, 795–96.

Younkins, Ronald. "Denise Levertov and the Hasidic Tradition." *Descant* 19 (1974): 40–48.

DENISE LYNCH

Denise Levertov in Pilgrimage

In the essay "A Sense of Pilgrimage" (*The Poet in the World*, 1973), Denise Levertov finds the theme of journey running throughout her poetry, at times aspiring to mythic force through religious symbolism and ritual. The enduring power of Christian myth to inform poetry is evident in two of Levertov's recent collections, *Candles in Babylon* and *Breathing the Water*. Here Levertov channels her political commitment and "rebellious *caritas*" (Gilbert 349) into conventional gestures of faith, and infuses the joy of spiritual community into the isolate poetic act. Levertov's observations in "Origins of a Poem" (*World*) seem particularly relevant to these collections: "The art of realizing inner experience in material substance is in itself an action *toward others*. . . . The Substance, the means, of an art, is an incarnation—not reference but phenomenon" (49–50). The most compelling poems take Levertov's pilgrimage into the mysteries of language and faith, where the Logos is revealed through the flesh of Christian tradition, and even the terror of a nuclear age yields to the numinous moment.

Levertov's professed faith in a "God revealed in the Incarnation" springs from an imagination which embraces "paradoxes too vast to fit our mental capacities and, thus, never perceived in their entirety" ("A Poet's View" 46–49). Her poems associate the creative act not only with hearing the Word, as does Velasquez's "young Black servant intently listening" to Christ ("The Servant Girl at Emmaus," *Breathing* 66), but with finding in the Incarnation creaturely assurance of redemption. The Venerable Bede's story of Caedmon, the unlettered cowherd who receives the divine gift of song, demonstrates how attentiveness to the material world empowers the imagination and kindles faith. Though Levertov's Caedmon (*Breathing* 65) is a "clodhopper" who breaks the gliding ring of his companions, he is mutely observant of nature's dance, "the motes / of gold moving / from shadow to shadow," and when heaven kindles his Christian

Reprinted from *Sagetrieb* 8, no. 1–2 (Spring and Fall 1989): 175–89.

imagination his voice is irresistibly pulled "into the ring of the dance." Caedmon's full participation in the human community requires that he give utterance to vision: that the Word become word. In "Candlemas" (*Breathing* 70) Simeon likewise finds "certitude" of redemption in the Incarnation, the "infant light" that allows him to turn "illumined / towards deep night."

Other poems in *Breathing the Water* attest to an affinity with the seventeenth-century poet George Herbert who, like Levertov, sometimes loses this assurance of God's love. In "Standoff" (67), for example, the speaker remonstrates against doubt: "Assail God's hearing. . . . / Cozen the saints. . . . / When shall we / dare to fly?" To reenact Incarnation is to imbue with life the stony recess of the heart, so that it becomes an encampment of poetic faith. Thus in "La Cordelle" (72–74), a poem reminiscent of Herbert's "The Altar," the uncarved block of stone standing within the chapel is transformed into an altar by the vibrant flowers placed in offering before it, "the entire bouquet / singing its colors / the livelong / empty day, the stones / resanctified." The poet's painterly imagination, transforming stones which held "memory of shame," affirms and "sustains" life.

"Mass for the Day of St. Thomas Didymus," the longest poem in *Candles in Babylon* (108–15), also finds hope in the gestures of faith and imagination. Structurally and thematically, this work realizes the synthesis of life and death Levertov admires in Rilke and achieves, as Joan Hallisey observes (289), a lyrical fusion of private and public voices. The poem is divided into six parts corresponding to sections of the liturgy of the Mass. Beginning with the "Kyrie" and ending with the "Agnus Dei," Levertov's persona participates in a redemptive pilgrimage of love that promises to find culmination in the Eucharistic banquet. The "Mass" is offered on the day honoring the Apostle who, in spite of his love for God, would not believe in the Resurrection until he touched the wounds of crucifixion. This is "doubting" Thomas the twin (Didymus), whose vacillations between belief and unbelief embody for Levertov the contemporary spiritual dilemma.

Levertov's comments on the genesis of her "Mass" suggests that its richly varied cadences and voices not only follow liturgical order but enact a private psychodrama of faith:

> My initial idea was just to use those forms which have been so nourishing as a structure for composers through so many centuries and see what I could do with them in poetry. So it started off, paradoxically, as an agnostic mass. In the process

of writing it, I moved somewhere . . . it gets to the incarnation. I now define myself as a Christian, but not a very orthodox one and I think that there is a way of looking at Christian faith as involving the cooperation of man. (Smith 603)

Juxtaposing quiet colloquies with the "deep unknown" with hymns of praise and anguished afterthoughts, the "Mass" captures the "rhythm of the inner voice" (*World* 24) and the *melos* of longing. In its synthesis of terror and hope, it lyrically affirms the redemptive power of imagination.

Hayden Carruth has used the term "spiritual imagination" to refer to Levertov's keen awareness of otherness: her sense of the subjectivity and holiness of all creation (145). That "spiritual imagination" is manifest in the "Mass," which checks the free-falls into dread with praise for the mystery, flux and plenitude of creation. Thus the "Gloria" celebrates the "unknown," all experience countering expectation or defying explanation ("Praise the wet snow / falling early"), all contraries of shadow and light, heat and cold, visibility and invisibility, earth and life. The "Credo" (110), a personal statement of belief and doubt, intones the holiness of every "minim mote" and identifies imagination with the elixir of faith: "Thou . . . / lover of making, of the / wrought letter, / wrought flower, / iron, deed, dream." In the alchemy of the creative act, the "common dust" of earth reveals a divine presence: "Drift, / gray become gold, in the beam of / vision." Every act of naming that springs from the imagination is holy and recapitulates the Incarnation, when—infinity found finite habitation. The "Sanctus" (111) reaffirms this in its exalted praise for

> all that Imagination
> has wrought, has rendered,
> striving, in throes of epiphany—
>
> naming, forming—to give
> to the Vast Loneliness
> a hearth, a locus—

Like childbirth, the labored utterance of those names ("throes of epiphany") is an act of faith claiming the void as a "harboring" rather than threatening silence. The "Benedictus" (111–13) offers thanksgiving for this power of naming, as well as for the things that can be named:

The name of the spirit is written
in woodgrain, windripple, crystal,

in crystals of snow, in petal, leaf,
moss and moon, fossil and feather,

blood, bone, song, silence,
very word of
very word,
flesh and
vision.

For Levertov, the Word manifests itself in all things fulfilling natural purpose ("Blessèd is that which utters / its being"), as well as in the poet's celebration of those things with language, the "flesh" embodying "vision."

In Levertov's "Mass," doubt repeatedly threatens to throttle this voice of praise. The poem parenthetically asks whether the Word can still inspire gestures of faith in an evil world, whether the spirit is "Yet to be felt / on the palm, in the breast / by deafmute dreamers" (112); the dread of global extinction is a "destructive vortex" diminishing our humanity no less than the instruments of violence themselves. The speaker's spiritual vacillation, deftly rendered in the "Benedictus" (113) by irregular line lengths, abruptly returns to fervent prayer: "Blessèd / be the dust. . . . / The word / chose to become / flesh. In the blur of flesh / we bow, baffled." The "Benedictus" thus allows its own recovered harmony to suggest the drowning out of evil's "cacophony." The final blessing of "dust" is an acceptance of language as a sacramental instrument of "vision," however much impaired.

The "Mass for the Day of St. Thomas Didymus" ends with the "Agnus Dei" (113–14), the prayer of inner peace preceding the liturgy of the Eucharist. Christ is the "lamb of God" in John 1:29, whose defenseless innocence poses a terrifying challenge to humanity. The "Agnus Dei" probes the relationship between God's name and essence and, by extension, between language and reality. Christ is not only "lamb" but "woolbearer, bleater, / leaper in air," delightful yet troublesome; the names signify both the phenomenon and mystery of Incarnation, the concreteness and elusiveness of language. Levertov also invests the iconography of white and red, traditional symbols of Christ's purity and Passion, with new immediacy; the playful lamb's vulnerability can be repugnant, "an innocence / smelling of ignorance, / born in bloody snowdrifts, licked by forebearing / dogs more intelligent than its entire flock put together," but it challenges us to discover the "milk" of compassion even within our "icy hearts."

Levertov's "Mass" asserts, perhaps more eloquently than any other poem in *Candles in Babylon,* the power of poetry to preserve this vision of compassion in an "age of terror." The final colloquy (115) replaces the abstractions of the "Kyrie" ("O deep unknown") with the image of the frail lamb, an incarnation of poetic faith:

> So be it.
>> Come, rag of pungent
>> quiverings,
>>> dim star.
>>> Let's try
>>> if something human still
>>> can shield you,
>>>> spark
>>> of remote light.

That "something human" is at once the mystery of Incarnation, the individual communicant receiving the Eucharist, the spiritual community participating in liturgy, and the language imaginatively wrought by the poet as she renders the illumined moment. The "Mass on the Day of St. Thomas Didymus" recalls Levertov's observation that the "music of poetry comes into being when thought and feeling . . . become Word, become Flesh" (*World* 17), for its contrapuntal voices of dread and joy blend into a song of praise having both public and personal resonance. By accepting the limitations of the word in the "downspin of time," Levertov also reaffirms her own poetic witness.

In *Breathing the Water,* Levertov turns to the fourteenth-century visionary Julian of Norwich for meditation on divine love. In May 1373 Julian, an anchoress at Norwich, was granted her earlier threefold request to suffer physically as a young woman, to understand Christ's Passion and to receive as God's gift three wounds, when she became gravely ill and experienced sixteen showings in one day. A record of her original account and later meditations on the showings over the course of twenty years, Julian's *Revelations of Divine Love* articulate the theme of pilgrimage central to Levertov's poetry. Although God is in all things, "concentrated as it were, in a single point" (chap. 11, 80), ubiquitous and therefore immeasurable, Julian also experienced Him within the city of her soul in another way: "as being as it were on pilgrimage; in other words, he is here with us, leading us on, and staying by us until he has brought us all to blessedness in heaven" (chap. 81, 206). The meaning of God's revelations to Julian is love, that of a Maker for His Creation and, in terms more accessible to humanity, the love of a mother for her child: "So we see that Jesus is the true Mother of our nature, for he made us. He is our Mother, too, by grace, because he took our created nature upon himself" (chap. 59, 168). Levertov imagines Julian's spiritual quest beginning in an idyllic childhood nourished by attentive motherly love, and the poem contains numerous images of enclosure that suggest a soul's gestation: "tall towers," "bowls," "hall," "bower," "two cupped palms," "nest," "small dark room," "under-water." In the tradition of the Benedictine St. Anselm's "Oratio 65" (Molinari 170), Levertov finds in the image of the Virgin's womb a compelling metaphor for God's protective love and indwelling presence: "waking each day within our microcosm, we find it, and ourselves." Like the "Mass," the poems inspired by Julian narrate a pilgrimage towards love.

In the *Revelations* Julian recalls envisioning the Virgin as a "simple humble girl" whose "profound reverence" for her Creator makes her wise beyond her years (chap. 4, 67). This wisdom lies in recognizing "the greatness of her Creator and the smallness of her created self" (67), an important theme of Julian's treatise and the basis for sections one to three of "The Showings." Although Levertov's persona shares with Julian the consciousness of living in "dark times," with "war, and the Black Death, hunger, strife, / torture, massacre" (81), she feels distanced from her medieval subject by the knowledge contemporary humanity shoulders:

> Julian, there are vast gaps we call black holes,
> unable to picture what's both dense and vacant;
>
> and there's the dizzying multiplication of all
> language can name or fail to name, unutterable
> swarming of molecules.
>
> (75)

Moreover, the limitations of language in naming and organizing an ever-expanding universe invites, rather than the "true dread" of reverence Julian exalts (chap. 74, 193–94), the false dread of fear: "All Pascal / imagined he could not stretch his mind to imagine / is known to exceed his dread" (75). The final phrase is provocatively ambiguous; does our knowledge exceed anything Pascal dreaded to imagine, or has our knowledge brought us dread exceeding his? Pascal lived in an age (1623–62) that sought to investigate and understand reality through mathematical reasoning. The scientific era had begun and for some the "dizzying" logical structures of Cartesianism threatened belief in God's existence. Pascal's response was to champion the truths of the heart and the mystery of faith. His wager on divinity transformed the doubt stemming from a fascination with the unfathomable reaches of the universe. Levertov's allusion to Pascal calls attention to the false "dread" of fear she experiences as one living in the late twentieth century, when the old heretical idea of infinite space seems vindicated by discoveries of subatomic particles and new galactic frontiers. "The Showings" records a pilgrimage from the dread of doubt aroused by the "unutterable" reaches of outer space, to the dread of reverence inspired by inner space, the Word within.

Accordingly, the poem redefines space as it shifts focus from "black holes" to the mundane objects of daily history and then to the metaphysical space embodied in a "little thing":

> And you ask us to turn our gaze
> inside out, and see
> *a little thing, the size of a hazelnut,* and believe
> it is our world? Ask us to see it lying
> in God's pierced palm? That it encompasses
> every awareness our minds contain? All Time?
> . . . .
> Yes, this is indeed
> what you ask, sharing
> the mystery you were shown: *all that is made:*
> a little thing, the size of a hazelnut, held safe
> in God's pierced palm.

(75)

For Julian this "little thing" manifests three truths: that God made the world, loves it and sustains it (chap. 5, 68). Paradoxically, one has to accept the littleness of creation to grasp the greatness of the uncreated God upon whom its existence depends. This is the medieval enigma that bodies forth all "awareness," all time and space, and argues for divine love in the midst of "dark times."

Levertov finds in the "mystic" Julian no rejection of the physical world, but a longing for "supreme reality" to reveal itself through the flesh, as the poet's metaphor might express vision. Julian writes that the soul becomes a city of God when it is breathed into sensuality, and that Christ is the Mother of both our essential being and sensual nature: "That wonderful city, the seat of our Lord Jesus, is our sensuality in which he is enclosed, just as the substance of our nature is enclosed in him as with his blessed soul he sits at rest in the Godhead" (chap. 56, 11). Yet our sensuality must be "raised to the level of our substance" through virtue, mercy, and grace if we are to attain "full knowledge of God" (chap. 56, 161). Reflecting these ideas, the pilgrimage of Levertov's Julian takes her beyond the human love cut short by destiny: "Whatever that story, / long since she had travelled / through and beyond it" (76). Reading calls her up into "tall towers / of learning" where she changes in time; ultimately, the longing to witness God outstrips all other needs:

> To desire wounds—
> three, no less, no more—
> is audacity, not, five centuries early, neurosis;
> it's the desire to enact metaphor, for flesh to make known
> to intellect (as uttered song
> > makes known to voice,
> > as image to eye)
> make known in bone and breath
> (and not die) God's agony.
>
> (76)

Incarnation links Levertov with her subject: *Revelations of Divine Love* and "The Showings" spring from the same longing to share knowledge of love.

Just as Julian frequently employs the traditional meditative practice of composing a mental image of her subject for analysis and prayer, so Levertov comprehends Julian by evoking the child's sensory wonder, and the world of lush natural beauty that might have provided countless stimuli for the imagination: "the dairy's bowls of clabber, of rich cream," "a cake of butter / set on a green leaf," the cuckoo "changing its tune" (77). Amid this plenty, Julian might have seen the image of crucified Christ emblazoned on the stained glass of the village church: "You could see / Christ and his mother and his cross, / you could see his blood, and the throne of God" (79). Julian's mature vision of the world as a "little thing, the size of a hazelnut" might have been rooted in one happy moment when her mother gave her "a sparrow's egg from the hedgerow" (78). In such a moment, the eyes might have led Julian to the "imaginative understanding" and "spiritual sight" she alludes to in *Revelations* (chap. 9, 76) and revealed love as the meaning of Incarnation:

> God for a moment in our history
> placed in that five-fingered
> human nest
> the macrocosmic egg, sublime paradox,
> brown hazelnut of All that Is—
> made, and belov'd, and preserved.
> As still, waking each day within
> our microcosm, we find it, and ourselves.
>
> (78)

Collective history merges with the "daily history" alluded to earlier in the poem, as the senses reveal to the inward eye the littleness of creation in comparison with the infinite dimensions of divine love.

"The Showings" dramatizes a level of spiritual assurance absent from "Mass for the Day of St. Thomas Didymus," where a consciousness of global peril threatens to stifle imagination and obscure the Word. Julian is a "pilgrim of the depths" whose understanding of God's protective love allows her to laugh in scorn at the Devil. In the thirteenth and sixty-ninth showings Julian narrates her triumphs over the Fiend's temptations by meditating on Christ's Passion. Although Julian in the first temptation does not see Christ's laugh, she intuitively recognizes His scorn for the devil's malice and laughs so heartily that those surrounding her sickbed also laugh: "I saw our Lord scorn such malice, and expose the emptiness of the Fiend's powerlessness; and it is his will that we should do the same . . . their laughter did me good. I thought I would have liked all my fellow Christians to have seen what I saw, that they might laugh with me" (chap. 13, 84). Levertov (79–80) brings the scene to life and captures the emotional currents of the occasion: how the room "quivered" in a contagion of laughter as Julian sees the "oafish, ridiculous" Fiend and then, as the others are left "stranded in hilarity," reflects on the price Christ paid to counter the devil's malice: "The deathly // wounds and the anguished / heart."

Levertov's persistent joy in the present and, in the words of

"An English Field in the Nuclear Age," her recognition that "to render that isolate knowledge, certain . . . / there is no sharing save in the furnace, / the transubstantiate, acts / of passion" (*Candles* 79) find in Julian's visions an apt vehicle. The medieval writer's impulse to seek God and clearly discern his presence comes from the gift of grace and is ultimately rewarded with ineffable comfort. In the second revelation, she recalls her spiritual submersion:

> On another occasion I was led in imagination down to the sea-bed, and there I saw green hills and valleys looking as though they were moss-covered, with seaweed and sand. This I understand to mean that if a man or woman were under-sea and saw God ever present with him (as indeed God is) he would be safe in body and soul, and take no hurt. Moreover, he would know comfort and consolation beyond all power to tell. (chap. 10, 77)

Described in "The Showings" (81) as a "walking under-water / on the green hills of moss, the detailed sand and seaweed," this inner pilgrimage offers the possibility of transforming the great evils that can shake a person, in a metaphor taken from Julian, "*sorrowfully, mournfully, / shaken as men shake / a cloth in the wind.*" The synthesis of imagination and faith, of outer and inner vision, offers Julian personal redemption through love, and a joy that, although fragile, commands witness:

>   you clung to joy though tears and sweat
>   rolled down your face like the blood
>   you watched pour down *in beads uncountable*
>   *as rain from the eaves:*
>   clung like an acrobat, by your teeth, fiercely,
>   to a cobweb-thin high-wire, your certainty
>   of infinite mercy, witnessed
>   with your own eyes, with outward sight
>   in your small room, with inward sight
>   in your untrammeled spirit—
>   knowledge we long to share:
>   *Love was his meaning.*
>
>   (82)

The ambiguity of "knowledge we long to share" expresses Levertov's desire to extract meaning from *Revelations* and simultaneously participate in a communal act of sharing. The line recalls the ending of "The Many Mansions": "For that the vision / was given me: to know and share, // passing from hand to hand. . . . // the amulet of mercy" (*Candles* 116). A similarly intimate voice repeatedly utters Julian's name in the final section of "The Showings" ("Julian, Julian— / I turn to you"), but becomes a collective ("we") voice; the solitary pilgrim travels here within a spiritual community knowing no boundaries of time or space.

Levertov's poems on Julian engage the reader in meditative exercises kindling imagination and kinship. "On a Theme from Julian's Chapter XX" (*Breathing* 68–69) ponders the meaning of the Passion, and of finite time, as does Julian's Revelations. Composing for meditation a vivid image of the crucified Christ ("hot wood, the nails, blood trickling / into the eyes") Levertov's speaker gradually understands the inadequacy of human time in measuring Christ's passion. The intellect can provide a knowledge of history, a taste of the ashes of the "long tormented," a breathing in of the "ancient dust of the world," but it cannot clarify our vision of the six-hour agony on the cross: "Torture then, torture now, / the same, the pain's the same, / immemorial branding iron, / electric prod." The mystic Julian, however, grasped that the difference between divine and human time lies in the paradox of Incarnation; the "*oneing / with the Godhead*" opened Him to an infinity of pain, an understanding of "*every sorrow and desolation*" throughout history.

Like "The Mass for the Day of St. Thomas Didymus," "On a Theme from Julian's Chapter XX" embraces this fusion of flesh and divinity as the prototypical creative act, in which imagination reveals a unity of being even through the lens of selfhood:

> The great wonder is
> that the human cells of His flesh and bone
> didn't explode
> when utmost Imagination rose
> in that flood of knowledge. Unique
> in agony, Infinite strength, Incarnate,
> empowered Him to endure
> inside of history,
> . . . .
> within the mesh of the web, Himself
> woven within it, yet seeing it,
> seeing it whole.

(69)

Levertov's search for "organic form," which she defines as "an intuition of an order, a form beyond forms . . . of which man's creative works are analogies, resemblances, natural allegories" (*World* 7), here enters the realm of sacred mystery, where Christian myth serves as the focus of contemplation.

Levertov's comments on contemplation and meditation in "Some Notes on Organic Form" anticipate the spiritual path her recent poems have taken. To meditate means to keep the mind in contemplation, so that "the heat of feeling warms the intellect" and the poet can "observe" and "regard . . . in the presence of a god"; "the poet stands openmouthed in the temple of life, contemplating his experience" (*World* 8). This sense of the poet as priest whose acts are sacramental and communal is conveyed with new depth in the poems on Julian, which recall Levertov's observations in "Origins of a Poem": "When the poet converses with this god he has summoned into manifestation, he reveals to others the possibility of their own dialogue with the god in themselves. Writing the poem is the poet's means of summoning the divine" (*World* 47). The Christian god summoned in Julian's *Revelations* and Levertov's poems on the anchorite embodies goodness and inspires a vision of community: "God, as I see it, is everything that is good; he has made the whole of creation, and loves all that he has made" (*Revelations,* chap. 9, 75). To "breathe the water" is to summon this God of infinite love amid the transient sufferings of a fallen world.

Like Julian, the pilgrim-artist can only "enact metaphor," experience mystery within the web of language and time. Yet this veiled "seeking" is for Levertov, no less than her medieval subject, its own reward. Similarly, Levertov's attraction to Rainer Maria Rilke's work rests partly in the joy he found in artistic process. In the essay "The Poet in the World," Levertov quotes from one of Rilke's letters a passage expressing the double satisfaction in work available to an artist: "even this most urgent realization of a higher reality appears . . . as a means to win something once more invisible, . . . a saner state in the midst of our being" (*World* 113). Visible and invisible elements exist in sacramental tension and exert their pull on the artist. Levertov's interest in the relation of outer to inner form is well known, and she finds in Rilke an artist whose interest in craft stems from a sense of the spiritual dimensions of creativity. Her recent poems reclaim Rilke's joy in "such inseeing, in the indescribably swift, deep, timeless moments of this divine inseeing" ("Rilke As Mentor," *Light Up the Cave* 288).

"Variation on a Theme by Rilke" (*Breathing* 71) expresses the idea of art as a communion of craftsman and observer, spirit and matter, vision and medium, the One and the many. Giotto, Rembrandt, all whose "inspired depictions" of God were not "a willed fiction" but testament of irrepressible faith, rendered truth. In Rilke's *Book of Hours,* book 1, poem 4, such painted images form a protective fortress around the heart's treasure: "We've built up images / like walls before you, / till now you're hemmed with thousands of ramparts" ("Wir bauen Bilder vor dir auf wie Wände / so dass schon tausend Mauern um dich stehn," *Das Stunden-Buch* 8). Levertov turns the walls into a sanctuary harboring an inner presence, rather than a fortress—a cathedral whose majesty rests in its marriage of outer and inner structures:

> The seraph buttress flying
> to support a cathedral's external walls,
> the shadowy ribs of the vaulted sanctuary:
> aren't both—and equally—
> the form of a holy place?

The stained-glass windows' ruby glow can be viewed from the inside, but only because of the light filtering through them. The artistic process is at once a private and public act: "Each, at work in his art, / perceived his neighbor," the individual artists executing vision yet conscious of otherness. In this synthesis of inner and outer truths, the artist manifests "grace," the condition of longing which for Julian "works to uplift, to regard, and ever to surpass all we desire or deserve" (*Revelations,* chap. 48, 136–37). Yet even the inspired truths of art are only "clues to His mystery," leading us on but never providing full knowledge of infinity.

The poems in *Breathing the Water* nevertheless register the hope that accompanies a sense of pilgrimage. Levertov's speaker repeatedly awakens to a renewed awareness of possibilities: echoing the bell that in Rilke's poem rings in the canonical hours "clear and metallic" ("Da neigt sich die Stunde und ruhrt mich an / mit clarem, metellenem Schlag"), Levertov's day grants both "honor and task"; in the first poem in the book, another "Variation on a Theme by Rilke" (3), she undertakes the quest with knightly zeal and faith in her own creative powers: "what I heard was my whole self / saying and singing what it knew: *I can.*" The wanderer of "The Spirits Appeased" (8) finds no one to receive him in the "forest hut," yet his attentiveness reveals an invisible presence affording replenishment. In the last poem in *Breathing the Water,* yet another "Variation and Reflection" (83) inspired by Rilke's *Book of Hours* (book 1, poem 7), the mind's craving for a "timeless moment" of "stillness," when the self might transcend the mechanistic laws of a physical universe and paradoxically contain "boundlessness," cannot be sated. The first part of Levertov's poem echoes Rilke's plaintive wish for a quiet moment of spiritual fulfillment: "If only stillness reigned, pure, elemental. / If silence fell on all that's accidental / and casual and the neighbor's laugh were quiet." ("Wenn es nur einmal so ganzstille ware. / Wenn das Zufallige und Ungefahre / verstummte und das nachbarliche lachen," *Buch* 9–10). But Levertov completes the implied syllogism in part two of her poem, which answers wish with reality. We can never get beyond the veil of happenstance; like Julian we can only receive wounds, and feel spirit "within the pulse of flesh" and "in the dust of being." The second part of Levertov's poem borrows the image of ringed flight from Rilke's second meditation: "Round God, the old tower, my gyres I perform, / and I've gyred there centuries long" ("Ich kreise um Gott, um den uralten Turm, / und ich kreise jahrtausendelang" *Buch* 7). While Rilke's "gyre" suggests creative empowerment, Levertov makes humanity the center of God's orbit; the circle becomes an emblem of both our spiritual longing and human limitation. Vision flies on the wings of time; the desire for "stillness" is at once the condition and cause of our pilgrimage:

> the wings of the morning
> brush through our blood
> as cloud-shadows brush the land.
> What we desire travels with us.
> We must breathe time as fishes breathe water.
> God's flight circles us.

For Levertov the mystery of Infinity circumscribes our lives and defines our common humanity.

The most moving poems in these recent collections achieve a synthesis of personal and cultural inheritance that Levertov finds in "myth-in-poetry at its most penetrating" ("Pilgrimage," *World* 83). They enact an artistic process that is both pilgrimage and incarnation, a seeking and sharing of spiritual knowledge. Mystery is rendered in the temporal rhythms of Christian worship, as in the haunting images of "Embrasure" (*Breathing* 15):

James with his cockleshell or Genevieve
a fraction westward move each day
in ruby beads,

. . . .

In cloud or dark invisible
yet moving always, and in light

turning—the circle
east by west or west by east
day after day

constant in pilgrimage.

The joy Levertov characteristically finds in "living in the moment" (*Light Up the Cave* 111) is now commingled with serene faith in a spiritual community beyond time and death: "dustmote congregations file / endlessly through the slanted amethyst." In the impulse to see the Word revealed through the flesh of language, Levertov uncovers the common ground upon which many poet-pilgrims have tread.

WORKS CITED

Carruth, Hayden. "What 'Organic' Means?" *Sagetrieb* 4 (1985): 145–46.

Gilbert, Sandra. "Revolutionary Love: Denise Levertov and the Poetics of Politics." *Parnassus* 12 (1985): 335–51.

Hallisey, Joan F. "Denise Levertov—'Forever a Stranger and Pilgrim.' " *Centennial Review* 30 (1986): 281–91.

Julian of Norwich. *Revelations of Divine Love.* Trans. Clifton Wolters. Baltimore: Penguin Books, 1966.

Levertov, Denise. *Breathing the Water.* New York: New Directions, 1987.

———. *Candles in Babylon.* New York: New Directions, 1982.

———. *Light Up the Cave.* New York: New Directions, 1981.

———. *The Poet in the World.* New York: New Directions, 1973.

———. "A Poet's View." *Religion and Intellectual Life* (Summer 1984): 46–53.

Molinari, Paul. *Julian of Norwich.* London: Longmans, Green and Co., 1958.

Rilke, Rainer Maria. *Selected Works.* 2 vols. Trans. J. B. Leishman. New York: New Directions, 1967.

———. *Das Stunden-Buch.* Leipzig: Insel-Derlag, 1931.

Smith, Lorrie. "An Interview with Denise Levertov." *Michigan Quarterly Review* 24 (1985): 596–604.

EDWARD ZLOTKOWSKI

In the Garden

A Place of Creation

a garden flowing behind a rooted house
"They Looking Back . . . ," *The Double Image*

I

In an essay entitled "The Untaught Teacher," Denise Levertov writes: "My principal efforts . . . were . . . to awaken [her students'] powers of sensuous observation . . . as the only foundation for technical development in the art of poetry" (*PW,* 173). For Levertov herself such powers were awakened at home at an early age:

> [My mother] taught me to look;
> to name the flowers when I was still close to the ground,
> my face level with theirs;
> or to watch the sublime metamorphoses
> unfold and unfold
> over the walled back gardens of our street . . .
>
> ("The 90th Year," *LF*)

"Looking" and "naming" were the lessons taught, and the place of instruction was the garden behind the poet's childhood home. Furthermore, the line "my face level with theirs" is to be taken at face value. For as another poem tells us, the "lessons" did indeed begin in "Earliest Spring":

> This is the earliest
> spring of my life. Last year
>
> I was a baby, and what I saw then
> is forgotten. Now I'm a child.
>
> (*LF*)

From this biographical beginning the image of the garden—both in a literal and in a more extended sense—grows into one of the most significant figures in Levertov's work. No other locale equals it in effective resonance or spiritual power.

II

The importance of the garden as creative base and psychological touchstone makes itself felt in Levertov's very first book, *The Double Image*. Indeed, the very first poem in that book opens with a scene that establishes many of the key associations this image will carry throughout her writings. For although "Childhood's End" does not begin with a garden in the strict sense, its opening scene does suggest a place of beauty, magic, and safety that constitutes a *hortus conclusus* in all but name.

> The world alive with love, where leaves tremble,
> systole and diastole marking miraculous hours,
> is burning round the children where they lie
> deep in caressing grasses all the day,
> and feverish words of once upon a time
> assail their hearts with langour and with swans.

As line 3 suggests, this natural but also intense and visionary world belongs especially to children—or at least to those who have not lost their ability to believe in wonders. It is, moreover, a world "alive" both with love and with transformation. As the poet, in a much later poem, says of her original childhood garden:

> Now as if smoke or sweetness were blown my way
> I inhale a sense of her [sister's] livingness in that instant,
> . . . .
> a young girl in the garden, the same alchemical square
> I grew in, we thought sometimes
> too small for our grand destinies—
>
> ("Olga Poems," 3, 2, *SD*)

The word "alchemical" carries great weight, for it marks the garden as a place of mysteries and miracles, "bells and flames" ("Earliest Spring," *LF*), a place where appearances become epiphanies, where sight becomes vision, where the alert imagination renders every phenomenon most real and every experience most intense. The second poem of *The Double Image* suggests as much—through the language of fairy tales:

the world grew,
a garden flowing behind a rooted house.

Trees in the park were wearing coats of mail:
the nightly fairy tale lived there by day—
flying Mary Anna,
little crying loaves,
the eight wonderful stones.
To bed by daylight meant a secret journey.

But this second poem also adds an important new association. For Levertov chose for its title a line from the conclusion of *Paradise Lost,* " 'They, Looking Back, All th' Eastern Side Beheld,' " and this reference, in turn, suggests that the garden—and all it signifies—can be compared with Eden. To be in the garden, to return to the garden, is to claim one's original birthright of joy, creativity, and proximity to the divine: "In the beginning was delight" ("Relearning the Alphabet," *RA*).[1]

But it is not just in Levertov's poetry that the garden and the gardenlike possess special resonance. In her various prose reminiscences the same constellation of concepts appears with a power and consistency that leaves little doubt as to its generative creative importance. For when Levertov was growing up, her hometown, Ilford, was still a relatively rural suburb of London. She had two great parks right next door, and her freedom from formal schooling left her much time to wander and explore—not just these parks but the surrounding English countryside as well. And in its gentle beauty, variety, and safety the latter quickly became a kind of extended "garden" to the adventurous child. Here, often accompanied by her older sister, she would set off on rambles which were the "grown-up" equivalent of her first walks with her mother: adventures in which both the eye and the imagination were intensely—and pleasurably—awakened.[2] Indeed, this extended gardenlike landscape eventually came to represent for Levertov the "place of origin,"[3] and its parameters are nowhere more lyrically and lovingly celebrated than in the poem "A Map of the Western Part of the County of Essex in England" (*JL*).

I am Essex-born:
Cranbrook Wash called me into its dark tunnel,
the little streams of Valentines heard my resolves,
Roding held my head above water when I thought it was

drowning me; in Hainault only a haze of thin trees
stood between the red doubledecker buses and the boar-hunt,
the spirit of merciful Phillipa glimmered there.
Pergo Park knew me, and Clavering, and Havering-atte-Bower,
Stanford Rivers lost me in osier beds, Stapleton Abbots
sent me safe home on the dark road after Simeon-quiet evensong,
Wansted drew me over and over into its basic poetry. . . .

Given this sense of the surrounding English countryside as a kind of "earthly paradise" ("By Rail through the Earthly Paradise, Perhaps Bedfordshire," *EP*), it is not surprising that in many of Levertov's autobiographical reminiscences it should reveal a creative and affective power that recalls the vivid natural pleasures of the young Wordsworth. One example is especially striking.

In a piece appropriately entitled "*MY* Prelude" (emphasis added), Levertov tells how "One spring morning, led by a surge of common sense and the hand of the Muse . . . I quit my ballet class never to return" (*LC*, 244). What follows is a true "conversion" account in that it presents the young poet finally and unequivocally awakening to the reality of her calling. And where does this conversion take place? By now we will recognize several familiar features.

When I slowed down and looked about me I saw it was spring. A chaffinch—I remember that it was a chaffinch because next day I looked it up in a bird book—was singing on a branch that overhung the lane in which I found myself. It had rained the night before, and now in mid morning the earth still smelled damp and fresh. Leaves and grass were that new light green I associated with the Middle Ages and with some of the earliest English poems. Rivulets rippled in the ditches, and there were small wildflowers in the hedgerows. Only a month or two before I had written sadly to my closest friend saying I felt I'd lost the intensity of sight . . . I'd had as a child. Now I realized I was taking in with restored vision all that I had thought was lost to me. I was released from a dull enchantment. (251)

That the older poet, looking back, should locate her "coming to her (creative) senses" in such a setting is hardly surprising, given her concept of a "place of origin." All the key elements of that first, "Earliest Spring" are here: the awareness of abundant, radiant natural beauty; the sensuous richness; a precision of seeing—and naming, intensity of vision; a feeling of sacred space and transformation; an elemental joy in being alive. And it is this same constellation of concepts that will return to characterize many other key moments and important turns in the adult poet's life—a signal, and a pledge, that the experience at hand represents inner growth, a further opening of the poet's ability to see.

III

But the interest that attends the garden in Levertov's work does not derive solely from its significance as a source of spiritual and creative power; it also derives from the fact that the garden—and all it represents—is imminently subject to loss. Indeed, the titles of the two early poems already referred to—"Childhood's End" and " 'They, Looking Back, All th' Eastern Side Beheld' "—clearly imply as much. For if the garden can be identified as the primary creative place in Levertov's world, loss of it can be identified as a primary fear. This fear, if we are to believe the poet's own testimony, goes back to the very beginnings of her psychic life. In a 1980 essay entitled "Interweavings: Reflections on the Role of Dream in the Making of Poems," Levertov recalls a dream she had when she was no more than six, a dream she still finds frightening.

> [It] was a kind of nightmare; and after it had recurred a number of times I found I could summon it at will. . . . Retrospectively, I see it as a mythic vision of Eden and the Fall: the scene is a barn, wooden and pleasantly—not scarily dark, in which the golden hay and straw are illuminated by a glow as of candlelight. And all around the room of the barn are seated various animals . . . and they look comfortable, relaxed. There's an atmosphere of great peace and well being and camaraderie. But suddenly—without a minute's transition—all is changed: all blackens, crinkles, and corrugates like burnt paper. There's a sense of horror.[4]

As Levertov herself notes, this dream can be interpreted as prophetic of "the nuclear holocaust we live in fear of," and indeed, ever since the Vietnam War, the potentially catastrophic power of human technology to waste the earth and its creatures has sounded as a major theme in her work.[5] Nevertheless, it is not technology that threatens the gardens of *The Double Image* and many subsequent volumes, but another danger—far less spectacular, though no less powerful: that ancient human "enemy," time. Indeed, even in " 'They Looking Back . . .' " with its implicit biblical associations, expulsion from Eden occurs, not because of any concrete act, but simply because "time grew hostile." The "Fall" is as natural, and inevitable, as any autumn.[6]

There are times in Levertov's work when the power of time to drive us from the garden—that place or state where life is intensely creative and deeply joyful—seems especially devastating. As the above may serve to suggest, this is certainly the case in many poems of the *The Double Image,* but it is no less true of the sequence of poems Levertov wrote on and around her mother's death in Mexico in 1977. Perhaps this should not be surprising, since no loss has touched her like this one.[7] After all, Beatrice Levertoff was not just her mother; she was, as we are told in "Death in Mexico" (*LF*), "the garden-maker"—she who first initiated the poet into the joys and mysteries of the garden. And so it is the final—albeit fitting—indignity that her mother's slide towards death should be most vividly marked by the neglect and dissolution of her last beloved garden.

> Even two weeks after her fall,
> three weeks before she died, the garden
> began to vanish.
> . . . .
>   Oh, there was green, still,
> but the garden was disappearing—each day
> less sign of the ordered,
> thought-out oasis, a squared circle her mind
> constructed for rose and lily, begonia
> and rosemary-for-remembrance.
> Twenty years in the making—
> less than a month to undo itself. . . .
>
>   ("Death in Mexico")

Natural dissolution—"is this how time / takes one?" ("Autumnal," *LF*) Unfortunately, time is not the garden's most tragic threat. Often allied to time, but more psychologically complex and multivalenced, is that other traditional threat to Eden: awareness, specifically, awareness of "evil," of life's dark side. Indeed, already running through many of the explicit and implicit dialogues of *The Double Image* is a debate between the desire to retain some kind of childlike openness and a dark "realism" that has "outgrown" such naivete.

But perhaps the clearest single example of how awareness can cancel delight occurs in the prose memoir "Growing Up, or When Anna Screamed" (*LC*, 3–11). Here Levertov describes in vivid detail one of those rare occasions when she and her sister allowed others to join them on a ramble through the English countryside. The journey is a magical one: "For many hours it seemed that we danced the day, danced it into being, created afternoon out of a chocolate bar, a rainstorm, and the emerging sungleams, and so would dance through life." Finally, the young people arrive at "a place that hushed us in wonder, a scene magically appropriate to such a day." It is an enclosed field full of browsing rabbits: "such a quiet, secret kind of place. One felt no one had passed that way for a long time. The sun was still quite bright, though slanting." And in a corner of this secret place, this place of marvels, they find an old barn.

> Up in the loft was a contained, warm ambiance. Light was pouring through the opening in a thick, almost palpable shaft, honey-gold and dense with motes. The place was filled with old but sweetsmelling hay—a huge mound, a mountain, of it.[8] Instinctively we dove into its tickly softness, in an instant we were bouncing and sliding in it. . . . It was the very peak of the day's joy, following on the mystery of the rabbits that had itself seemed a culminating marvel. Life was giving us a mode of utterance, a way to gesture delight with our whole untried bodies.

Though there are important differences between this "delightful" barn and the garden with its treasury of fresh flora, the present scene, "the very peak" of a daylong country ramble, is not unrelated. The protected natural setting, the spontaneity, the sense of mystery and marvels, the intensity of sensuous delight—all are characteristic of Levertov's Edenic locales. Indeed, the very language of this scene reveals a sonic intensity and density typical of Levertov's special moments of grace.

Suddenly, however, "from silent Anna, Anna the frowning one . . . unplayful Anna who today had played and joked . . . from silent Anna came a chilling scream." Buried in the mound of hay into which the group has been recklessly throwing itself appears "a shining, grinningly curved scythe blade." It is the serpent in the garden: a new knowledge of danger—and even death—that brings the entire idyll to an abrupt conclusion. Hence the piece's title: "Growing Up, or When Anna Screamed," for growing up involves precisely that awareness of the world's dangers that puts us on our guard, that teaches us to deflect vital energies from spontaneous openness and joyful intensity to critical distance and strategems of defense. Whether the danger that floods our awareness is as global as nuclear annihilation or as personal as emotional vulnerability, such defensive self-consciousness runs counter to what the garden represents.[9]

Hence, it is not surprising that in much of the poetry of the war years (1966–75), the accessibility—and even the relevance—of the garden as a state of mind and spirit is seriously qualified. This is not to say that the concept simply disappears. Nonetheless, its presence is often embattled or in some sense fragile. Nowhere is this more striking than in the poet's descriptions of North Vietnam, where America's bombs threaten to shatter a landscape almost fairy tale–like in its beauty and serenity. The much anthologized "What Were They Like?" (*SD*) is a case in point. In response to several questions about prewar Vietnam a voice explains:

> 1) Sir, their light hearts turned to stone.
>   It is not remembered whether in gardens
>   stone lanterns illumined pleasant ways.
> 2) Perhaps they gathered once to delight in blossom,
>   but after the children were killed
>   there were no more buds.

Gardens, blossoms, children, delight—given the almost Edenic qualities Levertov attributes to traditional Vietnamese culture, it is not surprising she fought so tenaciously against its destruction. Its rural base must have struck a deeply resonant chord.

But it is in Levertov's long journal poem *To Stay Alive* that we see, in its most developed and sustained form, the complex psychological and creative tension that can arise between what she at one point calls the "kindness / of the *private life*" and a "fearful / knowledge of *present history*." For here we find in the same person two very different tendencies: on the one hand, an English child with " 'roots in the 19th century,' " a child for whom the lush sensuousness of Keats's "Nightingale" and Hopkins's "gold-engrove" represent home (*SA*, 33–35), and, on the other hand, an antiwar activist whose awareness of human need and human brutality calls into question almost everything—including her own identity.[10] Given these contrary commitments, it is only appropriate that the events surrounding the Berkeley's People's Park should take on particular symbolic importance. For here Levertov found a special kind of "garden," a political Eden—the attempt to combine delight and justice, to create an urban park all human beings could share.

May 14th, 1969—Berkeley
Went with some of my students to work in the People's Park. There seemed to be plenty of digging and gardening help so we decided, as Jeff had his truck available, to shovel up the garbage that had been thrown into the west part of the lot and take it out to the city dump. (43)

She then goes on to describe her "happiness / in the sun":

> poets and dreamers studying
> joy together, clearing
> refuse off the neglected, newly recognized,
> humbly waiting ground, place, locus, of what could be our
> New World even now . . .
>
> each leaf of
> the new grass near us
> a new testament . . .[11]

But this urban garden was not to survive, and the police attack that stopped its reclamation proved to be a radicalizing experience of considerable power. The poet's eyes were now opened "to the whole system of insane greed, of racism and imperialism, of which war is only the inevitable expression" ("Author's Preface," *SA*, viii). Metaphorically speaking, one can describe a major task of Levertov's postwar poetry as the attempt to find a way to reenter and celebrate the garden without betraying one's historical and moral awareness.

V

For one cannot use the garden as an escape. Its significance is grounded in authenticity; its magic requires a heightening, not a clouding of reality. After all, this is the place of precise seeing and exact naming! The fact that the young woman of "Recoveries" is "vague," "accustomed to behave with dreamy rashness" (*LC*, 12–13), almost plunges her into personal tragedy, and when her near escape leads to

> the unfolding of a fuller, leafier springtime, she came to feel that reality, with its disasters, was not so alien to her nor she to it. It was as if she were wearing eyeglasses and finding that the images they revealed were not crude but brilliant in their clarity, and this brilliance had its own glamor, a precision compelling as the fuzzier, softer forms perceived by naked myopic eyes. (22)

Thus we come to a third and final way in which the experience of the garden can be lost. If we turn again to the prose piece entitled "My Prelude," we discover that the main reason the young poet seems to have "lost the intensity of sight [she'd] had as a child" was not the passage of time in and of itself nor even her being constantly beset by worries and demands. Instead, it was her failure to remain faithful to her imagination, to that primary creative self the garden nourishes and represents.

> My poetry had been at a standstill, blocked by the idea that I ought to create . . . but that summer I wrote out of what I *really* felt, really saw, instead of out of what I had been *trying* to feel and see. . . . From the day of my walk to Burnham Beeches there began to work in me—to ferment—a sense of what I couldn't do and could do: of who I was. (*LC*, 252–53)

Accuracy of vision and authenticity of voice—two signs of the true self. We recall once more those primary lessons Levertov learned from her mother, the "garden-maker." Unless one is prepared to see and speak accurately, with integrity, one will, like "The Old Adam" (*TS*), lose both the garden—and one's life. For "The Old Adam" is a figure who looks at his own past and sees

> A photo of someone else's childhood,
> a garden in another country—world
> he had no part in and has no power to imagine:
>
> yet the old man who has failed his memory
> keens over the picture. . . .

This is in some respects the most tragic—because the least excusable—way to forfeit the garden. The old Adam, the man of unredeemed imagination, loses his birthright out of spiritual sloth, greed, superficial ambition, personal cowardiceness, settling instead for a "life / unlived, of which he is dying / very slowly."[12] Hence, when the protagonist of "Recoveries" finally emerges from the haze in which she has lived, she is not only "taken unawares by a flood of joy." She also regains access to the "place of origin."

> A sense of absolute identification with her earliest memories, of seeing things when she was two or three years old with the self-same eyes she looked out of now, a feeling of the continuity of that past with the long future she was walking towards . . . exhilarated her. (*LC*, 21)

Indeed, consciously establishing access to this place can be seen as one important indication of Levertov's artistic maturation.

We noted above that the idea of loss through time is especially prominent in *The Double Image* and on the occasion of the poet's mother's death. Analogously, a concern with the dangers of inauthenticity is especially evident in the work of the late fifties and early sixties when the poet was at the point of finding her mature voice and establishing her poetic identity.[13] It is probably not coincidental that Levertov's turn from her own version of the short Williams lyric—the objective, image-dominated vignette of some present scene or object—to the more intense, subjective song for which she became famous was accompanied by a new reaching back into her own past for resonant scenes and figures. We have already seen how, in the poem "A Map of the Western Part of the County of Essex in England" (*JL*), the poet lovingly identifies herself as a child of the gardenlike Essex landscape. Here for the first time since her arrival in the United States "something forgotten for twenty years" presses itself into speech—an extended, detailed naming of the landscape of her youth:

ancient

rights of way where I walked when I was ten burning with
desire
for the world's great splendors, a child who traced voyages
indelibly all over the atlas, who now in a far country
remembers the first river,

. . . .

the walls of the garden, the first light.

Surely it is not coincidental that shortly after rediscovering this primary connection the poet first uses the phrase "place of origin" ("The Well") or that in the very next poem ("Come into Animal Presence") she goes on to proclaim the abiding power of what was once so efficacious.

> Those who were sacred have remained so,
> holiness does not dissolve, it is a presence
> of bronze, only the sight that saw it
> faltered and turned from it.
> An old joy returns in holy presence.

VI

With this critical rediscovery of "an old joy" Levertov might have gone on for the rest of her career delighting in the wonders of exact seeing and naming. However, by the time the sixties were only half over, first her sister's death and then America's escalating involvement in Vietnam led her to reclaim her "autumn birthright" ("A Lamentation," *SD*). And once the gates of grief had opened, a permanent chill threatened to wither the joys of "Earliest Spring." Indeed, the very first of the war poems opens with an image of "steel petals" blocking sight and song.

> Fair is the world.
> I sing.
> . . . . . .
>
> And before the song
> attains even a first refrain
>
> the petals creak and
> begin to rise.
> They rise and recurl
> in a bud's form
>
> and clamp shut.
> I wait in the dark.
>
> ("The Pulse," *SD*)

As we have seen, the "place of origin" seemed to recede during these years into an historical, geographical, and even spiritual distance. In "The Cold Spring" (*RA*), a poem of powerful and painful self-examination, Levertov laments:

What do I know?
>   Swing of the
>   birch catkins,
>   drift of
>   watergrass,
>   tufts of
>   green on the
>   trees,

. . . .

> It's not enough.

Hence, it would be hard to underestimate the significance of her first return to England after a twenty-year absence (1970). For as the psychological narrative of "To Stay Alive" makes clear, her return to England provided more than merely a welcome respite from the political and emotional turmoil of "Amerika." It also helped put her back in touch with that basic delight in simple, natural things that had always guided and nourished her imagination. And this, in turn, helped her find her way beyond the spiritual crisis brought on by the war. Nowhere is the significance of this return to England better summed up than in the title and final lines of a lyric that directly resulted from that trip, "By Rail through the Earthly Paradise, Perhaps Bedfordshire" (*FP*):

> no thirst for righteousness
> dries my throat, I am silent
> and happy, and troubled only
> by my own happiness. Looking,
>
> looking and naming. I wish the train now
> would halt for me at a station in the fields,
> (the name goes by
> unread).
> >   In the deep aftermath
> of its faded rhythm I could become
>
> a carved stone
> set in the gates of the earthly paradise,
>
> an angler's fly
> lost in the sedge to watch the centuries.

Back in the English countryside, back in "the earthly paradise," she again feels the power of the "place of origin" to stir her literally to her roots. But though she *could* become "a stone / set in [its] gates," she also admits "I don't want / to stay forever," and this passing contact with Paradise, this touching base—but then moving on, back into a world where darkness prevails—can be regarded as typical of the role of the garden in much of Levertov's later work.

For the great darkness to which the war opened her eyes clearly has not ended. The dangers of nuclear madness, of environmental suicide, of man's inhumanity to man—these and other horrors continue to impinge powerfully upon the poet's awareness. Indeed, imaginative integrity would seem to demand no less.[14] As a result, the garden's power to sustain her imagination grows more attenuated. For even the "place of origin," the actual parkland around her childhood home, has by now been defaced:

> The Wishing Well was a spring
> bubbling clear and soundless into a shallow pool
> . . . .
> This was the place from which
> year after year in childhood I demanded my departure. . . .

This was then. Now she discovers this same spring "filled to the shallow brim / with debris of a culture's sickness" ("The Stricken Children," *BW*). It would be hard to imagine, for Levertov, a more personal sense of violation.

And yet, the garden, the impulse to come home, still has not been destroyed. During the last decade Levertov's poetry has embraced an overtly Christian vision, and one important consequence of this development has been the increasing number of New Testament references and images in her work. On the one hand, this has resulted in an even greater hallowing of the "earthly paradise" as a reflection of God's goodness: "The spirit that walked upon the face of the waters / walks the meadow of long grass" ("Passage," *OP*). But to some extent, it has also helped "God" replace the "earth-gods" as the primary focus of her praise and the source of her deepest hope and consolation.[15] Hence, the last few volumes show a relative decline in the importance of the garden as idea-generating image.[16] The "earthly paradise" has been subsumed by a more purely spiritual conception. Intensity and delight seek out a more distinctly Christian context for their expression. Like St. John in "A Woodcut" (*DH*), we often move "above the earthly orchards," walking towards "burnished Jerusalem, thronged with the blessèd."[17]

And yet, many of the earliest images and scenes do continue to reappear in important new forms. The angel that comes to teach Caedmon to sing visits him in the sanctuary of a barn, among "the warm beasts, / dumb among body sounds," ("Caedmon," *BW*), and Julian of Norwich, the subject of Levertov's most ambitious recent poem ("The Showings: Lady Julian of Norwich, 1342–1416," *BW*), begins her life in a setting that by now must sound familiar.

> 'To understand her, you must imagine . . .'
> A childhood, then;
> the dairy's bowls of clabber, of rich cream,
> ghost-white in shade, and outside
> the midsummer gold, humming of dandelions.

From this beginning the poem moves us directly into the heart of one of Levertov's most lovely rural scenes. In other words, despite the new Christian focus, the function and identity of the garden/gardenlike as a place of intense delight, pronounced beauty, and natural creativity has by no means disappeared. Indeed, in this last example, it is not so much Julian as Levertov herself whose work demands we " 'must imagine . . .' / A childhood." For such a demand and such a scene are the poet's own invention—her own imaginative addendum to the "necessary" configuration of Julian's life.[18]

It is ironic that, in the end, that which most deflects Levertov away from the earthly paradise, the "garden flowing behind a rooted house" (*DI*), may turn out to be not so much the threat of darkness—or betrayal of the imagination or the irresistible march of time—but the discovery of an even higher, more powerful "magic." But as the spiritual sweep and intensity of her latest poetry indicates, if this should be the case, neither she nor we will be the poorer for the results.

> I am impatient with these branches, this light.
> The sky, however blue, intrudes.
> . . . .
> Because
> I know a different need has begun

to cast its lines out from me into
a place unknown. . . .

("Intimation," *DH*)

NOTES

I have employed the following abbreviations for Levertov's works:
*The Double Image: DI; Collected Earlier Poems 1940–1960: CE; The Jacob's
Ladder: JL; O Taste and See: TS; The Sorrow Dance: SD; Relearning the
Alphabet: RA; To Stay Alive: SA; The Freeing of the Dust: FD; Life in the
Forest: LF; Oblique Prayers: OP; Breathing the Water: BW; A Door in the
Hive: DH; The Poet in the World: PW; Light Up the Cave: LC.*

1. The pun here is not just on "de-light" for "the light," but also on
"delight" as the root meaning of "Eden." Indeed, "Paradise" literally
signifies an "enclosed park or garden." Note in this connection the
formulation that occurs towards the end of "A Daughter (II)" in *Life in
the Forest.* Here the "daughter," baffled by her once "vivid" mother's
lingering death, desperately asks: "is any vision / —an entrance into a
garden / of recognitions and revelations, Eden / of radiant comprehen-
sions, taking / timeless place in the wounded head[?]"

2. Hence, in a passage in the "Olga Poems," the citation "*In a garden
grene whenas I lay*" immediately suggests memories of Valentines Park.

3. This phrase appears in several works. See, for example, "The
Well" and "The Illustration" in *The Jacob's Ladder* and "Chekhov on the
West Heath" in *Life in the Forest.*

4. For a very telling variation on this "Peaceable Kingdom," see
"Caedmon" in *Breathing the Water,* where the "forest of torches, feathers
of flame, sparks upflying" represent Levertov's own addition to the
basic story and parallel the conflagration in her childhood nightmare.
However, what there exists as a source of terror and destruction here
serves as a seal of divine inspiration: Caedmon becomes the singer of
God's creation.

5. See, for example, "In California: Morning, Evening, Late Janu-
ary" (*DH*) where a "fragile paradise" of oak, eucalyptus, miner's let-
tuce, and grass is threatened by a "babel of destructive construction."

6. See, in this regard, the "Girlhood of Jane Harrison" (*CE*). Just as
Jane does a dance "to welcome the fall," so in "A Lamentation" (*SD*)
Levertov herself reclaims an "autumn birthright" she betrayed in order
to dance "*Summer.*" This reclaiming occurs in a context of both personal
and public grief: her sister's death and an intensification of the Vietnam
War.

7. Not only do the poems in *Life in the Forest* dealing with her
mother's death constitute an extended elegy. The subsequent volumes
also contain poems haunted by this loss. See, for example, "Visitant" in
Candles in Babylon and "The Mourner" in *Oblique Prayers.*

318

8. The scene reminds one of the "golden hay and straw" in Levertov's apocalyptic dream.

9. In the present case, it is not just awareness of the scythe that cancels this moment of childlike magic; it is also, in retrospect, awareness of the impending Holocaust. For Anna has come to England as a Jewish refugee and soon after chooses to rejoin her parents in "safe" Czechoslovakia. Note in this connection the dark irony of "The Peachtree" from "During the Eichmann Trial" (*JL*). Here Eichman begins his infamous career by murdering a Jewish boy "in a villa garden / the Devil's garden."

10. A major theme of part 1, 29–35.

11. It is interesting—but not at all surprising—that it is precisely this passage that Levertov chose to excerpt from *To Stay Alive* for her *Selected Poems*.

12. The phrase "the unlived life of which one can die" is a frequently quoted favorite of Levertov's and is taken from the Czech poet Rilke.

13. Levertov herself suggests 1959 as the point when "James Laughlin felt [she] had a voice of [her] own" and accepted her as "a New Directions author" ("Authors Note," *CE*).

14. As Levertov says in an unpublished essay entitled "Poetry, Prophecy, Survival," "But again, that profound impulse—the radiant joy, the awe of gratitude—is trivialized if its manifestations do not in some way acknowledge their context of icy shadows."

15. See "Of Gods" as well as the rest of section 4 of *Oblique Prayers:* "Of God and of the Gods." Here Levertov first explicitly explores this critical distinction. It is, of course, true that the garden as a locale favored by the gods [of nature] has always had an essentially numinous quality, and that "the unknown God of the gods" ("The God of Flowers") continues to smile warmly upon the natural world. Nevertheless, it would be a mistake to underestimate the significance of this explicit distinction. At the very least it ushers in a new vocabulary and a new iconography.

16. One particular exception to this observation is itself revealing. "Girls" (*BW*) presents us with a two-part vignette of a scene from the poet's youth. Here we immediately recognize most of the concepts we have come to identify with Levertov's "gardens." However, the present scene, unlike so many of its predecessors, is not asked to carry any particular spiritual charge or revelation. In fact, the "Girls" are repeatedly charged with "ignorance."

17. This, of course, is the general movement of Bunyan's *Pilgrim's Progress*. Note also the garden as "seductive way station" in Hans Christian Anderson's *The Snow Queen*. According to Levertov, both these works "most early affected [her] imagination" (*PW,* 66). The earthly garden as prelude to something even finer also appears in George MacDonald's *At the Back of the North Wind,* another favorite from Levertov's youth (*PW,* 74). Finally, note the poet's singling out a version of "Jerusa-

lem the Golden" as one of her two favorite childhood hymns (*PW*, 67). Thus this latest turn goes back itself to the "time"—if not the "place"—of origin!

18. Even in *A Door in the Hive* we continue to find expressive evocations of the "place of origin." See, for instance, "For Instance."

BARRY MAXWELL

A Selected Bibliography

Books by Denise Levertov (in chronological order)
The Double Image. London: The Cresset Press, 1946.
Here and Now. The Pocket Poets Series: Number Six. San Francisco: The City Lights Pocket Book Shop, 1956.
5 Poems. [n.p.]: The White Rabbit Press, 1958.
Overland to the Islands. Highlands, N.C.: Jonathan Williams, 1958.
With Eyes at the Back of Our Heads. New York: New Directions, 1960.
The Jacob's Ladder. New York: New Directions, 1961.
O Taste and See. New York: New Directions, 1964.
The Sorrow Dance. New York: New Directions, 1967.
A Tree Telling of Orpheus. Los Angeles: Black Sparrow Press, 1968.
In the Night. New York: Albondocani Press, 1968.
Three Poems. Mount Horeb, Wis.: Perishable Press, 1968.
The Cold Spring & Other Poems. New York: New Directions, 1968.
Embroideries. Los Angeles: Black Sparrow Press, 1969.
Summer Poems 1969. Berkeley, Calif.: Oyez, 1970.
Relearning the Alphabet. New York: New Directions, 1970.
A New Year's Garland for My Students. Mount Horeb, Wis.: Perishable Press, 1970.
To Stay Alive. New York: New Directions, 1971.
Footprints. New York: New Directions, 1972.
Conversation in Moscow. [n.p.]: Hovey St. Press, 1973.
The Poet in the World. New York: New Directions, 1973.
The Freeing of the Dust. New York: New Directions, 1975.
Chekhov on the West Heath. Andes, N.Y.: Woolmer/Brotherson, 1977.
Modulations for Solo Voice. San Francisco: Five Trees Press, 1977.
Life in the Forest. New York: New Directions, 1978.
Collected Earlier Poems, 1940–1960. New York: New Directions, 1979.
Light Up the Cave. New York: New Directions, 1981.
Mass for the Day of St. Thomas Didymus. Concord, N.H.: William B. Ewert, 1981.
Pig Dreams: Scenes from the Life of Sylvia. Woodstock, Vt.: Countryman Press, 1981.
Wanderer's Daysong. Port Townsend, Wash.: Copper Canyon Press, 1981.
Candles in Babylon. New York: New Directions, 1982.
El Salvador: Requiem and Invocation. Boston: Back Bay Chorale, 1983.

This bibliography is intended as a supplement to the contents of this volume. It does not repeat bibliographic information about the essays and reviews included; that information is given at the beginning of each text, except the essay by Edward Zlotkowski, which appears here for the first time.

Poems 1960–1967. New York: New Directions, 1983.

Oblique Prayers: New Poems with Fourteen Translations from Jean Joubert. New York: New Directions, 1984.

Selected Poems. Newcastle upon Tyne: Bloodaxe Books, 1986.

Poems 1968–1972. New York: New Directions, 1987.

Breathing the Water. New York: New Directions, 1987.

A Door in the Hive. New York: New Directions, 1989.

Evening Train. New York: New Directions, 1992.

New and Selected Essays. New York: New Directions, 1992.

Books or Dissertations Entirely or Partially on Denise Levertov's Work

Berke, Roberta. *Bounds Out of Bounds: A Compass for Recent American and British Poetry.* New York: Oxford University Press, 1981.

Block, Sandra Jean. "The Archetypal Feminine in the Poetry of Denise Levertov." Diss., Kansas State University, 1978.

Bowles, Gloria Lee. "Suppression and Expression in Poetry by American Women: Louise Bogan, Denise Levertov, and Adrienne Rich." Diss., University of California, Berkeley, 1976.

Christensen, Inger. *The Shadow of the Dome: Organicism and Romantic Poetry.* Bergen, Nor.: Department of English, University of Bergen, 1985.

Deren, Jane Martha. "Denise Levertov's Postmodern Poetic: A Study in Theory and Criticism." Diss., Temple University, 1977.

Duncan, Robert. Comment in Denise Levertov, *Overland to the Islands.* Highlands, N.C.: Jonathan Williams, 1958.

Elder, John. *Imagining the Earth: Poetry and the Vision of Nature.* Urbana: University of Illinois Press, 1985.

Felstiner, John. "Poetry and Political Experience: Denise Levertov." *Coming to Light: American Women Poets in the Twentieth Century.* Ed. Diane Wood Middlebrook and Marilyn Yalom. Ann Arbor: University of Michigan Press, 1985. 138–44.

Fesmire, Bonnie Lynn. "The Blaze Within: Forms of Pilgrimage in the Poetry of Denise Levertov, Anne Sexton, Sylvia Plath, and Adrienne Rich." Diss., Florida State University, 1981.

Foster, Heidi Anne. "The Poet's Voice: A Reevaluation of the Aims of Education." Diss., Boston University School of Education, 1980.

Gelpi, Albert. *The Tenth Muse.* Cambridge: Cambridge University Press, 1991.

Gould, Jean. "Denise Levertov." *Modern American Women Poets.* New York: Dodd, Mead & Company, 1985.

Howard, Richard. *Alone with America: Essays on the Art of Poetry in the United States since 1950.* New York: Atheneum, 1969; enlarged edition 1980.

Kammer, Jeanne Henry. "Repression, Compression and Power: Six Women Poets in America, 1860–1960." Diss., Carnegie-Mellon University, 1976.

Lacey, Paul A. *The Inner War: Forms and Themes in Recent American Poetry.* Philadelphia: Fortress, 1972.

Marquis, Harriet Hill. " 'Cries of Communion': The Poetry of Denise Levertov." Diss., Drew University, 1984.

Marten, Harry. *Understanding Denise Levertov.* Columbia, S.C.: University of South Carolina Press, 1988.

Mersmann, James F. *Out of the Vietnam Vortex: A Study of Poets and Poetry against the War.* Lawrence: University Press of Kansas, 1974.

Middleton, Peter. *Revelation and Revolution in the Poetry of Denise Levertov.* London: Binnacle Press, 1981.

Mills, Ralph J., Jr. *Cry of the Human: Essays on Contemporary American Poetry.* Urbana: University of Illinois Press, 1975.

———. "Denise Levertov: The Poetry of the Immediate." *Poets in Progress: Critical Prefaces to Thirteen Modern American Poets.* Ed. Edward Hungerford. Evanston, Ill.: Northwestern University Press, 1962.

Nelson, Cary. *Our Last First Poets: Vision and History in Contemporary American Poetry.* Urbana: University of Illinois Press, 1981.

Ostriker, Alicia Suskin. *Stealing the Language: The Emergence of Women's Poetry in America.* Boston: Beacon Press, 1986.

Phillips, Martha Jean Payne. "The Dissenting Voice: A Rhetorical Analysis of Denise Levertov's Engaged Poetry." Diss., University of Texas at Austin, 1975.

Pope, Deborah. *A Separate Vision: Isolation in Contemporary Women's Poetry.* Baton Rouge: Louisiana State University Press, 1984.

Rexroth, Kenneth. *New British Poets.* New York: New Directions, 1948.

———. *With Eye and Ear.* New York: Herder and Herder, 1970.

Rosenthal, Macha Louis. *The New Poets: American and British Poetry since World War II.* New York: Oxford University Press, 1967.

Rugoff, Kathy. "The Holocaust in American and British Poetry." Diss., Florida State University, 1983.

Sadoff, Dianne F. "Mythopoeia, The Moon, and Contemporary Women's Poetry." *Feminist Criticism: Essays on Theory, Poetry, and Prose.* Ed. Cheryl L. Brown and Karen Olson. Metuchen, N.J.: Scarecrow Press, 1978.

Sakelliou-Schultz, Liana. *Denise Levertov: An Annotated Primary and Secondary Bibliography.* New York: Garland Publishing, 1988.

Sautter, Diane. "Perception in Process: A Study of Denise Levertov's Poetic Practice." Diss., Syracuse University, 1980.

Slaughter, William. *The Imagination's Tongue: Denise Levertov's Poetic.* Portree, Scotland: Aquila, 1981.

Stauffer, Donald Barlow. *A Short History of American Poetry.* New York: E. P. Dutton & Co., 1974.

Stepanchev, Stephen. *American Poetry since 1945: A Critical Survey.* New York: Harper and Row, 1965.

Sutton, Walter. *American Free Verse: The Modern Revolution in Poetry.* New York: New Directions, 1973.

Thurley, Geoffrey. *The American Moment: American Poetry in the Mid-Century.* New York: St. Martin's Press, 1977.

Waggoner, Hyatt H. *American Poets: From the Puritans to the Present.* Baton Rouge: Louisiana State University Press, 1984.

Wagner, Linda Welshimer. *American Modern: Essays in Fiction and Poetry.* Port Washington, N.Y.: Kennikat Press, 1979.

———. *Denise Levertov.* New York: Twayne Publishers, 1967.

———. ed. *Denise Levertov: In Her Own Province.* New York: New Directions, 1979.

Weatherhead, A. Kingsley. *The Edge of the Image: Marianne Moore. William Carlos Williams, and Some Other Poets.* Seattle: University of Washington Press, 1967.

Williams, William Carlos. *Something to Say: William Carlos Williams on Younger Poets.* Ed. James E. B. Breslin. The William Carlos Williams Archive Series 1. New York: New Directions, 1985.

Wosk, Julie Helen. "Prophecies for America: Social Criticism in the Recent Po-
etry of Bly, Levertov, Corso, and Ginsberg." Diss., University of Wisconsin,
at Madison, 1974.

Articles on or Reviews of Denise Levertov's Work

Aiken, William. "Denise Levertov, Robert Duncan, and Allen Ginsberg: Modes
of the Self in Projective Poetry." *Modern Poetry Studies,* 10, nos. 2–3 (1981):
200–45.

Altieri, Charles. "From Experience to Discourse: American Poetry and Poetics in
the Seventies." *Contemporary Literature* 21, no. 2 (1980): 191–224.

———. "From Symbolist Thought to Immanence: The Ground of Postmodern
American Poetics." *Boundary 2* 1, 3 (1973): 605–41.

Berry, Wendell. "A Secular Pilgrimage." *Hudson Review* 23 (1970): 401–24.

Blackburn, Paul. "The International Word." *The Nation,* 21 April 1962, 357–60.

Blades, Sophia B. "Metaphors of Life and Death in the Poetry of Denise Lever-
tov and Sylvia Plath." *Dalhousie Review* 57 (1977): 494–506.

Bly, Robert. "The Work of Denise Levertov." *Sixties* 9 (1967): 48–65. This article
was written under the *nom de plume* "Crunk."

Breslin, Paul. "Black Mountain: A Critique of the Curriculum." *Poetry* 136, no.
4 (1980): 219–39.

Burns, G. Rev. of *To Stay Alive. Southwest Review* 57 (1972): 162.

Carruth, Hayden. "An Informal Epic." Rev. of *O Taste and See. Poetry* 105
(1965): 259–61.

———. "What 'Organic' Means?" *Sagetrieb,* 4, no. 1 (1985): 145–46.

Collecott, Diana. "Mirror-images: Images of Mirrors . . . in Poems by Sylvia
Plath, Adrienne Rich, Denise Levertov and H.D." *Revue francaise d'Etudes
Americaines* 30 (1986): 449–60.

Condee, Nancy. "American Poetry and the Political Statement: An Overview of
the Sixties and Seventies." *Zeitschrift für Anglistik und Amerikanistik.* Ed. Eber-
hart Bruning et al. Leipzig, East Germany, 30, no. 2 (1982): 232–43.

Cooperman, Stanley. "Poetry of Dissent in the United States." *Michigan Quar-
terly Review* 10 (1971): 23–28.

Costello, Bonnie. Rev. of *Collected Earlier Poems, 1940–1960. Parnassus* 8, no. 1
(1979): 198–212.

Creeley, Robert. "Here and Now." Rev. of *Here and Now. New Mexico Quarterly*
27 (1957): 125–27.

Crowder, Ashby Bland. "Modes of Marriage in Creeley and Levertov." *The
South Central Bulletin* 42, no. 4 (1982): 128.

Crowder, Ashby Bland, and John Churchill. "The Problem of Interpretation: A
Case In Point." *College Literature* 13, no. 2 (1986): 123–40.

Dargan, Joan. "Poetic and Political Consciousness in Denise Levertov and Caro-
lyn Forche." *CEA Critic* 48, no. 3 (1986): 58–67.

Driscoll, Kerry. "A Sense of Unremitting Emergency: Politics in the Early Work
of Denise Levertov." *Centennial Review* 30, no. 2 (1986): 292–303.

Duncan, Robert. "Letters for Denise Levertov: An A Muse Ment" *Black Moun-
tain Review* (Fall 1954).

Eagleton, Terry. Rev. of *Relearning the Alphabet. Stand.* Newcastle upon Tyne, 12,
no. 1 (1973): 77.

Economou, George. Rev. of *Oblique Prayers. Times Educational Supplement,* 15
May 1985, 430.

Ewart, Gavin. "Prohibit Sharply the Rehearsed Response." Rev. of *Relearning the Alphabet. AMBIT* 45 (1970): 46–50.

Friedman, Susan Stanford. "Creativity and the Childbirth Metaphor: Gender Difference in Literary Discourse." *Feminist Studies* 13, no. 1 (1987): 49–82.

Ginsberg, Allen. Rev. of *Light Up the Cave. American Book Review* 4, no. 9 (1982).

Gitlin, Todd. "The Return of Political Poetry." *Commonweal: A Weekly Review of Public Affairs, Literature, and the Arts,* 23 July 1971, 375–78.

Gitzen, Julian. "From Reverence of Attention: The Poetry of Denise Levertov." *Midwest Quarterly: A Journal of Contemporary Thought* 16 (1975): 328–41.

Gubar, Susan. "The Blank Page and the Issues of Female Creativity." *Critical Inquiry* 8, no. 2 (1981): 243–63.

Gunn, Thom. "Things, Voices, Minds." Rev. of *The Jacob's Ladder. Yale Review* 52 (1962): 129–38.

Hallisey, Joan F. "Denise Levertov— . . . 'Forever a Stranger and Pilgrim' " *Centennial Review* 30, no. 2 (1986): 281–91.

Harris, Victoria Frenkel. "The Incorporative Consciousness: Levertov's Journey From Discretion to Unity." *Exploration: Journal of the MLA Special Session on the Literature of Exploration and Travel* 4, no. 1 (1976): 33–48.

Hartman, Geoffrey. "Les Belles Dames Sans Merci." Rev. of *With Eyes at the Back of Our Heads. Kenyon Review* 22 (1960): 691–700.

Hunt, Jean. "The New Grief-Language of Denise Levertov." *The University Review* 35, no. 2 (1968): 149–53.

————. "Denise Levertov's New Grief-Language II." *The University Review* 35, no. 3 (1969): 171–77.

Ignatow, David. Rev. of *The Freeing of the Dust. The New York Times Book Review,* 30 Nov. 1975, 54–55.

Jackson, Richard. "A Common Time: The Poetry of Denise Levertov." *Sagetrieb* 5, no. 2 (1986): 5–46.

Kyle, Carol A. "Every Step an Arrival: 'Six Variations' and the Musical Structure of Denise Levertov's Poetry." *The Centennial Review* 17, no. 3 (1973): 281–96.

Lauter, Paul. "Poetry Demanding and Detached." Rev. of *With Eyes at the Back of Our Heads. The New Leader,* 15 May 1961, 22–23.

Lazer, Hank. "In Defense of American Poetry." *Ohio Review* 20, no. 3 (1980): 9–22.

Lynch, Denise. "Levertov's 'An English Field in the Nuclear Age.' " *Explicator* 46, no. 4 (1988): 40–41.

Marten, Harry. "Exploring the Human Community: The Poetry of Denise Levertov and Muriel Rukeyser." *Sagetrieb* 3, no. 3 (1984): 51–61.

Martz, Louis L. "Recent Poetry: The Elegiac Mode." Rev. of *O Taste and See. Yale Review* 54, no. 2 (1965): 285–98.

Montefiore, Jan. " 'What words say': Three Women Poets Reading H.D." *Agenda* 25, nos. 3–4 (1987–88): 172–90.

Mottram, Eric. "The Limits of Self-Regard." Rev. of *To Stay Alive. Parnassus* 1 (1972): 152–62.

Ostriker, Alicia. "In Mind: The Divided Self and Women's Poetry." *Midwest Quarterly: A Journal of Contemporary Thought* 24 (1983): 351–65.

Perloff, Marjorie G. "Beyond *The Bell Jar*: Women Poets in Transition." *South Carolina Review* 11, no. 2 (1979): 4–16.

Porter, Peter. "The Long Pilgrimage." Rev. of *Oblique Prayers. Observer,* 11 Jan. 1987, 23.

Rexroth, Kenneth. "Levertov and the Young Poets." Rev. of *The Jacob's Ladder*. *The New Leader*, 9 July 1962, 21–22.

———. "The New American Poets." *Harper's Magazine*, June 1965, 65–71.

Rosenfeld, Alvin H. " 'The Being of Language and the Language of Being': Heidegger and Modern Poetics." *Boundary 2* 4 (1976): 535–53.

Rosenthal, Macha Louis: "Dynamics of Form and Motive in Some Representative Twentieth-Century Lyric Poems." *ELH* 37, no. 1 (1970): 136–51.

———. "In Exquisite Chaos." Rev. of *With Eyes at the Back of Our Heads*. *The Nation*, 1 Nov. 1958, 324–27.

Sautter, Diane. "Tacit and Explicit Tulips." *Pre/Text: Inter-Disciplinary Journal of Rhetoric*, Eastern Illinois University, 2, nos. 1–2 (1981): 45–61.

Seidman, Hugh. "Images, Artifacts, Entertainments." Rev. of *Life in the Forest*. *The New York Times Book Review*, 8 July 1979, 14.

Sisko, Nancy J. "To Stay Alive: Levertov's Search for a Revolutionary Poetry." *Sagetrieb* 5, no. 2 (1986): 47–60.

Smith, Lorrie. Rev. of *Oblique Prayers*. *Sagetrieb* 4, nos. 2–3 (1985): 335–42.

Sorrentino, Gilbert. "Measure of Maturity." Rev. of *The Jacob's Ladder*. *The Nation*, 10 Mar. 1962, 220–21.

Sutton, Walter. "Denise Levertov and Emerson." *Notes on Modern American Literature* 1, no. 1 (1976): n.p.

"Symposium on Postmodern Form." *New England Review and Bread Loaf Quarterly* 6, no. 1 (1983). Cf. especially pp. 7ff, 31ff, 35, 51.

Tomlinson, Charles. "Dr. Williams' Practice." Rev. of *1967—Penguin Modern Poets*. *Encounter*. London, 29 Nov. 1967, 66–71.

Viator, Timothy J. "Levertov's 'Pleasures'." *Notes on Contemporary Literature* 18, no. 4 (1988): 2–3.

Wagner, Linda Welshimer. "Levertov and Rich: The Later Poems." *South Carolina Review* 11, no. 2 (1979): 18–27.

———. "Matters of the Here and Now." Rev. of *The Poet in the World*. *The Nation*, 22 June 1974, 795–96.

———. Rev. of *The Freeing of the Dust*. *The Nation*, 14 Aug. 1976, 121.

Wallace, Ronald. "Alone with Poems." *Colorado Quarterly* 23 (1975): 341–53.

Wright, James. "Gravity and Incantation." Rev. of *The Jacob's Ladder*. *Minnesota Review* 2 (1962): 424–27.

———. "The Few Poets of England and America." *Minnesota Review* 1, no. 2 (1961): 248–56.

Younkins, Ronald. "Denise Levertov and the Hasidic Tradition." *Descant: The Texas Christian University Literary Journal* 19, no. 1 (1974): 40–48.

Zweig, Paul. "Magistral Strokes and First Steps." Rev. of *Relearning the Alphabet*. *The Nation*, 21 June 1971, 794–95.